THE LAND OF
HAUNTED CASTLES

LUXEMBURG CITY
Ancient gate on the road to the City of Emperors

THE LAND OF HAUNTED CASTLES

BY

ROBERT J. CASEY

ILLUSTRATED WITH
MANY PHOTOGRAPHS

"Dim with the mist of years, gray flits
the shade of power...."
—Byron.

Fredonia Books
Amsterdam, The Netherlands

The Land of Haunted Castles

by
Robert J. Casey

ISBN: 1-4101-0138-X

Copyright © 2003 by Fredonia Books

Reprinted from the 1921 edition

Fredonia Books
Amsterdam, The Netherlands
http://www.fredoniabooks.com

All rights reserved, including the right to reproduce this book, or portions thereof, in any form.

In order to make original editions of historical works available to scholars at an economical price, this facsimile of the original edition of 1921 is reproduced from the best available copy and has been digitally enhanced to improve legibility, but the text remains unaltered to retain historical authenticity.

To
MARIE

CONTENTS

CHAPTER		PAGE
I	GRIMM REALITY	1
	The Case of Lady Gretel	2
II	DRUID AND ROMAN	13
	The Ancestry of the Fairies	14
III	GHOSTS	29
	Who They Were and Where They Came From	30
IV	THE FAIRY MELUSINE	49
	Peeping Siegfroid and the Mermaid Godiva	50
V	TIME'S FOOTPRINTS	65
	A Love Eternal	66
VI	PATHS OF GLORY	75
	Royal Purple	76
VII	JOHN THE BLIND	93
	The Wandering King of Bohemia	94
VIII	SWORD AND TORCH	109
	The Emperor Charles Quint	110
IX	THE CAPITAL	139
	City of Cloak and Sword	140
X	ANSEMBOURG	159
	The Lady of the Spinning Wheel	160
XI	HOLLENFELS	175
	The Hollow Rock and Its Dream of Fair Women	176
XII	MARIENTHAL	197
	The Flying Horseman	198
XIII	SCHOENFELS	209
	The Little People	210
XIV	MERSCH AND PETTINGEN	219
	Coffins and Centurions	220
XV	ETTELBRUCK	233
	The Bahnhof and a Cinemadventure	234

CONTENTS

CHAPTER		PAGE
XVI	VIANDEN	257
	The Dice of the Devil	258
XVII	DAHNEN	299
	The Wise Men of Gotham	300
XVIII	ECHTERNACH	311
	Where Thousands Dance for the Glory of God	312
XIX	A GARDEN OF THE GODS	330
	The Tale of a Three-Legged Cat	331
XX	BRANDENBOURG	343
	The Hunted Huntsman	344
XXI	BOURSCHEID	353
	The Restless Crusader	355
XXII	ESCH-SUR-SURE	363
	Ghost Bells in Fairyland	364
XXIII	CLERVAUX	377
	Et Get Fir de Glaf!	378
XXIV	BEAUFORT	385
	The Splendid Romance of Jean Beck	386
XXV	HERRINGERBURG	395
	The Lady of the Magical Voice	396
XXVI	LA ROCHETTE	407
	Four-and-Twenty Blackbirds Baked in a Pie	408
XXVII	CHRISTNACH	423
	Swanhilde and the Love of Rodoric	424
XXVIII	PASTELS	431
	The People of the Toy-Kingdom	432
XXIX	THE FIREMEN	445
	Guardians of Society	446
XXX	MARRIAGE	459
	The Bride and Her Garter	460
XXXI	A FAMOUS VICTORY	473
	We are the Salt of the Earth	474
XXXII	THE END OF THE ROAD	493

LIST OF ILLUSTRATIONS

Luxemburg City—Ancient gate on the road to the City of Emperors	*Frontispiece*
	FACING PAGE
Luxemburg City—In this spot where an isolated rock arose in a narrow valley, rival empires stubbed their imperial toes for a thousand years	17
Luxemburg City—Approach to the Great Rock where Siegfroid and the Fairy Melusine built their stronghold	32
Luxemburg City—The Grand Ducal Palace. A relic of the Spanish Occupation	53
Luxemburg City—Detail of the old fortification	60
Luxemburg City—At the foot of the Bock	69
Luxemburg City—View from the Bock—Looking across the lower town and the Viaduc du Nord	76
Luxemburg City—Road from the Bock to the Lower City showing part of the fortifications begun by Siegfroid and his fairy and perfected by Vauban for Louis XIV of France	97
"New" Château Ansembourg—Main entrance of the Sixteenth Century Château	112
"New" Château Ansembourg—The Garden	112
Luxemburg City—The Lower City	129
Luxemburg City—The Suburb of the Grand, the Upper Town	129
Château Berg—The Grand Ducal Country Seat	144
Old Ansembourg—Where the "Lady of the Spinning Wheel" wove the wedding gown that was her shroud	168
Old Ansembourg—From the Spinning Wheel Lady's Window View from the corner tower of Old Ansembourg	168
Hollenfels—Windows of the Chapel	177
Hollenfels—Looking from the Rampart	177
Hollenfels—Altar—Hollenfels Chapel	192
Hollenfels—Salle des Chevaliers	192
Schoenfels—From the rocks of the Little People	213
Mersch—To the left is the new basilica, in the center the spire of the ancient church that was built upon a foundation of Frankish coffins, to the right the square tower of the old castle	220

LIST OF ILLUSTRATIONS

	FACING PAGE
ETTELBRUCK—This city was called for the "Scourge of God," "Attila's Bridge." It is a "new town" without great interest on its own account, but the meeting of the valleys in which lie the castles	245
BOURSCHEID—About these walls rode the ghost of a crusader in battered armor. He ceased his vigil when Palestine fell to the British	252
VIANDEN—It defied armies and the elements but succumbed at last to the insidious junk man	261
VIANDEN—Outer wall, chapel and gables of the immense Salle des Chevaliers	268
VIANDEN—The Watch Tower	277
VIANDEN—Underground Passage	277
VIANDEN—Inner Court	284
VIANDEN—The Double Chapel	289
VIANDEN—Remains of Upper Floor	289
VIANDEN—Roman Ovens	304
VIANDEN—Roman Kitchens	304
MARIENTHAL—From the Precipice	321
MARIENTHAL—Vale of Eternal Tranquillity	321
BRANDENBOURG—Here a small garrison made a gallant stand against the torchmen of Louis XIV—and strange things have been happening ever since	336
BOURSCHEID—The castle was one of the strongest in the duchy but was dismantled by Louis XIV when he set Vauban to strengthening the works of Luxemburg City, inland Gibraltar	357
ESCH-SUR-SURE—The crusading graf hung a Saracen's head to the ramparts in testimony of his prowess . . . even now can be heard the noises of the men at arms, the clanking of heavy armor and the jingle of chain-mail	364
BEAUFORT—The château is remarkable chiefly for its excellent masonry. It is one of the duchy's finest examples of medieval military architecture	392
LAROCHETTE—Above the town on its high rocks sits the castle. Much of the village is built within the line of its dismantled outer circle of defenses	420
FROM THE RAMPARTS OF HOLLENFELS—Hundreds of feet above the spot where the toes of the castle crag dip into a little river	465
LUXEMBURG CITY—German artillery in retreat through Luxemburg City—November, 1918	480
LUXEMBURG CITY—The German retreat of November, 1918	480

CHAPTER I
GRIMM REALITY

The Case of Lady Gretel

> The same that ofttimes hath
> Charm'd magic casements, opening on the foam
> Of perilous seas, in faery lands forlorn.
> —Keats

THE LAND OF HAUNTED CASTLES

CHAPTER I

GRIMM REALITY

GRETEL passed on through passages of crystal and rooms of silver,—spacious chambers, empty and silent. Before a golden door she halted, suddenly afraid, as from the wall to the right of her seven crimson birds in seven wicker cages spoke to her in solemn warning: "Turn back, turn back, there is blood on the ring."

Thus the Brothers Grimm, those great historians of human imagination, wrote of one of the castles that sprang up centuries ago between Germany and France. Their fairy stories of princesses captive in great eagles' nests of rock, of enchanted princes buried in the forgotten donjon-keeps, delightful though they have been to every child who has ever learned to read, have never been regarded as scientific accounts of the life and politics of the era with which they are concerned. They are fairy tales, wholly fairy tales, and nothing but fairy tales. So of course no one believes them.

If one is seeking the plain, unvarnished truth, whether about castles or cabbages, he must go to an unbiased

THE LAND OF HAUNTED CASTLES

source. He cannot expect facts from a spinner of fairy tales. Imagination has wrecked more than one scientific inquiry before now. All men are liars,—some good, some bad, some consciously and some unconsciously. Hence, the ideal informant should be a man with intelligence enough to remember what he has learned, but totally lacking in the invention that would add untruthful embellishments.

The Teutonic peasant, by nature as patiently dull and unimaginative as the great over-developed Belgian horses that he follows in the fields, is humanity's closest approach to this ideal. He is intensely practical, as any one who has watched his careful outlay of hard-earned marks will testify. He is not overburdened with intelligence, but has been educated in very efficient grade schools, has heard of modern progress, is acquainted distantly with the telephone, more closely with the electric light, has traveled a little, reads the provincial newspapers, and harbors a few dim political opinions. An average twentieth-century sort of person he seems to be, and in him, if anywhere, should be the truth.

Under the crumbling walls of a medieval stronghold he hoes his potatoes, a perfect copy of a Millet painting. He was brought up in the little stone house down the white road,—the one under the beeches, sir. The house is older than the memory of man. The peasant's father lived there, and his great-great-grandmother, and before her other ancestors who heard the artillery and saw the torches of Louis XIV.

Can he tell you of the castle? Of course he can. The history of the country-side is at the tip of his tongue:

"It was an accursed castle, sir. It was built by Hermann the Strong as a fortress against his many enemies. Here came the Princess Gretel and the Prince Siegfroid her husband for shelter. The Prince Siegfroid was a Frank, sir. He looked upon Hermann as a friend. Which was very foolish. The Princess Gretel did not like the place. You can see, sir, that it was large and rough. She and the prince were quartered in that old north tower that now makes an excellent shelter for the pigs.

"There were strange noises in the castle. Every night the wailing of a woman could be heard above the moaning of the wind in the crevices.

"Hermann laughed at them and said that prowling animals from the forests of the Ardennes had very sorrowful voices. Siegfroid and his princess were reassured.

"One day Siegfroid went out to hunt with Hermann and failed to return. A party of horsemen, retainers of the Baron von Alpenburg, had waylaid them and Siegfroid had died in the fighting. So Hermann said. And no one ever knew to the contrary. I would not venture to state the opinion that perhaps Hermann, in whose eyes the Princess Gretel was very beautiful, had accomplished the killing without the help of the baron's retainers.

THE LAND OF HAUNTED CASTLES

Some people have said so. But there must always be gossips.

"The princess remained at the castle. After a time Hermann consoled her and asked that she marry him. She agreed, poor thing. What else was there for her to do? The date was set for the wedding and the engagement was made the occasion for a grand celebration in the salle des chevaliers of the castle.

"Hermann the Strong and his men-at-arms were very good drinkers. But the heady vintages of the Rhine and Lorraine flowed like water and by midnight all of them were stretched under the long tables.

"Gretel, who had tasted very little of the wine, arose to go to her room.

"She passed out of the salle des chevaliers to another long hall that used to stand where now you see that fertilizer tank. Then suddenly she heard the crying woman again; only now the wailing was so weak that it scarcely could be noticed among the noises of the wind. She followed it toward an iron door.

"A voice within her—a very strange thing it was, sir,—seemed to call out to her to look at the ring that had been given her by Hermann the Strong. She removed it and became sick at heart.

"There was blood on the ring, sir. It is hard to believe, nowadays, that such things could happen.

"She opened the iron door. It was very terrible.

GRIMM REALITY

There before her was a dungeon. In it, chained to a wall and dying from a sword cut over her heart, was a woman. It was the wife of Hermann the Strong, sir. He had been forced to get rid of her before his second wedding-day because even in those times one wife was enough for a man and a monk had told him that the curse of God would punish bigamy.

"Gretel fled. But it was winter-time and she died from exposure in the woods yonder. They say that even now the wailing of the wife of Hermann the Strong and the cries of the princess who died trying to escape him can be heard about these ruins. A strange story, is it not, sir?"

So speaks the simple twentieth-century peasant, pausing in his narrative as an automobile siren interrupts him from the road at his right and a shrill locomotive whistle sounds across the fertile valley. So is heard the voice of unbiased history speaking through the lips of this educated modern. It is as consistent as if the Archbishop of Canterbury should rise up in his pulpit to expound the theological truth of Ovid's metamorphoses.

The case of the Princess Gretel is not an exaggeration. Admitted that she is a mythical character introduced here for the first time on any stage. But she is typical. So is the whole-souled man with the hoe who tells of her. Hermann the Strong is no more romantic a figure than Henry the Red, who, in the depths of Vianden, has been shaking dice for centuries to save his soul from the devil. Gretel

THE LAND OF HAUNTED CASTLES

is in no detail more fanciful than the White Lady of Beaufort. The whimsical philosophy that provides the motive for the slaying of Hermann's wife is no more overdrawn than is the explanation of the miraculous escape of the Flying Horseman of Marienthal.

You may shape, you may fashion a man as you will, but somewhere back in his cranium is a sneaking liking for fairy tales, with its accompaniments, a fear of the supernatural and a belief in ghosts.

There will always be folk-tales. And there will always be folks engaged in manufacturing new ones. There will always be vivid dreamers,—and a market for Ouija boards.

Many a Poilu knows that Napoleon came back to save France at the first Battle of the Marne. An equal number saw the shade of Joan of Arc at Verdun. As the years give imagination time to mellow, the actual spots where they appeared will be charted and tourists will be taken to them, for a price. Maimed veterans will tell how they saw the apparitions and a future generation will learn that troops of lancers in chain mail turned back the German horde before Paris and that it was not the "seventy-fives," but the ghosts of the guns that failed at Waterloo that stopped the rush on the Meuse.

We need not wander so far afield. The legends of our own Catskills, resting-place of Rip Van Winkle, are diversified enough to have suited even the Brothers

GRIMM REALITY

Grimm. We used to have a number of cases of diabolical possession in New England; and it was only yesterday that a New York woman rode in her own automobile to a prosaic police court to charge a neighbor woman with witchcraft.

Where there has been history there is certain to be legend. Fairy tale follows fact as an echo trails the blast of a trumpet. The louder the trumpet, the greater the echo. The more picturesque and romantic the historical incident, the more strangely fascinating and more generally accepted the folk-lore.

It is only natural that there should be haunted castles in the Grand Duchy of Luxemburg. It is the most beautiful country in northern Europe. It has been the home of a dozen races, the battle-ground of a score of wars. It has been for a thousand years a sort of great Chinese wall between two powerful ententes. The bones of Roman legionaries have given calcium to its soil. The sarcophagi of crusaders are in its gray-green churches. Its people carry in their blood an atavistic stoicism in the presence of death, fortified by a practical faith in a life beyond the grave. And the past intrudes itself upon them subconsciously in the thousand mysterious relics that cling to the crags in successful defiance to time and the elements.

Through Luxemburg swept the Goths, the Visigoths, and the Huns, the Romans, the Belgæ, the Franks, the

THE LAND OF HAUNTED CASTLES

Gauls, the Spaniards, and, more recently, the Dutch, the Germans, and the French.

The people lived on the brink of a sort of military volcano that erupted periodically and with dire results.

Sword and fire, pestilence and famine, and the constant influx of rival races over one frontier or the other by turns decimated and reinforced the population. Its national language swung from one dialect to another. Its racial characteristics changed with each succeeding epoch of wars. That is the price a people must pay if they live on the highway between two mighty forces.

Sometime shortly after Tubal Cain, or whoever it was, pounded out the first sword, Luxemburg became the strategic center of Europe, the gateway by which the tribes of the half-starved North and East might enter the fertile fields of the South and West, and, since a gate swings two ways, a similar convenience for the men-at-arms of Southern conquerors.

It was across the old Luxemburg that the troops of Kaiser Wilhelm II passed into Belgium and thence to France. Through Luxemburg marched the great tides of *feldgrau* that cast up a flotsam of death on the beach of war at Verdun.

Once Luxemburg city, the capital, was a stronghold conceded to be as impregnable as Gibraltar. Lesser fortresses—grim, imposing, romantic—look down with majestic aloofness from every peak of rock, at the head of

GRIMM REALITY

every cañon. Age has not lessened their grandeur nor dimmed their glamour. If ghosts must walk the earth, they could find no spot on the globe where their appearance would be more natural, or better understood.

CHAPTER II
DRUID AND ROMAN

The Ancestry of the Fairies

The night is long that never finds the day.—Shakespeare

CHAPTER II

DRUID AND ROMAN

IT would be difficult to say just when the fairies came to Luxemburg. They seem always to have been there, like the rocky hills, the wars, the robber barons, and the other products of the Ardennes soil. Many of the country's legends bear the stamp of Druidic origin. Some hark back to the priests of Baal.

The relics of the Celts are strewn the length and breadth of the land, strewn more numerously and with greater abandon at the points where the race came into close contact with the better-armed Teutons. The sacrificial stones of the Druid priests, oriented after the fashion of the ruins of Stonehenge, the blood-vats, imperishable adjuncts to human sacrifice, have stood through the ages, grim guardians of the mysteries of haunted woods. Temples of Diana and Venus are in the glades hard by the shrines of Christian saints. It is hardly remarkable in view of this evidence of religion conquering religion and race succumbing to race, that legend, folk-tale, philosophy, and creed should have become inextricably intertwined in the minds of the people.

If some one were to tell us that the woods at Diekirch echoed nightly with the shrieks of sacrifice and that the

THE LAND OF HAUNTED CASTLES

ghost fires of forgotten priestcraft still glowed among the crags, we might find it hard to disbelieve. For to a civilized mind it would seem that poetic justice is lacking in the world if the barbaric horrors of the Druids can ever die.

That the ghastly curse of them remains upon the country-side where they were wrought seems easily credible.

There were people in Luxemburg prior to the coming of the Celts, of course, but what sort of savage existence they led can only be imagined. They bequeathed to posterity few records of their régime save in the catacombs of the dwarfs at Schoenfels and in the crude weapons and implements of an early stone age uncovered at widely separated points in the Ardennes.

The Celts—or, more properly, the Gauls—were a high-minded race of killers who probably had some virtues. All that is known of them does not combine to produce any great sorrow that they have vanished. They were only a short distance removed from the animals that furnished them with food and clothing, and in disposition the animals appear to have had the better of the comparison.

The Gauls sprang from the same Aryan stock as the Teutons, but the Teutons sprang farther.

Tacitus in his annals makes it appear that the Germanic tribes were little brothers of the Angels,—honest,

LUXEMBURG CITY

In this spot where an isolated rock arose in a narrow valley, rival empires stubbed their imperial toes for a thousand years

intelligent, and chaste; great warriors, and souls of a marvelous simplicity. It has been pointed out by interested persons that Tacitus was something of a politician, and might have attributed all attainable virtue to the Teutons by way of proving that Rome under certain administrations had dropped some distance from the fundamental civilization of savagery. It has been hinted that the Germanic tribes were but little different from the Gauls and that both of them were stupid beasts. Historical light on the subject, unless we are prepared to take the bull's-eye illumination of the ardent Tacitus himself, is very dim.

But, judging the two tribes by the result of their coalition, it appears that the Teutons had a better start toward culture than had the Gauls. They defeated the Gauls. Hence it appears that they were better armed or better trained.

They founded, through the amalgamating process that always followed such conquests in the dawning of the world, the sturdy races of Europe,—intelligent and strong, simple, religious, basically good. The descendants of the Gauls and the Teutons, despite their continuous wars, displayed little of the savagery of either of their progenitors. For the most part they were peaceable, kindly, and Christian, content to till their fields and live in peace and amity with their neighbors. Professional armies did the fighting. The bulk of the people, save

THE LAND OF HAUNTED CASTLES

those of the invaded countries, knew of wars only as vague rumors were brought to them by passing travelers and were for the most part unaffected by them, until the atavistic debacle of 1914 which plunged civilization to its neck in bloody horror.

Europe had traveled a long way from the Gauls before it reached the Marne. And then it suddenly returned to them, doubly terrible in the sacrifice of its acquired ideals. It is significant that the Teutonic strain which built up the old world was the influence that attempted to tear the structure down.

The Celts, lacking tools and brains and the other requisites of building, lived in caves or rude huts or in skin tents or under the open sky. But despite their losing struggle with the housing-problem, they left one notable contribution to the architecture of medieval Europe.

It is a noticeable fact that a reed wall will not stop a man-eating bear, nor serve long as a barrier to a hungry wolf. And there were many such animals, none of them too well nourished, in the Ardennes. Blasting-powder was then several eons still in the future, as was cement. Masonry was an art undreamed of. Ordinary ingenuity that might have made use of the rocky chips, or the boulders that afterward were incorporated into the outer cinctures of the castles was lacking. But a spark of invention glowed dimly behind the low brow of the Gaul. He discovered that bears and wolves and their ilk got

DRUID AND ROMAN

into difficulties immediately they stepped off of dry land.

Of this observation was born the *mardelle*. The mardelle was the ancestor of the moated castle and was about ninety-nine per cent. moat.

It was an artificial lake, a deep pit perhaps fifty yards wide, in the center of which a hut was built on stilts. Here the first ladies of the lake could go boating or fishing or even bathing without fear. At night the overlord of this castle was lulled to sleep by the purling of the waves under the floor of woven willow and the baying of disappointed wolves upon the shore.

Traces of the mardelles still are to be found in the valley of the Sure. They went out, probably, when the tyrannical Druids were overthrown and the remnants of the Gauls learned to make metal tools and to use the other materials that favored permanent construction.

The Gauls appear to have been an easy-going race, fairly good-natured and agricultural, fierce fighters in their way, but lacking the genius for planning the mob warfare of their day and the stamina for prosecuting it. The Teutons, their neighbors, were less tractable. For all their varied virtues as set forth by the enthusiastic Tacitus, they were monomaniacs and bloodshed was their obsession.

Just what refining influence may attach to war has not yet been made clear, but ethnologists agree that the Gaul in his pastoral simplicity was one of the most naturally

THE LAND OF HAUNTED CASTLES

peaceful and most woefully ignorant creatures of which history has any record. Cæsar ascribes to him a shocking immorality transcending in bestiality even the polyandry of the South Sea islands. The Roman in his commentaries declares that whole communities lived under one roof and shared their women in common, and other writers whose opinions have been based more or less upon hearsay describe the life of the Gaul as one long orgy of sexual excess.

In justice to the reputation of these little-known savages it might be well to present in passing a different picture of their habits as painted by Winwood Reade.

Reade, who attempted to make out a case for the Druids, and more particularly the forgotten ancestors of the British race, finds the Gauls to have been quite as lovable creatures as the Teutons of Tacitus. He says:

> They feared nothing, these brave men. They sang as they marched into battle and perhaps to death. They shot arrows at the heavens when it thundered; they laughed as they saw their own hearts' blood gushing forth.
> And yet they were plain and simple in their manners; open and generous, docile and grateful, strangers to low cunning and deceit, so hospitable that they hailed the arrival of each fresh guest with joy and festivities, so warm hearted that they were never more pleased than when they could bestow a kindness.
> Their code of morals, like those of civilized nations, had its little contradictions; they account it disgraceful to steal but honorable to rob, and though they observed the strictest chastity, they did not blush to live promiscuously in communities of twelve.

DRUID AND ROMAN

This extraordinary custom induced Cæsar to assert that they enjoyed each other's wives in common; but in this he is borne out by no other authorities, and indeed there are many instances of this kind among barbarous nations, who love, apparently, to hide their real purity under a gross and filthy enamel.

Richard of Circencester (probably alluding to Bath, the aquæ solis of the ancients) mentions, however, some salt and warm springs used by the ancient Britons, from which were formed hot baths suited to all ages, with distinct places for the two sexes; a refinement which was unknown in Lacedœmon.

And Procopius writes:

"So highly rated is chastity among these barbarians that if even the bare mention of marriage occurs without its completion, the maiden seems to lose her fair fame."

So much for the morals of the Gaul. Concerning his other characteristics there seems to be less controversy. Reade declares that the British Celts were so inquisitive that they would compel travelers to stop and exchange gossip with them and listen with rapt attention to merchants who appear to have been the ancestors of town criers.

The strain of credulity that was the Gaul's remains in the modern nations that he fathered,—a credulity that under some conditions makes for a trustfulness, frankness, and honesty far removed from the savage faith that was born of ignorance.

If some antiquarian some day can read in the oriented ruins about Diekirch and Vianden and Echternach the story of the religion that the sons of Noah established on

THE LAND OF HAUNTED CASTLES

the European continent, he will be able to produce a book of surpassing interest and worthy of preservation so long as the art of reading shall endure. A number of instincts inbred in the white races of the world to-day are directly traceable to Druidic influence. And no architects of human destiny are shrouded in deeper mystery than these same Druids.

Reade, after a study of the ruins and folk-lore of Stonehenge and Wales, advances the belief that the Druids were the offspring of the Hebrew patriarchs. He says:

> They worshiped one God, and prayed to him in the open air; and believed in a heaven, in a hell and in the immortality of the soul.
>
> It is strange that these offsprings of the patriarchs should also be corrupted from the same sources and should thus still preserve a resemblance to one another in the minor tenets of their polluted creeds.
>
> Those pupils of the Egyptian priests, the Phœnicians, or Canaanites, who had taught the Israelites to sacrifice human beings, and to pass their children through the fire to Moloch, infused the same bloodthirsty precepts among the Druids. As the Indian wife was burnt upon her husband's pyre, so on the corpses of the Celtic lords were consumed their children, their slaves, and their horses.
>
> And like other nations of antiquity, the Druids worshiped the heavenly bodies and also trees, and water and mountains and the signs of the serpent, the bull and the cross.
>
> As far as we can learn, however, the Druids paid honors rather than adoration to their deities, as the Jews revered their archangels and reserved their worship for Jehovah. . . .
>
> The Druids possessed remarkable powers and immunities. Like the Levites, the Hebrews and the Egyptian priests they were ex-

DRUID AND ROMAN

empted from taxes and military service. They also annually elected the magistrates of the cities. They educated all children of whatever station, not permitting their parents to receive them until they were fourteen years of age. Thus the Druids were regarded as the real fathers of the people.

The Persian Magi were entrusted with the education of their sovereign; but in Britain the kings were not only brought up by the Druids but relieved by them of all the odium and ceremonies of sovereignty.

These terrible priests formed the councils of the state, and declared peace or war as they pleased. The poor slave whom they seated on a throne, and whom they permitted to wear robes more gorgeous even than their own, was surrounded not by his noblemen but by Druids. He was a prisoner in his court and his jailors were inexorable, for they were priests.

There was a chief Druid to advise him, a bard to sing to him, a sennechai, or chronicler to register his action in the Greek character, and a physician to attend to his health and to cure or kill him as the state required.

. . . The Druidic precepts were all in verses which amounted to 20,000 in number and which it was forbidden to write. Consequently a long course of preparatory study was required and some spent so much as twenty years in a state of probation.

These verses were in rime, which the Druids invented to assist the memory, and in triplet form from the veneration which was paid to the number three by all the nations of antiquity.

Concerning the weird ceremonials of these strange priests virtually nothing is known. Some of their magic has been preserved to posterity by tradition, but, as is usual in such cases, it is the outlandish fairy tale that has survived rather than an authentic history of customs. Reade cites the case of the "serpent's egg":

THE LAND OF HAUNTED CASTLES

It was supposed to have been formed by a multitude of serpents close entwined together and by the frothy saliva that proceeded from their throats. When it was made it was raised up in the air by their combined hissing, and to render it efficacious it was to be caught in a clean, white cloth before it could fall to the ground—for in Druidism that which touched the ground was polluted. He who performed this ingenious task was obliged to mount a swift horse and to ride away at full speed pursued by the serpents from whom he was not safe until he had crossed a river.

The Druids tested its virtue by encasing it in gold and throwing it into a river. If it swam against the stream it would render its possessor superior to his adversaries in all disputes and obtain for him the friendship of great men. . . .

The eggs were made of some kind of glass or earth glazed over, and are sometimes blue, green or white, and sometimes variegated.

There is a peculiar custom at Vianden. On Easter Sunday it is customary for a courted maiden to give her swain an egg. If it be dyed black he knows without further explanation that his suit is dismissed. No one in Vianden knows where the custom originated, but the egg that rendered a man superior to his adversaries and the egg by which a maiden betokens her freedom of choice seem somehow related. And Vianden was once a center of Druid worship.

The Druids vanished from Luxemburg as other inhabitants of the Ardennes had vanished before them. They succumbed to the superior forces of the Romans in Gaul as they did in Britain. And new conquerors and new deities came to occupy the narrow valleys.

Such traces of prehistoric life as have been excavated

DRUID AND ROMAN

in the Ardennes tend to show that the Luxemburg district, by every characteristic of topography suited to be a buffer between the tribes of the Rhine and the tribes of the Seine, was always an independent unit. It was not always independent in the sense that it was autonomous, but in defeat or victory it preserved its identity.

The Scourge of God with his seven hundred thousand barbarians swept down out of the North, leaving his calling-card in the name of Ettelbruck (Attila's bridge) Hunsdorf, Hunswold, etc.

The Vandals, the Goths, the Franks, and the Visigoths carried the merciless warfare of their times across the country-side, leaving upon the people the indelible impress of oppression and miscegenation.

With the Romans came a new mythology that kept alive the native superstitions even in the process of civilization. That the inhabitants of the country about Lucilinburhuc took kindly to education and the arts is evidenced in the monuments of that era which survived the destructive influences of poverty, the elements, a dozen wars, and the greed of conquerors. Treves a thousand years ago was more populous than it is to-day,—the center of a densely settled community. It is obvious that modern housing and living-conditions alone made such a city possible.

Roman roads, built by Luxembourgeois under the engineers of Cæsar and Julian, are still the principal passage-

THE LAND OF HAUNTED CASTLES

ways across the Ardennes. Traces of Romanesque pottery have been discovered in the ruins of native kilns to the north. The names of Roman goddesses are decipherable on the foundation stones of crumbling altars, the length and breadth of the duchy.

The Romans pass on and the old traditions are preserved and new ones manufactured by a new group of dictators operating a new system of civilization.

The castles and the feudal system may be said to be developments from the same source.

Chaos came with the decaying of the Roman Empire. Although new conquerors arose and flashed briefly across the historical firmament, the control of the rulers over their scattered subjects became looser and looser. Armies were recruited and the law, such as it was, administered through the nobles. And the nobles through centuries of despotic rule found themselves the overlords of petty kingdoms.

They built the castles as fortresses rather than homes and fought hundreds of wars too insignificant to find a place in history but of terrible moment to the Rhine country and the illustrious Ardennes.

Every district had its private king. Every king had his own battle preserves and resented any incursions by his neighbors into the zones where he reserved the right of pillage, murder, and loot.

People gathered naturally under these robber barons

for the protection which they despaired of getting from the vague authority of an emperor or real king. They may not have enjoyed serfdom and its obbligato of hard labor with few comforts, but the system had points of superiority over private enterprise in competition with the numerous destructive forces that made life a burden for one who was prosperous. The serf did n't own the land that he tilled, and his recompense was slight, but usually he got three meals a day; and in rural Luxemburg, which is prosperous if any section of Europe may be called prosperous, he gets but little more out of the free and enlightened life of to-day.

Serfdom is born in the peasant. His love of liberty and intense patriotism may, after all, be merely an atavistic instinct of rebellion,—the urge of the iron-collared slave against the yoke of a feudal master, outcropping in the slave's descendant. Human nature, if we may judge from the evidences of all the epochs that are traceable in Luxemburg's rocky hills, has changed but little in two thousand years. Old ideas remain, old stories are told, and old ghosts walk abroad in the land.

CHAPTER III
GHOSTS

Who They Were and Where They Came From

> The knight's bones are dust, and his good sword rust;
> His soul is with the saints, I trust.—COLERIDGE.

CHAPTER III

GHOSTS

ANY study of history here must necessarily be sketchy,—a brief page or two from a chronology that details in the story of a toy nation the entire progress of the human race, from bloody savagery to cultured modernity. But some of it is necessary. Only in the understanding of the stock from which the castle ghosts are sprung can one appreciate the immortality with which long-accepted tradition has endowed them.

Ghostly itself is the history of Luxemburg,—ghostly and ghastly,—with a past peopled by strange races first cousins to the characters of the piquant myths that are their sole bequest to the unimaginative present, with a modern existence unalterably linked with the destinies of the world.

Luxemburg at present comprises 998 square miles of territory and about a quarter of a million inhabitants. At the time of its greatest glory it was but little larger. But for centuries it has been the axis about which the affairs of Europe have turned. It has been as definite an influence in the life of Americans as was Plymouth Rock. For America sprang from Europe and the threads of fate

THE LAND OF HAUNTED CASTLES

that governed the formation of European racial stock were spun in the Ardennes.

> For thirteen hundred years before Rome was built, stood Treves; may it stand in peace forever.

Thus read an inscription in Latin upon a house in the ancient city of emperors. If it may be accepted at face-value, it is an indication that in this region Rome built her civilization upon the foundations of a civilization that had gone before. Treves remains to-day, despite the zeal of German archæologists who have obilterated its romantic connections with the mysterious past, a bit of Italy hundreds of miles and dozens of centuries out of place.

Here as ever comes legend.

It is said that the city was founded by Trebeta, stepson of Semiramis, Queen of Assyria. But the native imagination, which does not hesitate to describe the color of Satan's cloak or give a name to any lost soul that moans among the crumbling rocks of a castle ruin, is silent when called upon to tell more of this story of how Treves came to exist.

Whether Trebeta brought with him sufficient Assyrians to found a colony or merely impressed upon the nomads of the vicinity the force of his leadership, is as unexplainable as his coming itself. The tribe that inhabited the lands adjacent to Treves was known as the Treviri, but it would be difficult to say whether the tribe was named after the city or the city after the tribe.

LUXEMBURG CITY

Approach to the Great Rock where Siegfroid and the Fairy Melusine built their stronghold

GHOSTS

That is something for the historian to worry about; and he will have his share of worry, for there are no written records to lend him aid. Not until Julius Cæsar of facile pen and ready strategy came into the land with the eagles of Rome does the actual story of Luxemburg and its environs emerge from its slim chapters of conjecture into the more enduring passages of a great egotist's military notebook.

"Omnia Gallia divisa est in partes tres."

So begin the commentaries. So begins the history of the haunted castles and the men who made them.

Cæsar's mention of the bravery of some of the Gallic tribes, particularly of the Belgæ, whose habitat was northern Luxemburg and Brabant, indicates that the melting-pot had been in potent operation some generations before he tested its product with battle-ax and lance. The warlike Teuton already had left the imprint of his prowess upon the Celts, stirring them from their laziness, bequeathing to them his stamina and his will. The Gauls of Cæsar's day were tribes of fighting-men whose accomplishments upon the battle-field are better judged by the Romans' pains to subdue them than by the half-praises grudgingly given them in the commentaries.

The proprietorship of the illustrious Luxemburg was divided, at the time of Cæsar's coming, between the Treviri on the south and east and the Eburones on the north and west. The line dividing their domains is clearly

THE LAND OF HAUNTED CASTLES

defined, geographically and ethnologically. It traverses the table-land between the Alzette and Sure rivers and is dotted along its entire length with villages, the names of which end in "scheid," which signifies a divide or a parting.

For all that they were sprung from the same stock, the Treviri and the Eburones did not get along too well together. The Eburones were a Gallic tribe and made no bones about it. The Treviri were intensely proud of their Teuton ancestry and refused to be classed with the Celts, who were their cousins. Cæsar, looking upon them with an eye unbiased by any ancestral pride, classifies them as Gauls.

The wily Cæsar was quick to recognize the advantages that might come to him through the attitude of the Treviri toward their neighbors.

After the death of Indutiomar, his implacable enemy, he declared the Treviri to be a free people. The extent of their "freedom" was problematical. For there were always sufficient legions in Gaul to maintain a proper respect for the Roman eagles should occasion arise. But the compliment was accepted at face-value by the Treviri. Although their leaders had been divided in the debate over whether it might not be better to fight the Romans than aid them, and though many a young man of the Trevirians had lost his life in maintaining one side or another of that unsettled issue, the declaration of freedom was followed by a prompt and unanimous alliance with Rome. If credulity was, as has been said, one of the outstanding characteristics of the ancient Celts, this Roman alliance alone would seem to place the brand of Gaul upon the Treviri.

They paid Cæsar for the compliment he had bestowed upon them. They fought for him in his invasion. They arrayed themselves against Pompey at Pharsalia. They became an integral factor in the Roman military establishment.

And this brought them a new reward. They were admitted to Roman citizenship, with new rights to bear arms for Rome. They functioned ornamentally as well as usefully in the Prætorian Guard and even sent a few of their number to the senate. Treves became a Roman colony and the Ardennes region, the forest Arduenna of Cæsar's commentaries, became a sort of distant suburb of Rome.

The products of Belgica—notably the smoked pork of the Ardennes—became famous in Rome. The vineyards of the Moselle entered into successful competition with those upon the slopes of Italy. Ardenne, the conquered. was preparing to undo its conquerors by supplying them with luxuries.

Then Cæsar fell at the base of Pompey's pillar.

Augustus, who did not understand the Belgæ,—or, if he did, rated them too low to warrant consideration,—

THE LAND OF HAUNTED CASTLES

steadily decreased their privileges and drove them into revolt. They were crushed. And more liberties disappeared in the crushing.

There came Claudius Civilis and the Batavian revolt. The Bructerian witch, a necromancer of great power and deep divination, is said to have caused the uprising. Dead Gauls counseled the ferocious thrust against the Roman yoke and after that there were more dead Gauls to bear them company.

The Romans stayed on and what privileges the Belgæ received were those that the Romans chose to give them.

The foundations of Luxemburg were receiving a firm grounding in the ashes of defeat. The Gallo-Teuton races of the district were being purified with a new reagent, fortitude. Love of country had a real meaning for them, for it is notable among peoples of a Celtic strain that oppression solidifies them. Civilization, acquired unconsciously from their conquerors, was fitting them for a rôle in the world's affairs.

From the second to the fourth century Rome, with no new worlds to conquer, turned its attention to the betterment of the peoples already under its control. Treves at this time came to the height of its glory,—a place remarkable for its museum, its baths, its amphitheater, the palace of Constantine, and the Porta Nigra. Military roads were constructed between the numerous fortresses and camps built by the Romans at the high tide of their invasion. One ran from Treves to Rheims, past the great rock that was to furnish the site of Luxemburg city. Arlon, Namur, Cologne, and Metz were linked with broad highways, the same roads that carried the bulk of the German advance against France nearly two thousand years later.

Vast stores of Roman relics—accoutrements, household utensils, temple requisites, and coins—found their way into rubbish-piles, one day to be excavated and counted as treasure-troves. One realizes that the big copper medallions of the period might have been difficult to carry about. At any rate, the soldiers apparently attached little value to them, for they have been found in quantities wherever there are traces of military encampments. Hundreds of them have been unearthed in the moat about the ruins at Pettingen, leading archæologists of the grand duchy to believe that these walls are among the oldest in the neighborhood.

The Roman legions themselves revolted in 263 and the Ardennes woods were full of petty imperators. Chrokus came with a band of Suevi, Franks, and Alemanni, setting a style in murder, rapine, and pillage that was little improved upon by the sundry and divers barbaric chieftains who followed the Romans. Aside from this incursion, which resulted in the taking off of whole villages, the century closed without incident.

The amphitheater at Treves was put to use by Constantine, it is reported, in the red execution of several thou-

THE LAND OF HAUNTED CASTLES

sand Frankish prisoners. But they were Franks and did n't count. The star of Rome was setting in a crimson sea.

The French nation got a foothold upon the continent of Europe in 419 through combinations of Frankish tribes that forced recognition from the tottering empire.

Some thirty years later Asia the great and mysterious let loose a terrible plague, the Hun,—half a million of him,—the original militarist, pushing European civilization toward the Atlantic with fire-brand and scimitar. At Chalons, fated spot, he was driven back. The retreat of this bloody savage was almost as efficient in the creation of chaos as the work of the men-at-arms of cultured European nations that only a few years ago marched into Flanders in his age-old tracks.

A few years later the Empire of the West came to the end that had been in sight for a century. The Germanic tribes of the Northeast moved, sometimes like a sluggish stream, sometimes like a hurricane-driven flood, across Luxemburg, toward the Meuse. The peoples of the West swung back against them.

The Franks of Brabant spread out unopposed, embracing the Meuse, the Scheldt, and lower Germany. Luxemburg, incorporated as part of the Province of Austrasia under the Merovingian dynasty, became a dim entity for the first time in written history and was ruled by a count, whose authority appears to have been problematical.

GHOSTS

Yet the Franks occupied no great place in the scheme of the world's development. They were brilliant fighting-men for their times, brave and intelligent. But they lacked internal unity and leadership. They percolated, rather than conquered, the territory that Julius Cæsar wrested from the Gauls by bloody strategy. How far they might have gone had the Germanic tribes not been engaged in their own business at the time, can only be guessed. Before real opposition had developed against them there arose Clovis, one of the greatest plunderers of all time.

In his own bailiwick he had reduced the ancient and honorable profession of assassination to an exact science. As a youth he succeeded to the leadership of the Salian tribe in Batavia and displayed a talent for intrigue, politics, and war that could not but be recognized. His first notable act was the coalition of his own forces with those of his neighbor and relative Ragnacaire for a campaign against the Roman Patrician Syagrius, who ruled at Soissons.

Syagrius fled for protection to Alaric, King of the Visigoths, but Clovis was nothing if not persistent. He astonished even his own followers by threatening to drive down through what is now France and take the Roman by force of arms,—a large order for the captain of a nondescript troop of half-trained axmen. But Alaric, peaceable when he saw nothing to be gained by war, turned over his guest to the gentle Clovis, who promptly executed him.

There is a legend still current in Luxemburg, where Clovis is looked upon as one of the chief factors in the determination of the duchy's racial individuality, that the Bishop of Rheims, St. Remi, was indirectly responsible for the quick growth of his power.

In the looting of Syagrius's domain a vase of great size and beauty was taken by the Franks from the church at Rheims. St. Remi, who had been on good terms with the young king, requested that this portion of the plunder at least be restored. When the division of the spoils was begun at Soissons, Clovis claimed the vase, "over and above the share apportioned to him by lot." All his followers agreed except a surly lieutenant, who had coveted the vase himself. He promptly struck the vase with his battle-ax, shouting: "Thou shalt have naught but what is given thee by the lots."

Clovis took the insult with a forbearance remarkable even in one so good-humored. Some months later he held an inspection. When he came to the warrior who had smashed the vase he commented impartially upon the condition of his lance and battle-ax, observing that in all his years as a military leader he had never seen any equipment quite so foul and unfit for service.

He jerked the man's ax from his grasp and threw it on

GHOSTS

the ground. As the warrior stooped to recover it, Clovis raised his own ax and split his skull.

"This is for the Soissons vase," he observed. After that implicit discipline was one of the characteristics of his army.

Clovis afterward became a Christian and was baptized at Rheims, but he does not seem to have allowed his Christianity to interfere with his other business. Other Frankish tribes joined his standard and he carried out his threat to push down through Gaul. He defeated Alaric and was halted in his attempt to dominate the whole of Europe only through the intervention of Theodoric the Great of Italy.

He left to the Merovingians, his successors, all Gaul, from western France to the Rhine, and a number of the Alps provinces.

The Franks, however, experienced the fate of the various hordes that have conquered China. They were absorbed. Their Germanic language could not supersede the Latin that was Europe's heritage from the Roman dynasty. Little by little was evolved that softened, simplified Latin, the *Lingua Franca*, whence in the ninth century came French as we know it now.

But about Treves, and in the Moselle region generally, tongues and tonsils were more suited to the Teuton idiom that Roman teaching never quite succeeded in displacing. Germanic names and Germanic root-words remain to-

THE LAND OF HAUNTED CASTLES

day as they were when the Teuton tribes first put their impress upon the country.

The Franks were primarily fighters. Their arts were military. Their epics they carved out of nations with sword and battle-ax. The nomadic impulses of their Asiatic forebears were in their blood and the open country was their home.

The traces of the Merovingians in Luxemburg are principally graves. Nominally, at least, the Franks were a Christian people and they gave their dead a Christian burial not unmixed with the pious practices of an instinctive paganism.

Their departed brothers in arms were laid in vaults in coffins of wood or stone. The rows of graves in their cemeteries ran north and south and the dead were placed in them with their feet to the east. This custom was Christian or Druidic, depending upon the motive which prompted it. Combined with the orientation of the dead was a ceremonial founded upon a pagan belief that the life to come would be merely a recurrence of the present, —a place or state of warfare, pillage, love, and feasting on a sublimated scale. So the dear departed Frank went to his last resting-place with a complete equipment.

This necessitated the building of large coffins. Even in the largest of the stone boxes, the corpse was cramped by the drinking-horns, armor, shields, lances, and what not piled in beside it. With such mortuary relics Luxemburg is strewn from end to end. The duchy in parts is underlaid with a sort of giant's tiling of stone caskets.

Frankish inability to digest what it had devoured resulted in due time in the division of Europe into Austrasia, or Austria, whence developed Germany, and Neustria, the cocoon of modern France. There were numerous dissensions and reunions on the part of the Merovingian rulers, but it was not until the latter part of the eighth century that the great Frankish empire once more became a tangible unit. This time the coördination was effected by Austrasian princes. They sent their "mayors of the palace" to Soissons as their personal representatives. The mayors of the palace in time furnished royal stock for new empire.

There were many such princely agents chosen from the Moselle district. One may be mentioned, Pepin of Heristal.

Pepin remembered the place of his origin. In his work for the revival of the old Frankish nationalism and the Christianizing of the pagan tribes beyond the Rhine, he found time to bestow favor upon the region from which he had sprung. There he built his hunting-lodges and magnificent country seats and opened an era of prosperity for the Luxemburg region that continued during the reigns of Charles Martel and the great Charlemagne.

Christianity had been readily accepted in the Pagus Mosellanus when the cross of Constantine replaced the eagle as the standard of Rome. The peculiar blending of Teuton and Celt had developed a race by instinct adaptable to Christian tenet,—homely folk, simple and conscientious. The gods of Rome, that tribe of deified passions and impassioned deities, were received as an improvement upon Druidism; and so they were, as voodooism might be said to be an improvement upon the worship of Moloch. But their woeful ineffectiveness was realized as much by the new converts as by the Roman legionaries who had ceased to respect them. Treves and its neighbors were awaiting Christianity.

St. Helena lived for a time at Treves. It was in her honor that the great amphitheater was reddened with the massacre of the pagan Franks. The great Constantine, her son, made the city his second capital and took all the Christians of the vicinity under his imperial protection.

When the Franks succeeded Rome, albeit their own Christianity was nominal,—a faith of convenience rather than ultimate salvation,—they did not allow their apathy to hinder the work begun under the Romans. St. Eucherius, first Bishop of Treves, received his appointment to the see at the hands of St. Peter. He was followed by St. Agritus and St. Maximin, whose missions flourished.

The temples of Diana and Venus that had sprung up in the groves where the Druids conducted their sacred abattoirs were converted into churches. The simplicity with

GHOSTS

which wooden panels adapted the altars of the pagan goddesses to Christian uses and crude images of the saints displaced the lares and penates in the newly civilized households is typical of the manner in which the two religions merged.

In the scattered villages of the Ardennes paganism retained its followers, just as the sacrificial fires in the Druid forests continued to glow long after Julius Cæsar —two-fisted theologian that he was—had brought his arguments of iron and brass to advance the cause of Zeus against the priests of Baal or his local representative.

And pagan practices never died entirely. Some of them have received a Christian significance. Some of them are looked upon as harmless superstitions, but in many localities in the duchy a reincarnated Phœnician might find himself at home in the ceremonial of a Christian festival day and a Druid might view the honoring of a patron saint and whet his knife to take part in it.

When Pepin died he left two widows, but one of them, whose title was not recognized by the church, had small part in shaping the destinies of the community in which she wore her mourning.

The other, Plectrude, gave royal favor to a monastery at Echternach, religious capital of Luxemburg, and built better than had her intelligent husband. The Echternach abbey for thirteen hundred years carried the torch of civilization in the Moselle region. It taught the

THE LAND OF HAUNTED CASTLES

people mutual dependence, a grace they sorely needed; the amenities of a social existence, which they lacked no less; and the best methods of agriculture, which assured them of a lasting livelihood.

The Anglo-Saxon St. Willibrord and his contemporary St. Hubert divided the Ardennes, north and south, between them and carried on a zealous work, humanizing as well as Christianizing, patiently laboring in a difficult vineyard.

Across the Rhine, results were not so simple. The Saxons, serene in their paganism, did not take kindly to missionaries. Charlemagne, witnessing the futility of linguistic argument, tried new tactics. He hanged forty-five hundred of them as proof of the error of their ways. But the Saxons were an ignorant people. They stubbornly refused to see the connection between this hangman's field-day and the truth of the Gospel. Instead of embracing the cross they retired to their hidden altars and offered sacrifices to their heathen gods, with an ungenerous prayer for the prompt removal of Charlemagne. Naturally incensed, the great emperor decided to make them their own missionaries.

He assembled ten thousand of the more active recalcitrants and scattered them through the Moselle provinces for the benefit of example, better climate, and social intercourse with their intellectual superiors.

The plan seems to have worked out all right and Lux-

GHOSTS

emburg received a new leaven. Sassenheim, Sassel, and Sasselbach are names on the map of the grand duchy that recall their visit. The "English" words that run through the native vocabulary are their gift to the people with whom they were thrown into unwilling contact.

The Normans, who paid a naval visit to the duchy, sailing up the Rhine and Moselle in their shallow-draft boats, added their bit to the great melting-pot. They conquered all who opposed them between Coblenz and Metz, and retired a few months later. But for all the brevity of their visit, their traits have come down to the posterity of the fair Austrasian women whom they found there.

Early in the eighth century had come Charles Martel the Hammer, fresh from his victory over the Saracens on the Loire,—a bit crude as a Christian, despite his fame as the savior of Europe. He fell ill at Treves. The monks, who were the only physicians of their period, undertook to cure him, and to that end laid his pain-racked body on St. Maximin's tomb. The Hammer recovered, and in gratitude willed four of his Austrasian districts to the convent.

Here comes the first approach of Luxemburg to nationality, for one of the districts, Wismaris Ecclesia, known locally as Weimerskirch, bounded a ruined fort atop a great rock in the valley of the Alizontia (Alzette). Lucilinburhuc it was called,—a name coined by the thick-

THE LAND OF HAUNTED CASTLES

tongued Franks from their *Latin culinæ* and German idiom. The title meant "Little Outpost."

The poly-racial humanity of Europe then set about demonstrating that Charlemagne had lived too long before his time. His empire proved to be a great engine that his incompetent successors could neither understand nor manage. The magnificent unity that he had welded was divided up into small parcels, one of which was named Lotharingia, or Lorraine, after its ruler, Lothaire II. A succession of half-witted kings left to history nothing but a list of comical names and presently there came a revolt in Lotharingia and the district passed under the domination of the East Franks, or Saxons.

The administration of the affairs of Lorraine, such as it was, was taken up by the dukes of Lorraine, whose power sprang from appointment by the German Emperor. About 930 A. D. lived Count Wiric or Ricvin, whose name, spelled either way, meant "rich in wine." He was the father of Siegfroid, and Siegfroid was the father of Luxemburg.

CHAPTER IV
THE FAIRY MELUSINE

Peeping Siegfroid and the Mermaid Godiva

> Fairy elves
> Whose midnight revels by a forest side
> Or fountain some belated peasant sees,
> Or dreams he sees, while overhead the moon
> Sits arbitress.
> —Milton.

CHAPTER IV

THE FAIRY MÉLUSINE

SIEGFROID was a quiet builder. Most of the world of his own time never heard of him or of the noble house of Ardenne, of which he was the chief. Succeeding ages knew of him only as one lofty ambition after another tripped over the stumbling-block he had left for them. Compact histories of the Christian era pass him by without a word, and for that matter so do some of the more voluminous. But Siegfroid, "unwept, unhonored, and unsung," sat amid his own little rocks and hammered out a future for Europe. The Druid priests of his skin-clad forefathers in the weirdest of their divinations could not have foretold the distance that Siegfroid's long arm would stretch forward into the centuries.

Directly, his influence ended with the war of 1870. Indirectly, it is still abroad over the shell craters of the Meuse Valley and the alien bayonets at the Rhine bridgeheads, and no one can guess where it will end.

Siegfroid was the first prince of a long and illustrious line. Of his blood were Cunegunde, saint and empress; Ermesinde, Countess of Luxemburg, patroness of religion, and administrative genius; Henry VII, Emperor of Germany; John the Blind of Bohemia, a kingly knight errant, at once the most picturesque, the most heroic, and

THE LAND OF HAUNTED CASTLES

the most pathetic figure of his time; Charles IV, head of the Holy Roman Empire; Sigismund, another emperor; and William the Silent, founder of the Dutch Republic. As the progenitor of this great dynasty alone he would have merited an immortal memory.

But Siegfroid made one other contribution to the world's affairs.

From Wiric he inherited a number of isolated properties of small individual importance. They were as much of a domain as a number of building-lots are a city. Siegfroid might have remained Count of Ardenne as his father before him had been, complacently accepting the world's goods amid unprotected holdings that presently would fall into the hands of some barbarian invader. But never would he have been much more than a rich country gentleman, loved or hated in his own county and unknown save to the peasants of his own lands. The young count, however, had ambitions.

He decided that only in the union of his territory could he hope to make himself a power and he speedily set about the task of coördination. In the center of his lands, on the road from Arlon to Treves, was a barren spot that appealed to his latent military instincts as an excellent place for an administrative capital. It was part of a tract deeded to the Abbey of St. Maximin at Treves by Charles Martel more than two hundred years before. Siegfroid was the owner of more desirable lands near

LUXEMBURG CITY

The Grand Ducal Palace. A relic of the Spanish Occupation

THE FAIRY MELUSINE

Feulen and these he traded for the part of the Weimerkirch territory needed as the keystone in his ducal edifice in 963 A. D.

From that purchase dates the history of Luxemburg as a distinct and autonomous nation.

Luxemburg was built about the great rock that juts into the valley of the Alzette,—the mighty Bock. Had there been no Bock there would have been no intense rivalry for its possession as a fortress, other strategic points would have taken up the attention of the free-fighting combatants, and the twentieth century would have seen other boundary arrangements upon the maps of Europe.

But the rock was there. Centuries before Christ it had become an important fort on the road from Rheims to Treves,—a commanding position that might well control any attack sweeping from the Rhineland toward the Meuse or from Holland toward the valley of the Moselle. Lucilinburhuc ("little fortress"), the prehistoric Celts had named it. The Romans conceded the title apt. They added a few decorations of their own to the great rock, strengthened it at the points where nature had not provided made-to-order moats and enceintes, and settled down to hold it during the five hundred years of their occupation.

It was old Herr Fischbach who told me the interesting chronicle of the Bock's later history.

THE LAND OF HAUNTED CASTLES

As related by Vauban—the engineer of fortifications who, under Louis XIV, made the natural rock the strongest inland military post in all the world—the story is the intriguing narrative of the development of a mass of rock upon which the peace of Europe was wrecked time after time during a thousand years. It needs no embellishment to stand forth as one of the most remarkable tales that have come up from an age of glittering romance.

As related by Herr Fischbach it becomes what such history would naturally be among a people of Gallic ancestry,—a whimsical recital of epic legend, a fairy tale comprising all the elements of the enchanted castle, the test of love, and the sleeping beauty. The narrator did not believe the tale himself, but he might have had difficulty in explaining why he doubted it. The inborn respect for tradition that he had acquired in his mother's arms was in his voice as he stood looking down upon the plain of Clausen, where once the splendid turrets of the Château Mansfeld, home of a Spanish intruder, who governed the district for Philip II, reared themselves under the protecting eyes of Siegfroid's Gibraltar.

"As you see, Monsieur, this was a wonderful city," he told me. "It has been so within my memory. As a small boy I watched the engineers tearing down the ramparts. I cheered when the Prussian garrison departed, and I

THE FAIRY MELUSINE

trembled with the rest of Luxemburg when they came back two years later to conquer France.

"They say, Monsieur, that Siegfroid could not have built his fort without supernatural help and many legends have sprung from his work. Some say that he sold his soul to the devil and then redeemed himself, but that is not a pretty story.

"If I were to believe any of the tales, I should choose that of Mélusine, the good fairy now locked up in the depths of the great rock, who holds the destiny of the city in her hands. "They say that Siegfroid met Mélusine when he first began to build his castle upon the ruins that the Romans had left. She was beautiful and he was young. He was brave and strong and she was more than half mortal. They fell in love.

"But she foresaw the danger that lay in marriage with a being of flesh and blood and tried to avoid him. That shows, Monsieur, that even a fairy cannot be omniscient, for repulses are no barrier to a strong man's love. He importuned. She listened to her heart. She consented to marry him upon condition that she might spend every Saturday in the privacy of her own room and that he would not intrude upon her nor ask her questions.

"Siegfroid agreed to the conditions. He would have agreed to anything to hasten their nuptials. And so they were married, the fairy and the mortal chieftain, with all the blessings of the church.

THE LAND OF HAUNTED CASTLES

"The next morning, when Siegfroid stepped forth from his modest house in the valley of the Alzette to look at the progress of his work upon the great Bock, he discovered to his wonderment that the rock had brought forth fruit. A great château, strongly and beautifully fashioned, crowned the summit. It was Mélusine's wedding-gift to her husband.

"Siegfroid did not question the miracle, for that was the age when such wonders were not uncommon. They became very happy, Monsieur, so happy that Mélusine forgot the danger that lay ahead of them. They had several fine children, all of them perfectly natural mortals with no trace of their semi-preternatural ancestry. And Mélusine was a good mother to them, except that she left them every Saturday in the care of her ladies in waiting while she retired to her own suite.

"There is no mention of how long this went on. It probably was a long time, for we know that Siegfroid's family was large. But one day he became suspicious. It is the way of men—and women, too. They are inquisitive. Siegfroid, after all, was merely a descendant of Mother Eve.

"That fatal Saturday he went to her apartments. Her bedroom was empty. So was that of her personal attendant. Siegfroid went on to the end of the wing, where Mélusine had built for herself a Roman bath fed by a natural spring. The door of this room was partially open

THE FAIRY MELUSINE

and Siegfroid, forgetting the promise that he had given in all honor, looked in.

"Horrible sight! There in the crystal waters of the bath sported Mélusine. Her thick golden hair fell in shimmering masses over her ivory shoulders. But her beautiful body, so wonderfully proportioned, had changed. Her legs, which tradition says were the most delicately molded limbs that ever carried a goddess sculptured in the flesh, were gone. In their place writhed the horrible tail of a mermaid. The soft, pink skin of Mélusine had been replaced by the green scales of a fish.

"In spite of himself Siegfroid cried out.

"Well, that was the end of it, Monsieur. The nymph cast one look of anguish toward the door. Then with a clap of thunder her bath sank into the earth, carrying her along with it. The dazed and horror-stricken count stood gazing through an open doorway upon the surface of the rock, as barren as it had been on the day when he espoused the beautiful Mélusine. It is said that he nearly died of grief. But grief does not bring back those whom we love, nor repair the damage wrought by our folly. He never saw Mélusine again.

"They say that she is still in the rock, a prisoner of evil enchantments, a victim of powers that resented her Christian marriage.

THE LAND OF HAUNTED CASTLES

"Every seven years she comes back, sometimes as a beautiful woman, sometimes in the form of a serpent, in either event holding in her mouth a small golden key.

"Whoever has the courage to take the key from between her teeth will find a marvelous creature in his embrace, Monsieur. For Mélusine will be free.

"Between her visits to the scene of her disastrous mortal love, Mélusine works upon a chemise of linen, taking one stitch every seven years. Not a rapid work, you will say, but it is important. If the chemise is finished before she is rescued from the rock, the earth will open and the Bock, the fortress, and the city of Luxemburg will be swallowed up. A single thunder-clap will mark their passing.

"A strange story, Monsieur. But I suppose there is some truth in it. There is some truth in everything."

To my notion the old man's summary of the situation was as accurate as it was concise: There is some truth in everything. Admitting that, one can understand the grand duchy and the beautiful faith of its people.

It might puzzle some how the mermaid came to wander so far afield and how, unless she were a very shallow-draft mermaid,—she managed to keep her fins moist in the rocky hills. But dozens of legends have it that she did. She came several hundred kilometers with the salt of the sea glistening in her green-gold tresses. Of course

THE FAIRY MELUSINE

she must have; otherwise, how could Siegfroid have found her there in the valley of the Alzette?

But, although Mélusine will ever be a principal character in Luxemburg city folk-lore, other legends attribute the rise of Siegfroid to influences entirely outside the sphere of his sea-going wife.

It is said—with bated breath and fearsome glance, but still convincingly—that Siegfroid rented his soul to the devil for aid in building the château and its rocky cinctures.

Thirty years was the term of the lease, to be followed by a permanent transfer subject to such terms as might be worked out at that time. The medieval Satan may have been totally evil, but it must be confessed that he was lacking in brains, for all his hundreds of years of acquaintance with the human race and its failings.

As soon as Siegfroid had completed the manufacture of the fortress that was to prove the curse of his country and the nations adjoining, he set about to make the best of the "joker" clauses in the contract. He promptly turned his attention to the religious pursuits that he had ignored in the signing of his base compact. He surrounded himself with pious companions, endowed monasteries and convents, including Echternach and Princess Irmene's hospital, and became studiously pious. He conducted a little private reformation in his own domains, ousting a number of lay brethren at the Echter-

THE LAND OF HAUNTED CASTLES

nach abbey who had leanings toward ecclesiastical revenue rather than priestly sacrifice, and replacing them with Benedictine monks who restored to the abbey the standard of morality that had distinguished its founders.

What the holder of the lease was doing all this time can hardly be imagined. He appeared, however, on the day appointed, while Siegfroid stood conversing with a holy monk of Treves, whose abbey he represented as advocate. The evil one struck at Siegfroid's unprotected neck, but the monk interposed his crucifix. At that same instant a puff of smoke arose from the top of the count's head and traveled in a widening ring through the open window and up into the cloudless sky. This was taken to indicate that the landlord of Siegfroid's soul had been a bit too late with his eviction proceedings and that the tenant had escaped replevin via a sort of injunction.

The devil, who must have felt a good deal of an ass to have been so completely taken in, promptly disappeared and did not come back until decades afterward, when he compromised on the loss of the count by taking a sort of small-change payment in the person of Henry the Damned.

Whatever the supernatural relationships of Siegfroid, it is certain that he left a tangible imprint of his personality upon the ages.

Lucilinburhuc, the ruined Roman outpost, became a burg, or fortified city. Conscripts from his adjoining lands

LUXEMBURG CITY
Detail of the old fortifications

THE FAIRY MELUSINE

were brought in to throw a heavy wall about the great château, a wall protected in turn by an artificial fosse isolating the great Bock from the plateau behind it. Caravans passing along the ancient road from Treves to Rheims took note of this growing stronghold and advertised its fame. Peasantry came to look and stayed to work. They discovered that Siegfroid as a leader was something of an improvement upon the robber barons of the period. They swore allegiance to him, placed themselves under his protection, and unloaded their lentil bowls and maces in the valley of the Alzette and in the gorge of its tributary the Petrusse.

So was formed the nucleus of a kingdom, much as other kingdoms were forming elsewhere through necessity of the world's changing policies and politics.

A wooden bridge was thrown across the chasm, seven square towers set in the outer wall to guard the city, and the burg that succeeded Lucilinburhuc was called by the name's equivalent in the current idiom, Lutzelbourg. Time and the varying fortunes of the language changed Lutzelbourg to Luxembourg or Luxemburg.

The interesting Siegfroid had other adventures beside his marital fiasco and soul-marketing experience. He fought a little war with King Lothair of France, who cast jealous eyes upon the seven-towered fortress of Lutzelbourg, and was captured. He was taken to a stronghold on the Marne and locked up in a rocky dungeon,—a fitting punishment, one would think, in view of the fact that his broken word had condemned the beautiful Mélusine to a similar fate.

Mélusine, however, did not desert him. Though she could not help herself, she had acquired an expert knowledge of prisons during her stay in the depths of the Bock and she communicated some of her useful information to her captive spouse. One day his jailer appeared with the daily ration of bread and water to find the dungeon empty and the brave Count Siegfroid miraculously flown. It was very disconcerting to Lothair of France, and likewise to the jailer, who lost his head as a consequence.

Siegfroid returned to the County of Lutzelbourg in 985 and lived there for thirteen years, a benefactor of the church and the clever organizer of a country. His accomplishments were worthy of a descendant of Charlemagne, for he lived to see the barons of the Alzette, Sure and Our united under his direction, and the spreading of the name Lutzelbourg over the domains of a dozen fortified cities.

He was survived by five sons and four daughters. The eldest daughter was Cunegunde, sainted empress, the wife of Henry II of Germany. The dynasty which he founded continued until the middle of the fifteenth century, when the House of Burgundy superseded it.

The early descendants of Siegfroid were a peculiar lot, who contributed much to the excitement of living in their

THE FAIRY MELUSINE

vicinity but little to the improvement of their own condition or that of their vassals.

Arthur Herchen in his "Manuel d' Histoire Nationale" says of them: "They were for the most part men of a fierce disposition, covetous of fame, booty, and occasionally vengeance. Also their wars were frequent, above all with the City of Treves. The history of their reigns is monotonous and fatiguing and not worth a detailed study."

To one who is interested in the steps that mark the development of the Luxembourgeois from savagery to their present-day estate, however, their careers have a certain significance. They represented a development of character. Children they were, just emerging from a nursery to a monarchic power that they had not been taught to use, creatures of whims and passions, swordsmen and benefactors, killers and saviors, robbers and crusaders. They were self-satisfied, vainglorious, pompous, kind, chivalrous, or cruel as the spirit moved them. Withal they were heroic and a bit comical.

Of seven of these counts, history makes detailed mention of only two. Giselbert (1047–59) found himself cramped in the quarters constructed by the illustrious Siegfroid. He directed the building of a new wall to take in ten times as much territory as Siegfroid had found necessary for the original city. It was guarded by twelve towers and pierced by six sally-ports. Conrad I,

THE LAND OF HAUNTED CASTLES

Giselbert's successor, made a name for himself through the establishment of the Abbey of Altmunster, a Benedictine institution which for three centuries exercised a monopoly over education in the eastern portion of the county.

Despite the quarrels of the seven, Luxemburg grew and was fairly prosperous. Every school-boy in the duchy knows why: Mélusine, whose blood flowed through their veins, was watching over them, preventing the extermination which ofttimes threatened them in the hope that some day they would bring about her rescue.

Poor Mélusine! She is still watching and still hoping.

CHAPTER V
TIME'S FOOTPRINTS

A Love Eternal

None shall part us
  From each other,
One in life and love are we.
—W. S. Gilbert

CHAPTER V

TIME'S FOOTPRINTS

SO a thousand years have passed and feudalism is sounding its lordly trumpets before the portcullis of Luxemburg. The illustrious and storied country has advanced that incalculable step which lies between an existence purely geographical and true nationality.

From Julius Cæsar to Siegfroid and the fairy Mélusine, Time has trodden a queer pathway. The sands from his hour-glass have spilled upon a road paved dim centuries ago by the flamens of the Druids and the sacrificial altarstones of the cult of Wotan. The shadows of successive springs have fallen across the sculptured shrines of Roman goddesses, the stone coffins of the Franks, the flagged courtyards of robbers' roosts, the modest chancels of Christian chapels, the ash-strewn trails of destructive invaders, the happy streets of villages built by empire, the wreckage of desolation.

Along that road to the dawn of the world are countless landmarks. About the landmarks cling scores of romances that have found no favor with the makers of books.

One knows something of the habits of the early Celts,

THE LAND OF HAUNTED CASTLES

of whom no contemporaneous word has been written, through the implements and monuments that they left behind in dying. The grim mysteries of the Druids are made real through the crop of strange rocks, planted in fire and irrigated with blood, still hidden in all their terrible secretiveness in shadowed groves and silent marshes.

Had Cæsar never written his one-sided commentaries, the magnificence of the empire that he helped so much to build would be realized from the burial hillocks along the magnificent highways constructed for his armies.

"Treat legend kindly," observes Guizot in his History of France. He quotes the opinion of Monsieur Fauriel of the Academy of Inscriptions concerning historical fables: "Whatever may be their authorship the fables in question are historic in the sense that they relate to real facts of which they are a poetical expression, a romantic development, conceived with the idea of popularizing kings with their Gallo-Roman subjects." And he disagrees with this paraphrase of the adage "Where there is smoke there is fire"; "It cannot be admitted that this is a sufficient and truthlike explanation of these tales. They have a graver origin and contain more truth than would be supposed from some of the anecdotes and sayings mixed up with them."

Guizot speaks concerning a fanciful tale regarding the marriage of Clovis with Clotilde, niece of Gondebaud, King of the Bergundians. But what he has said of one

LUXEMBURG CITY
At the foot of the Bock

anecdote is applicable to all. Few myths, from the Haida Indian stories of Raven, which are preposterous, to the Homeric epics, which sound almost plausible, are manufactured out of whole cloth.

Episodes of the Roman occupation still make fireside conversation in some quarters of Luxemburg among people who could not tell you Cæsar's first name. They have remained green in the memory while dates and places have grown hazy.

Children still are frightened in the Bouillon district —once part and parcel of Luxemburg—with threats of the Black Woman who has been roaming the Ardennes since long before the stanchest oak was yet an unsprouted acorn.

Details of her appearance are not lacking. She is nude, black, wild, a terrible sprite with matted hair who practises strange rites about a fire in the rocks. And these details give clew to her identity.

To-day she is a myth, a children's bogey. Forgotten ages ago, when she had her beginning she was probably a Druid priestess, lingering after her time, practising her strange cult for the secret edification of backwoodsmen who refused to be proselytized by the gods of Rome. She was seen by some pious villager who knew nothing of her connections, and her spirit has lived in the vestal fires of tradition through centuries which her power of divination could not have penetrated.

THE LAND OF HAUNTED CASTLES

History, penned by the Romans in the bitterness of personal experience, tells us that the Swabians came out of the Black Forest,—a hundred thousand blond reincarnations of the great Hercules, destroyers relentless and terrible. The legions of Rome itself were powerless to stop them as they put the Rhineland on the pyre, a sacrifice to the great god Wotan. The Swabians were driven back to the Rhine, eventually, for they were a raiding-party on a magnificent scale rather than an army. Where they might have been a great racial influence they became vague figures in a half-forgotten incident. So much is a matter of the written word.

The Nennig mosaics, as interpreted by Passmore, tell a simple story of love, the same then as now, and intrigue, that has changed hardly a bit in international relationships, as it existed during the Roman occupation of the Rhineland.

There was a patrician at Treves. The stone records of his ornate career show him to have been something of a fop. Act One of the Nennig drama places him in the midst of luxurious surroundings in the City of Emperors. A sybarite he appears to have been, and a patron of the arts as represented by carvings of ingenuous nymphs in garments of refreshing frankness.

Enter his daughter. She flashes upon the stony picture in a scene of affectionate greeting, a display of sentiment contrasting prettily with the sensuous selfishness of the earlier scene.

The daughter is blonde, petite, and wilful. She shows the latter quality when the next slab of the cinema is unfolded to discover her flatly refusing to wed the son of a Roman governor. She points disdainfully to his oiled hair and anointed beard and announces that by no means will she sacrifice her life to such a nonentity. She does not like the way in which he wears his clothes, nor the disposition that the style of his hair so patently indicates.

Comes the dénouement in the next marble. It represents the golden-haired daughter in a clandestine meeting with a tall, brawny guard of the palace forces,—a captain of the household troop and the son of a Northern chieftain. He loves her. The scene is dainty and complete.

But the road of love, even the stony love of a couple in mosaic, is rough. In every plot is the obstacle that must be surmounted before the iris closes upon the last scene. In this bit of Roman picturization it appears in the shape of a father, a superstitious soul, bound body and soul to the nefarious Druids.

A black-bodied priestess looks upon a "serpent's egg" and tells him of his son's liaison with the daughter of a hated enemy.

The climax is developed swiftly. There is a picture which shows the fanatic father in conference with the chiefs of the Swabians, a barbarian pest still in their ice-locked cocoon of the North. And revenge, the basic motive of the mosaic plot, is quickly outlined.

The last of the vivid tablets shows the Swabians in their flight across Europe,—a sanguinary plague only too happy to find an excuse to sweep out of their barren fatherland into the more fertile plains of the Rhine country, crushing down by sheer weight of numbers the better-trained troops of Rome.

Steel is in their right hand and flame in their left. And their objective is the booty-filled villa of the Roman patrician.

The mosaics end here, exasperatingly incomplete. The film has snapped and the house is in darkness at the point where the fortunes of the wilful Roman heroine and her semi-savage lover should be definitely settled. Whether she perished as the Druid father intended that she should, in the drive of the Swabians, or escaped to the crags of the Alzette with the captain of the guard is a matter of conjecture. After all, her individual case is an affair of no moment. She is merely one of many mysteries and unimportant. United with him and happy, or separated and heartbroken, she would have been dead long centuries ago, anyway. Only love is eternal, and the weaver of the stone tapestries of Nennig seems to have realized this, cementing into his colorful blocks the dominant issue and forgetting the characters as the drama reached its dénouement.

Love is stronger than death.

Read the proof once more in the grave-mounds along the Roman road from Arlon to Treves.

Recently one of these hillocks was opened. The bones of him who had been buried there had long since given up their original elements to the soil. His trappings and armor, green with the corrosion of ages, an urn or two, a sculptured tablet, and a crystal tear-phial alone remained to mark the spot where he had been laid, a stranger far from home, for his last long sleep.

Reverent antiquarians removed these evidences of his visit,—to the museum at Luxemburg city, where one may see them and ponder upon the past of two thousand years ago that somehow seems very near.

But the crystal tear-phial fell to the lot of the man of science. A chemist at the capital opened it, poured the contents into a test-tube, and began his inquisitive round of qualitative tests. When the last reaction had been recorded in his laboratory note-book, he looked at the tube with a feeling very close to awe.

The contents of the phial were really human tears, —tears shed two thousand years ago!

There is something epic in those tears. Who shed them? A widow burying the enduring token of her grief with her husband,—a part of herself, as a sort of civilized suttee? A daughter left comfortless, unprotected and alone, hundreds of miles from the seven hills? Or did they fall from the eyes of a soldier and a patriot moved from his professional stoicism as he was cut down in his prime with his life-work unfinished, his loved ones a poignant memory?

Ask the curator at the museum about it. He shakes his gray head sadly and confesses that the legend which some day will explain the matter in full detail has not yet been evolved.

"It is a mystery, Monsieur," says he. "It is droll, a bit pathetic that the soldier of the legion is gone, his bones scattered dust in the soil of a foreign country. The empire that he helped to build is gone. Vanished are the traces of the nations that conquered it. And all that remains of his memory are a bit of all-enduring bronze and some human tears.

"I like to think of those tears not as souvenirs of a great grief, Monsieur, but as pearls born of a great love. For tears are the part of love. *Eh bien!* it was so two thousand years ago. It is so now."

He smiles as he says it. The Teuton strain in him rebukes his French enthusiasm and makes him a bit ashamed. But it is not difficult to see that he believes in his own pretty sentiment.

CHAPTER VI
PATHS OF GLORY

Royal Purple

Sceptre and Crown
Must tumble down
And in the dust be equal made
With the poor crooked scythe and spade.
—Shirley

LUXEMBURG CITY

View from the Bock—Looking across the lower town and the Viaduc du Nord

CHAPTER VI

PATHS OF GLORY

THE rise to power of the counts of Luxemburg, more through the advantageous position of their capital than because of any exceptional accomplishments as diplomats and men of arms, brought about a corresponding strengthening of their fiefs.

Spear-pointed crags, the length and breadth of the country, bristled with thick-walled outposts. In union the unscrupulous found comforting support, and strength of numbers brought them more plunder. Power and riches came to them simultaneously and the improvement of their station in life was reflected in the embellishment of their castles. Walls thickened, moats deepened, battlements were lifted to commanding heights above the narrow moraines.

The château of Mélusine became the scene of a remarkable court. There came armored knights in jingling chain-mail, with great two-handed swords slung across their shoulders and strange devices on their polished shields. There came princesses with golden hair and smiling eyes whose Gallic ancestry was sculptured in the splendor of their figures,—beautiful women, for the rob-

THE LAND OF HAUNTED CASTLES

ber barons who acquired their chatelaines as they acquired their riches, by right of conquest, would have no other kind. There came brilliantly robed prelates of the church, and scarred messengers of emperors, and hard-bitten errants, and gaunt but vigorous free-lances. The fame of the counts of Luxemburg and their court grew out of all proportion to the tiny district in which they ruled.

The direct male line of Siegfroid ended in 1036, with the death of Conrad II. Henry of Namur, grandson of Conrad I and cousin of Conrad II, inherited the title. Henry's advent, although he was of the blood of Siegfroid, generally is recorded as the beginning of the régime of the house of Namur.

Henry, the fourth of his name, better known as Henry the Blind and Unlucky, ruled the country for sixty turbulent years. He recovered to Luxemburg the fortress of Bouillon, captured by Count Renaud of Bar, and defeated Henry III of Limbourg in a quarrel over the rights to Arlon. The last years of his reign were spent in a sanguinary war against his nephew, Baudoin the Courageous, Count of Hainaut, who had aided him in the unpleasantness with Renaud and Henry of Limbourg.

For all that Henry the Blind was a crochety person, the record of whose morals indicates that he is little entitled to sympathy, this internecine strife of his declining years was not entirely his fault. It was misfortune that caused it,—misfortune and Mélusine.

Henry did not marry until he was sixty years old. That was the beginning of his misfortune. Laurence, daughter of the Count of Flanders, was his first wife and she died childless. The rheumatic bones of the sightless Henry were none the more comfortable because of the life he had led in districts where the wine flowed freely and the women were fair and kind, and he took the death of his wife as a warning that his days were numbered. In preparation for the end, he willed his possessions in Namur, Laroche, Durbuy, and Luxemburg to his sister Alix, Countess of Hainaut, and Baudoin her son. All of which was paving the way for greater misfortune.

Of Henry might have been written the famous doggerel:

> When the devil was sick
> The devil a saint would be.
> When the devil was better,
> The devil a saint was he.

Henry's mourning for the departed Laurence was cut short by the sudden stoppage of his rheumatic twinges. His prospects for a long and useful career accordingly became brighter, and he married a second time. His choice was Agnes of Nassau, sister of the Count of Gueldre.

This romantic attachment went the way of romances

THE LAND OF HAUNTED CASTLES

of its kind. The fair Agnes was young and Henry IV was seventy-five. They were divorced a short time after the ceremony and remained on the outs for fifteen years. So far as can be learned Henry did not miss his wife greatly during all those years. The rheumatism bothered him only intermittently and he was not the person to grieve.

He believed that in his arrangements with his sister Alix he had provided well for the future of Luxemburg. But he reckoned without Mélusine.

The fairy, imprisoned in her rock, knew all that was going on. She knew also that ten rulers of Siegfroid's line must occupy the throne before she could hope for rescue. She did not propose to allow a winebibbing, skirt-fancying old reprobate to condemn her to an eternal captivity. So she obtained a brief release on parole and interfered.

In his ninetieth year Henry was stricken with an illness that brought him to the edge of an untimely grave. He took the visitation as a warning and sent out messengers to bring back the wife he had divorced. Agnes was found, so legend has it, not far from Siegfroid's château and brought without delay to the bedside of the blind Henry. The reconciliation was complete.

A year later a daughter blessed their union,—Ermesinde, who was destined to bring renown to her country and trouble to her parents. Henry withdrew his promise that Baudoin should succeed him and the Count of Hainaut took up arms by way of protest.

Henry the Blind at ninety-seven found that he was not so young as he used to be. Warfare tired him and he lacked the genius for strategic manoeuver that had made him a fearsome power in his earlier days. He proceeded against Baudoin with a coalition of loyal princes and was decisively defeated at Noville sur Mehaigne.

Baudoin took over the County of Namur. Luxemburg, however, remained the fief of the Emperor Henry VI.

Henry retired to the abbey at Echternach to prepare for death, which overtook him there two years later.

The Countess Agnes remained with her daughter until Ermesinde was ten years old. Then she disappeared. Prosaic historians say that her body was laid beside that of her spouse at Echternach. Legend, ever more ready with explanation, refers again to the fairy Mélusine.

It was Mélusine, say those who tell the story, who came to Henry's bedside when he was calling for Agnes. It was Mélusine, in the form of the divorced countess, who returned to become the mother of Ermesinde,—a scandalous story but a deed in keeping with the airy, fairy conscience of Mélusine.

Ermesinde came to the throne, a baby, at a time when Luxemburg had fallen upon evil days. It appeared that despite the interference of Mélusine the country that

THE LAND OF HAUNTED CASTLES

Siegfroid had founded was doomed to fall to the first aggressor. But Ermesinde's fairy and exceptional gifts of intelligence did not desert her.

She was married when fourteen years old to Thibaut of Bar—to-day Bar-le-Duc—who set about to restore to Luxemburg the territories lost through the gay policies of the late Henry. After some negotiations with Henry VI, Thibaut obtained a renunciation of the emperor's claim to the country upon payment of a cash indemnity. He made war on Philip the Noble, Baudoin's successor, in an attempt to win back the lost province of Namur, and though he was unable to penetrate the citadel of Namur, he defeated Philip's troops so decisively that the treaty which closed the war gave to Ermesinde all of the county of Namur situated east of the Meuse, as well as her lost properties in Durbuy and Laroche.

Ermesinde was only eighteen years old when Thibaut died, but by that time she had learned the ins and outs of government. She was married a year later to Waleran of Limbourg, who brought to her as a wedding-present the district of Arlon. From this acquisition dates the bilingual nature of the duchy, for it gave to Luxemburg two distinct sections, the German on the east and the Walloon on the west.

Waleran died in 1225, at which time Ermesinde was twenty-eight years old and a match for the dozens of petty rulers who turned covetous eyes toward her patrimony.

She instituted many reforms, founded convents and abbeys at Clairfontaine, Useldange, Luxemburg, Marienthal, Bonnevoie, and Differdange, established a cabinet and council of state through the appointment of vassal knights to portfolios similar to those of the court of France, enfranchised a number of cities, increased the privileges of the bourgeoisie in the courts and in their relations with the seigneurs of their communities, lowered taxes, and established a universal military responsibility whereby all males able to carry arms were subject to call.

Under Ermesinde the County of Luxemburg enjoyed one of the most prosperous periods in its history. She died in 1247, at the age of fifty-one years, and was buried at Clairfontaine, the abbey which legend says she built at the direction of Our Lady herself.

Henry Blondel, her son, succeeded her and made a bit of history and tradition on his own account. He went to the crusades with St. Louis, added to the fame and fortune of Luxemburg in his own neighborhood and farther afield, and returned home to become a sort of militant pacifist who preferred the plowshare to the sword but kept his war-horse saddled and his battle-ax handy.

Under his administration occurred the Great War of the Cow,—the *guerre de vache* of a dozen legends.

THE LAND OF HAUNTED CASTLES

Unfortunately this war was not, as its name might imply, a war fought between cows. The cow served merely as a cause and thirty thousand men died in a three-cornered conflict to prove her status.

Tradition says that a farmer of Namur stole the cow from a resident of Ciney in the Principality of Liège. The Count of Namur refused to permit the extradition of the peasant and the Bishop of Liège mustered his burghers for an attack. The Count of Namur appealed to his father-in-law, Henry Blondel of Luxemburg, for aid and for three years (1275-78) the argument over the cow continued. Thirty villages and fourteen castles were burned. In the meantime the thieving peasant had been executed. Luxemburg's personal contribution to this zoölogical controversy was fifteen thousand lives.

Henry VI, eldest son of Henry Blondel, known by the picturesque if giddy title of Henry the Damned, got into trouble at the start of his reign by establishing a tollhouse on the Moselle to the discomfiture of the Archbishop of Treves.

There was nothing particularly new in this venture. It had been tried repeatedly before. Like the Panama Canal tolls of more recent memory, it was a prolific source of trouble. Imposts on Moselle shipments gave promise of an excellent revenue to Luxemburg and at the same time of a speedy end to the commerce which was the life of Treves.

PATHS OF GLORY

The Archbishop of Treves called upon Henry to remove his custom-house. Henry declined and was excommunicated, hence his cheerful title.

Later he kidnapped the Bishop of Liège, for causes concerning which historians do not agree, and held him prisoner six months in a dungeon until he had paid a substantial ransom.

In view of his pleasant disposition, it is not to be wondered at that he became involved in a war of considerable proportions.

After various changing connections—one of which had been with the County of Luxemburg—the Duchy of Limbourg was claimed in 1283 by Renaud of Gueldre, husband of the Duchess Ermengarde—whose death precipitated the controversy—and Adolphe of Berg, Ermengarde's cousin by marriage.

The claimants, with the wisdom born of experience in the fruitlessness of such arguments, promptly sold their "rights" and let the purchasers fight out the question of succession. Adolphe marketed his claim to John, Duke of Brabant. Renaud, supported by the Archbishop of Cologne, retired in favor of Henry of Luxemburg and his brother Waleran of Ligny.

Every prince in the lower Rhine country, Northern Lorraine, and Bergundy invited himself to a place in the inevitable fight that followed. The principal alignments were Renaud, the Archbishop of Cologne, and the two

THE LAND OF HAUNTED CASTLES

Luxemburg brothers on one side, the Duke of Brabant and the fiefs of Bergundy on the other.

The armies, which were two of the largest that had met on any European field since the overthrow of the Roman dynasty, established contact on the plains of Woeringen near Cologne, the flower of medieval chivalry was present for the grand clash and the Rhineland witnessed a stupendous pageant on a tragic scale. Woeringen was one of the most spectacular battle-fields in European history,—a great plain across which, as far as the eye could reach, squadrons of armored men on splendidly accoutred chargers dashed against one another with sword and lance—a colorful cinema of death. It was also one of the bloodiest, for some historians place the loss during three hours of fighting at twenty thousand men.

Henry the Damned fought like the fiend that tradition declared him to be. He continually sought the forefront of the battle for a hand-to-hand encounter with the Duke of Brabant, determined to settle with a personal argument the debate over the Limbourg succession. Three times they met. Three times they were separated in the terrible milling of horses and men.

They met a fourth time, hurled together by a sudden veering in the currents of the attack, and brought their deadly joust to fitting climax.

PATHS OF GLORY

Henry was unhorsed, but in falling struck the Duke of Brabant with his lance and unseated him.

The battle might still have gone on had not a retainer of the duke seized the opportunity, as Henry lay stunned, to drive a sword through a joint in his armor into his back. Brabant cried out in protest, but too late.

"Dog!" he shouted to his unfortunate vassal. "You have this day killed the bravest warrior in all Europe." He swung to his horse and once more the battle surged to and fro over the plain. Waleran also was slain in the fighting, but, like most conflicts of its sort, the hacking and slashing continued after the principal cause had been removed. Henry's body, mashed by the iron shoes of the horses, was unrecognizable and found a grave in common with the others of the twenty thousand on the red field under the open sky where the vultures were already circling.

The royal line of Luxemburg came close to extinction that day, for Henry of Houffalize and Baudoin, brothers of the count, also fell under the maces and lances of the Brabançon cavaliers.

"Their valiance and their glorious death brought high honor and renown to the chivalry of Luxemburg," says Herchen. "The death of Henry ended the war (though not the battle itself) and Limbourg was the prize of triumph for the Duke of Brabant."

Perhaps no battle in all the red annals of the middle

THE LAND OF HAUNTED CASTLES

ages could so well have served as the model for that later conflict which prompted little Peterkin's query: "What good came of it at last?"

Henry VII was only seventeen years old when his father's imperfect armor-plate cost him his claim to Limbourg and his life at a single sword stroke. His mother, Beatrix of Avesnes, administered the affairs of the county until he had attained his majority. During the four years of his preparation for the throne he was instructed in the arts of war and is said to have entertained ambitions to pay the Duke of Brabant for the memory of Woeringen.

But the medieval overlord was a strange creature. His wars usually were merely quarrels and all his quarrels were wars. Where later two gentlemen engaged in a dispute of a serious sort might have applied for a judgment of God in the form of a duel, and in present times the pair might settle their differences in a fist fight, the knights of the middle ages could not exchange personalities without involving everybody in the neighborhood. Serfs were cheap and armies readily recruited. Battles were fought without basis and the bloody results of them cheerfully forgotten.

So it was with Woeringen. While Henry was learning from his mother the gentle arts of sword-made government, the Duke of Brabant and Renaud of Gueldre were patching up their differences. Presently the duke made similar overtures to the widow of Henry VI. The outcome of this treaty was that all the Limbourg contestants still alive forgave one another with a magnanimity that had little effect upon the status of the twenty thousand dead on the banks of the Rhine, and Henry VII married Marguerite, the daughter of his father's enemy.

Henry VII took over the government in 1292. He began inauspiciously by setting out to acquire a curse similar to that visited upon his illustrious father. He built a new tollhouse on an island in the Moselle and resurrected the ancient argument with the clergy of Treves.

This time he supported his tariff policy by invading the Treverian territory. He burned a path from the Moselle boundary of Luxemburg to the west and visited his knightly wrath upon such vassals of Treves as attempted to oppose him. Then the war came to an end with an anticlimax. The reconciliation was effected before instead of after the principal encounter. The combatants of both armies threw down their arms before Treves and rushed into one another's embrace. The bishops of Treves admitted Henry to the city as they might have admitted any other distinguished guest and offered him a treaty whereby the long-disputed rights of Moselle navigation, imposts, and indemnities were amicably settled. It was a great surprise to the gentry of

THE LAND OF HAUNTED CASTLES

the period. Why either side should seek to avoid a war when such an excellent opportunity offered was a little beyond the philosophy of the Rhineland.

Thanks to his father's reputation and his own graces, Henry VII was chosen, in 1308, King of the Romans and head of the Holy Roman Empire and appears in subsequent history as Emperor Henry VI. Historians generally concede him to have been of an intelligence and justice far in advance of his times.

In one respect at least he is remarkable to moderns. He established so efficient a police force in Luxemburg that, despite the disorderly tendencies of the age, crime was reduced to a minimum. Theft disappeared so completely that Henry throughout his reign held himself ready to reimburse out of his own treasury all victims of robbery.

As emperor one of his first official acts was to convey to his son John the Kingdom of Bohemia, which, it is whispered, he had no right to cede. Bohemia was in a state of anarchy and the Bohemians were not much concerned with the nationality or identity of their ruler so long as some one actually gave them a government.

John married Elizabeth of Bohemia, daughter of Wenceslaus III, a Bohemian ruler who had been assassinated by an admiring subject. This strengthened his claim to the throne and thereafter he successfully combated all movements to depose him.

PATHS OF GLORY

Henry abdicated as Count of Luxemburg in favor of John and departed for Italy, where he contracted the malarial fever that killed him. Despite the fact that he was a man of talent and an emperor fitted for his office, his death was a matter of only passing concern to his people. His son John, the greatest adventurer and swashbuckler of his age, had already begun to make romance, and it is natural for countries as for individuals to prefer romance to the matter-of-fact usefulness of history in the building.

CHAPTER VII

JOHN THE BLIND

The Wandering King of Bohemia

Shall victor exult, or in death be laid low,
With his back to the field and his feet
    to the foe,
And leaving in battle no blot on his name,
Look proudly to heaven from death-bed
    of fame.

—Campbell.

CHAPTER VII

JOHN THE BLIND

JOHN THE BLIND was a stormy petrel of trouble. He spent little of his time at home, for in his day the scenes of war were elsewhere. A born fighting-man was John, with a sword that was never more than half sheathed, and a disposition that adapted itself more readily to the hardships of a campaign than to the comparatively luxurious pursuits of peace.

John sought to prepare the way for his own election to the throne of empire by personal advertising and he narrowly missed his goal.

His black plume was to the forefront in the sanguinary disputes with the Saracens. He was an exponent of Christianity militant in Egypt. He was a power and a terror in the little wars that enveloped Bohemia, and he swung an energetic mace in Flanders and Bergundy.

No other character in history approaches more closely the ideal of the medieval chevalier, fighting other people's battles while his own country groaned under the burden of his expenses, ever seeking wrongs to right and in the process making a few that despaired of righting, brave to the point of fanaticism, a religious zealot, a gentle knight, and a merciless killer. It seems to have been in the atmosphere of the middle ages that men should be made up of such diverse instincts. John appears to have been all things to all men.

He did nothing for Luxemburg except choose it as his birthplace. He was known as the King of Bohemia rather than as the Count of Luxemburg. He sold much of his domain to pay his expenses in adding to the fiefs of a friendly prince. He raised the taxes of his own people that he might lower those of strangers.

But for some reason Luxemburg worshiped him as it has worshiped no other ruler. His subjects felt that they shared in the glory of his achievements. They enshrined him as a native son upholding the honor of his race among distant peoples. Of all the figures in the duchy's variegated and multiform traditions, he is still supreme.

There is a pathetic strain in the romance of John of Bohemia. His eyesight began to fail shortly after he attained his throne. From that time until the day of his death, his career was one long pilgrimage from battle-field to physician and from savant to battle-field. He did not allow his personal afflictions to interfere with his business of war, but he dreaded the approaching darkness more than the thrust of a lance or the crash of a battle-ax.

An Arabian physician of remarkable reputation treated John's left eye. The treatment had prompt results. The prince could barely see with it when he consulted the Arabian. After four applications of secret herbs and

LUXEMBURG CITY

Road from the Bock to the Lower City showing part of the fortifications begun by Siegfroid and his fairy and perfected by Vauban for Louis XIV of France

the usual accompaniment of mystic incantation, the sight of the eye was completely gone.

John took the learned physician to the Oder River and threw him in.

His monocular vision interfered with his swordsmanship, but he did not allow that to check his ambitions. He went forth to new wars and in between battles consulted surgeons, magicians, and learned monks regarding the properties of medicines and charms that might help him to keep the remnant of his sight.

But the Arab's method had been thorough and speedily an infection developed in the right eye. The lure of the field of arms was passing for John of Bohemia. The panoply of mailed foot-men, the gleam of the sun upon the shields of the cavaliers—wonderful pageant of a glorious barbarity—were fast becoming mere streaks of light against a deepening gray, seen by the warrior-king only with exquisite pain. He went as a last resort to a Bergundian scientist.

The work of the monk who applied the soothing decoctions was quite as good as that of the Arab but no better. John discovered one morning that he would never again see the break of day. He would never again be counted a formidable swordsman. He would never be emperor.

The tragic climax of John's history is better known.

Blind, almost helpless, but a warrior still, he rode

forth to meet the English on the plains of Crécy, to help his friend of many campaigns, Philip VI of France.

His retainers escorted him forward to the center of the battle line and shouted to him directions for the wielding of his terrible sword. Pressed back by the troops of Edward III, they called out to him to save himself, but John scorned the advice.

"It does not please God," he replied, "that John of Bohemia should take flight and turn his back to the enemy."

And so he died, weapon in hand, struck down by a foeman whom he could not see. All of his suite except two men died with him.

A cross was raised to his memory on the field of Crécy. His casque and plumes, found by the Black Prince of Wales, were taken by the prince as his own, a delicate if somewhat superstitious tribute to the man who had lost them. John's heraldic device "Ich Dien" became a part of the coat of arms of the Prince of Wales.

The vicissitudes of John after death are scarcely less remarkable than his journeyings in life. His subsequent career is an excellent exposition of the motives that drive ghosts to seek peace away from the graves of their bodies.

On the morning after the Battle of Crécy, Edward III sent John's body to Prince Charles. In accordance with the blind king's will, the remains were taken to the church of Altmunster and laid in a crypt already prepared to receive them. When the Abbey of Altmunster was destroyed by the French revolutionists John's mortuary perigrinations were resumed. He was taken to the little church in the Grund of Luxemburg city where a monument was placed over him. Twice after that his nomadic bones wandered to new resting-places in Luxemburg. In 1795, when the French stormed the city, they were moved once more and fell into the hands of vandals who sold them to one Boch, a crockery merchant at Metlach on the Sarre.

How had the mighty fallen! For many a year all that was left of the great John of Bohemia was exhibited as a curiosity in Boch's chinaware museum. Frederick IV of Prussia ended this desecration. He built a beautiful mausoleum on the rocks overlooking the Sarre and there the oft-shaken dust of the blind hero of Crécy was given a suitable shelter.

There is reason to believe that his more recent resting-place will prove permanent. John probably will lie here until he hears the trumpet of the Angel Gabriel and will find no new experience in arising to answer it.

The news of John's death was received with a panic of sorrow in the country of his birth. Word of the fatal outcome of the Battle of Crécy came to Luxemburg as the great tent-fair which he had instituted was at the height of its interest. Traders from all parts of Lorraine and the Rhineland, from distant England and farthest

THE LAND OF HAUNTED CASTLES

France had traveled to Luxemburg with their wares. Buyers from the petty courts of a score of petty princes were present with well-filled purses to buy silks for the ladies of far-flung castles, Toledo armor, and Indian jewels. But the dreadful news spread in a flash. The people went home and locked themselves in their houses and the traders folded their tents and went away. By the title "Sorrowful Kermess" the successor to this fair is known to this day.

According to the will prepared by John long before his death, the title to the County of Luxemburg passed to Wenceslaus, his younger son. Charles the older—according to the Salic law the successor to John in all his titles—was given the Kingdom of Bohemia as his portion. John's death, despite this arrangement, brought about more trouble in the administration of Luxemburg.

Wenceslaus was under age. His brother Charles, who, thanks to the reputation and machinations of his illustrious father, became Emperor of Germany under the name of Charles IV, took over the government as regent and assumed the full prerogatives of office, including the title, and then proceeded to sell as much of the territory as necessary to provide him with funds for his activities in the empire.

He was thorough about it. Pawn, barter, sale, and gift,—every known method of raising money on property was employed by Charles, with the result that a country

JOHN THE BLIND

already impoverished through the spendthrift talents of John the Blind became a bit more wretched.

Charles retained the throne after Wenceslaus came of age, but the younger brother does not seem to have worried about it. Some historians argue that John had made a codicil to his will, bequeathing the property to Wenceslaus but giving the right to sell it to Charles,—an excellent arrangement.

The country was not particularly happy in its prospects in those days. And yet it had seen worse times and was to see others.

There was a streak of the pawnbroker in Charles as history represents him. He was a modern in that more than any public figure of his time he recognized that the ducat is a useful and highly satisfactory weapon. What he wanted he bought, carrying this policy out even to the purchase of the German electoral college and the Holy Roman Empire for his son. The money he required for such deals in high finance he obtained by the simple process of hypothecating a security. That some of the security was not precisely his own and that some of it had been previously mortgaged were merely the details that lifted his transactions out of the class of petty barter and trade.

He scorned the sword. Battle he considered a form of debate wholly unnecessary to a good salesman. Thus his reign was peaceful and marked by a thorough application of the policy of amicable adjustment in international affairs, and Charles IV was rated as a good emperor and a shrewd politician.

His influence was felt to a larger extent by the seigneurs of the castles than that of any of his predecessors on the throne of the Holy Roman Empire. He organized a "league to enforce peace" among the dukes and counts of the Moselle and Meuse and placed his brother Wenceslaus at the head of the association to stamp out the outlawry of the robber barons and their marauding retainers. Here is the germ of a league-of-nations idea. It is interesting as the first recorded experiment of its kind, but it does not appear to have been particularly successful.

As a tardy compensation for the financial difficulties which he had brought to Luxemburg, Charles issued a decree establishing it as a duchy and conferring upon its rulers the distinguished right to hold the emperor's horse. Then, as was customary with the Luxemburg nobility who had stepped into power elsewhere, he seems to have forgotten its existence.

Wenceslaus, despite his handicaps, refused to stay within the limitations prescribed by his advance notices. He took over the title of duke and set about making his coronet stand for something. Bit by bit he recovered his lost acres. A timely marriage brought him the duchies of Brabant and Limbourg and freed the territory of Luxemburg and other fiefs from a plaster of mortgages.

JOHN THE BLIND

It was during his reign that Luxemburg reached the acme of its territorial greatness. Its domains reached from the Moselle almost to the banks of the Meuse and from the northern Ardennes to the suburbs of Metz. A representative of its ruling house was at the head of the Holy Roman Empire. Its vassals were among the strongest in Europe. Its court was a marvel of splendor and culture. Its fighting-men were among the most highly esteemed of all the trained warrior forces of a continent.

But its glories were not unmixed with tragedy. The Black Death ravaged Europe and depopulated the Ardennes. A tremendously cold winter finished the work that the plague had started. Famine followed pestilence and whole villages disappeared. It is estimated that sixty thousand persons lost their lives in Luxemburg alone, a serious loss for a county so small.

Although Wenceslaus was known by his title as Duke of Brabant rather than Duke of Luxemburg and made his residence at Brussels instead of in the city of Siegfroid, he was not like other absentee rulers. In a time of national calamity the duchy could have had no better friend. He was just, modest, conservative, a skilful executive, the sort of governing head most needed by a people who had known too much of the jolly-good-fellow type of prince. His administration gave promise of better days for the duchy.

But the line of Siegfroid was riding for a fall.

THE LAND OF HAUNTED CASTLES

Wenceslaus died childless. Luxemburg passed to another Wenceslaus, his nephew, the son of Emperor Charles IV. Wenceslaus II was the prince who had profited by Charles's purchase of the German electoral college. He had already succeeded to the title of his dead father when Luxemburg unfortunately fell into his hands.

Wenceslaus II appears to have had little to make him remarkable except a thirst that distinguished him in a court of two-fisted drinking-men. That and a disposition to keep his money in circulation brought him as close to bankruptcy in 1388 as a jovial emperor can be expected to get. There was always a way out of debt for a ruler of Luxemburg, however. He promptly sold the duchy to his cousin Jost, reserving the right to buy it back. Thus Jost became in the parlance peculiarly suited to this industry of jobbing in small kingdoms, the *engagiste* of the country. The property passed at the death of Jost to Elizabeth of Goerlitz, his niece.

Historians generally place the end of the Luxemburg dynasty in 1443, thirty-two years after Elizabeth with her crown of debts and her scepter of mortgages came to occupy the throne of Mélusine. But the end of Luxemburg as a nation may be dated at the moment of her accession.

Whatever the duchy had lacked in previous régimes, through lack of attention from its rulers, was more than

JOHN THE BLIND

compensated in the plurality of governors that followed. Nobody knows what Elizabeth spent her money for. Certainly it was not for the maintenance of her territory. Piece by piece the counties and provinces upon which she held a lien passed into the hands of royal or ecclesiastical money-lenders, some of it for advances pitifully small.

Wenceslaus, deposed by the German electors, retired to Bohemia and died suddenly of apoplexy or poison, as you will. His brother Sigismund fell heir to his option on Luxemburg, his title to the Kingdom of Bohemia and eventually to his throne as Emperor of the Germans. He also inherited a number of political woes in the midst of which the debt of 120,000 florins for which the duchy had been pledged seemed a matter of small moment. Sigismund could not or would not raise the money to liquidate the debt and Elizabeth remained engagiste in the midst of an anarchy of her own manufacture.

The numerous persons to whom she had pawned the duchy began to press her for possession, so she evolved the worthy idea of cheating them all at once. There was only one person strong enough to execute the coup for her, for her husband, a nonentity in her interesting reign, had died of poisoning some years previously. There was but one hope,—her nephew, Philip the Good, Duke of Bergundy and Flanders, who was even then attempting

THE LAND OF HAUNTED CASTLES

to build the empire later known as the United Netherlands.

A word here, while the star of Luxemburg is setting. Sigismund, feeling the pinch of his imperial poverty, sold his rights to the Province of Brandenburg to Frederick of the High Zollern, or Hohenzollern, and thus a new family took its first step to power in the world's affairs.

Had the disposition of Elizabeth of Goerlitz been a bit sweeter and her financial transactions a bit more scrupulous, Sigismund might have found a way of redeeming the pledged Duchy of Luxemburg, for it is easier to treat with one claimant than with a dozen; and with Luxemburg redeemed there would have been no necessity for his transfer of Brandenburg to the Barons of the High Zollern. There is a subject that one might ponder upon amid the ruins of Rheims or in Hell's Half Acre in front of Verdun.

Sigismund died without leaving male issue. Albert of Austria, husband of Sigismund's daughter Elizabeth, was interrupted by death in an attempt to obtain a settlement of the tangled claims to the duchy.

The widow of Albert transferred her rights to her kinsman William of Saxony, who marched upon Luxemburg with eight hundred men. The people rose en masse to welcome William and betrayed their emotional regard for the genial Elizabeth of Goerlitz by driving her beyond the walls.

JOHN THE BLIND

Then came Philip the Good from Dijon with twenty-five hundred mercenaries, a tried fighting-man at the head of as fearless a band of cutthroats as ever wielded mace. The fortress that Siegfroid had begun might have withstood the armies of Europe in open conflict, but it was no protection to the followers of William against treachery.

Philip's soldiers were in the darkened streets of the capital before the defending garrison suspected that they had left Dijon. So the wonderful story of medieval Luxemburg came to an end in rapine and pillage. Booty for the mercenaries, a sop of money for William of Saxony, an annuity for the illustrious Elizabeth, a new pawn in an imperial chess game for Philip the Good.

What an end for a romance that began with Mélusine!

CHAPTER VIII
SWORD AND TORCH

The Emperor Charles Quint

The glories of our blood and state
  Are shadows, not substantial things;
There is no armour against fate;
  Death lays his icy hand on kings:
          —James Shirley.

CHAPTER VIII

SWORD AND TORCH

WITH the coming of gunpowder and artillery the styles in castles had changed. True, the handsomely engraved bronze guns of the period were not particularly dangerous. Their range was short, their aim inaccurate, and their effectiveness something less than might be considered worth the trouble of dragging them with an army. But the wily barons of the crags saw in the coming of the cannon the doom of walled citadels. They realized several centuries earlier than did the builders of the gun-emplacements at Liège, Dinant, and Namur, the inevitable superiority of explosives over fortification.

Their conviction that no man-made rock pile could long withstand the battering of solid shot brought with it the realization that castles might be made comfortable dwelling-places as well as strongholds. This new policy brought massive buildings of architectural worth,— among them Beaufort with its finished masonry, Schoenfels, and the new Ansembourg. But it substituted no new means of defense for the old. The ancient and modern continued to perch on hill and in hollow as if

THE LAND OF HAUNTED CASTLES

undecided as to what preparation they had better make for the test between gunpowder and stone that was certain to come. The ruins tell the story of the failure of the grafs to solve the problem.

The story of Luxemburg from the time of the accession of Philip to its next incarnation as an independent nation is largely the story of other countries and alien rulers who had advanced further in the science of destruction than had the Low Countries in the art of building.

It is a story of oppression, suffering, undying national pride, and gentle forbearance,—an epic in itself that can be treated here only in briefest outline. Philip the Good, better known to the Luxemburgers as Philip of the Long Legs, seems to have merited the title descriptive of his high moral qualities in much the same fashion as many a ward heeler of later days has come to be known as "Honest John."

He undid most of the work of enfranchisement done by Ermesinde in the dawning of the country's existence. A board of governors was substituted for the sovereign in the administration of the duchy, and Luxemburg became an integral part of the possessions of Bergundy.

Charles the Bold succeeded Philip and proceeded to carry out his dream of empire. He hoped to complete the solidification of his wide domains by harassing France in upsetting the alliances of Louis XI with the house of

MAIN ENTRANCE OF THE SIXTEENTH CENTURY CHATEAU
Three of the four "parts of the world" struggling against the shackles of the oppressor are seen in the colonnade. The building was rebuilt in its present form in 1719

THE GARDEN
"NEW" CHATEAU ANSEMBOURG

SWORD AND TORCH

York. He made one fatal error, however: he took in too much territory. Instead of starting off for England while the disorganized Lancastrians still were willing to renew the War of the Roses, he delayed to "punish" the Swiss confederates for a fancied affront and to wrest Lorraine from René, the troubadour king.

Charles suffered three principal defeats. He died at Nancy, whether as the result of wounds received in battle or an execution at the hands of the Vehmgericht—that great Ku-Klux Klan of the Rhine, dreaded by high and low alike in the days of the Holy Roman Empire—is still a matter of dispute among those who find the point worth arguing.

With the fall of Charles the Bold, grim anticlimax to a melodrama of empire, there fell also the last barrier in the march of France to destiny. Charles's disappearance from the European arena definitely aligned the peoples of France against the peoples of Germany in a titanic struggle for dominance, and it was purely as a factor in this endless contest that the rock of Luxemburg attracted the attention of the envious contenders.

Each decade was adding to its strength, each year was increasing its menace to the peace of Europe. An imperial Germany could not afford to have a French Gibraltar at its frontiers. A growing, ambitious, and valorous France could not sleep securely at night if a German banner floated over the Bock.

THE LAND OF HAUNTED CASTLES

The strategic importance of Luxemburg at that time is indicated by the fact that neither Germany nor France coveted it so much as a useful possession, but each craved possession to keep the other from getting it. And so came wars,—wars innumerable, bloody and inexcusable.

Marie of Burgundy, a girl still in her teens, succeeded the redoubtable Charles, her father. Louis XI sought to annex her possession by betrothing her to his son. But she had a mind of her own, a mind already formed so far as Louis and his royal house were concerned. She refused his offer and married Maximilian I of Austria, later emperor of Germany. She foresaw the inevitable result and strengthened the Great Rock with a number of walls and towers.

While the improvement was in progress Maximilian took up arms to defend the territory of his wife and carried the argument to Louis by invading Hainaut, then in the hands of the French. He would have gone on into France itself had not Louis sued for an armistice (1478).

A year later Marie's foresight was vindicated when the Duke of Amboise at the head of a French army suddenly appeared at Luxemburg. The French succeeded in breaching the walls, but were stopped by the cannon with which the place bristled. In the meantime Maximilian and his forces came to the rescue of the beleaguered capital by night and day marches. Amboise manoeuvered for

SWORD AND TORCH

position in "the green valley" near Mersch. Maximilian attacked and defeated him.

A fall from a horse on a hunting expedition caused Marie's death shortly after the beginning of her promising reign, but not before she had restored many of the privileges taken from the Luxemburgers by Philip the Good of the long legs, and Charles the Bold.

Marie's son, afterward known as Philip the Fair, was only four years old at the time of her unfortunate accident. He was brought up under the regency of Maximilian and married at sixteen years to Jeanne, daughter of two monarchs whose names stand at the beginning of American history, Ferdinand of Aragon and Isabella of Castile. That was four years after Isabella had pawned her jewels and Jeanne was rated as the wealthiest heiress in Europe,—how wealthy no one in the Old World could have realized, for the vastness of Christopher Columbus's discovery was unknown even to Christopher himself.

But, however good this match was for Philip, it was unlucky for Luxemburg. Ferdinand and Isabella died and Philip the Fair chose Spain, of all his possessions, as his own residence and capital. The duchy and Belgium were placed under the administration of a governor-general. Philip died shortly thereafter, his wife lost her mind in grieving for him, and his vast heritage passed to his son, the able Charles V, a Hapsburg, whose advent to power at the time of the reformation foredoomed him

THE LAND OF HAUNTED CASTLES

to a dubious position in the eyes of latter-day historians.

Charles V is either a blood-stained bigot or defender of the faith, a war-mad zealot or a militant advocate of peace, a poseur or a hero, a strong supporter of ideals and the law or a tyrant who recognized no law save his own stubborn will, depending upon the point of view of the historian who tells about him. Whatever his talents or his faults, he painted his career with a wide brush and the world remembers him.

He was twenty years old when he was elected Emperor of Germany and he brought to his new task a number of political ideas that made trouble for him. For one, he felt that although he was ruler of Germany, he himself was a Spaniard. For another, he was a foe of compromise. These two traits, plus his faith in the old church as opposed to the creed of Luther, paved the way for the Thirty Years' War that from 1618 to 1648 made Europe a shambles.

Charles kept a more watchful eye upon Luxemburg than had the other emperor-dukes of her history. He has been rated by Motley as one of the most skilful generals of his time and as such was fully aware of the importance of the fortress on the Alzette. He strengthened it until it seemed to have approached the ideal of impregnability, but Francis I of France overturned his work in 1542 with an army under the command of the dukes of Orleans and Guise. The imperial armies took it back, however, and except for a few thousand negligible halberdiers and lancers killed, the *status quo ante* was restored.

It was during the reign of Charles V that William de la Marck, the "Wild Boar of the Ardennes," made his noisome debut in the affairs of Luxemburg. Feared, hated, loathed, this wild boar exercised a power over the northwestern part of the province little short of that of a king. The other robber knights of his vicinity recognized in him the sublimation of their cheerful profession and accorded him marked respect, while his excesses set a stamp upon the country-side that remains to this day. It was he who betrayed the Low Countries to the French and who aided the troops of Francis in their invasion. The boar was hanged later in his career as befitted so worthy a character.

It has been said that Charles's religious zeal was in direct ratio to political expediency and perhaps the charge is well made. Historians of his own faith have declared that he would unhesitatingly have supported a Hottentot for the papacy if by doing so he could have furthered the personal and varied interests of Charles. He recognized Protestant coalitions in Germany while he was oppressing the Protestant Netherlands. He was lenient in some districts, an extortioner in others, and withal a great man. There was something of a Charlemagne in him, as witness his ability to keep the reins of government over all of the civilized world except England and a part of

THE LAND OF HAUNTED CASTLES

France. Governments in feudal times were unstable things and while many an ambitious vassal aspired to empire, only the strong survived as emperors.

Charles resigned in 1555. His brother, Ferdinand I, became Emperor of Germany, and his son Philip II succeeded to his territories in the Netherlands and his castles in Spain. Charles retired to the monastery of Yuste in the valley of the Estremadura to meditate upon the purpose of life and to amuse himself in the manufacture of clocks. It is said that he made very good clocks.

Philip II was a gentler personage than his father and succeeded, temporarily at least, in uniting the Catholic and Protestant elements of the Netherlands. But such an association could not last. William the Silent, product of the house of Vianden, hammered together from the seven northern provinces of the Netherlands the great Dutch Republic, and war that seemed destined never to end began.

Luxemburg, free from taxes which the Dutch resented, and in full sympathy with the laws governing religious worship, remained with the provinces which may roughly be called "Belgium," although better known through two centuries of subsequent history as the Spanish Netherlands.

France took the opportunity to strike at Philip II, who drew upon German troops for aid. Luxemburg from end to end became an armed camp.

SWORD AND TORCH

As usual it was the duchy that furnished the battle-fields, the drill-grounds, and the subsistence for most of the forces involved. Populations of whole towns emigrated to avoid troops, whether friend or foe. Artillery is no respecter of personal property and the buildings that were under French and Dutch fire to-day were subjected to a no less thorough bombardment to-morrow in the counter-attacks of the Spanish.

But during the hostilities the capital prospered. Spain was completing her conquests of Mexico and Peru and to Luxemburg city came the nobles who had shared in the loot, the nouveau riche of their day, wealthy beyond the dreams of sixteenth-century avarice and free of purse.

Count Mansfeld, the governor of the duchy for Philip, built a castle amid terraces and gardens in the valley of the Alzette that would have aroused the jealousy of Mélusine. He was responsible for the erection of a hôtel de ville in the style of the Spanish renaissance seen to-day as part of the grand-ducal palace. And though his marvelous château is dust and its treasures scattered, his memory is kept bright at the capital through the survival of a score of public improvements for which he was responsible.

Philip II looked upon his northern possessions as a place of exile and finally went back to Spain, leaving the government of Luxemburg and the remainder of the Netherlands to his half-sister, Marguerite of Parma. In

THE LAND OF HAUNTED CASTLES

1598 Philip saw death approaching and married his daughter Isabella to Archduke Albert of Austria, viceroy of such of the Netherlands as remained, and conferred upon them full rights of sovereignty with the condition that should they die childless the district should return to Spain.

When the envoys of the provinces met at Brussels that same year, to do homage to their new ruler, the Luxemburgers were singularly honored. They were placed at Albert's right hand immediately after the Knights of the Golden Fleece and raised only one finger in taking their oath of allegiance, whereas the other delegates were obliged to raise two. When the two-fingered envoys protested against such rank favoritism Albert set them in their places with a scathing rebuke.

"You have nothing to complain of," he declared. "You have rebelled against your God and your king. The men of Luxemburg have remained faithful to both. Of their loyalty the lifting of an eyebrow would be warranty enough for me."

In the meantime the war with the rebellious Netherlands continued. Albert, defeated at Nieuport, called the royalist provinces to a convention at Brussels and demanded funds for the carrying on of the conflict. The Luxemburgers showed an independent spirit, declaring that any subsidy they might vote him must not be considered as a precedent, that a canvass of population

SWORD AND TORCH

should be completed before additional taxes were assessed upon them, and that their participation in the meeting of the council should not be taken as indicating that they renounced any of their rights to individuality or their ancient objections to assimilation.

Albert conceded the point. He was voted thirty thousand florins and Luxemburg mobilized at his call in Flanders for an assault upon Ostend, the only Flemish town in the grasp of the Dutch government. Albert advanced to besiege the town and Isabella vowed that she would not change her chemise until he met success. Ostend did not fall until three years later.

Luxemburg came to look upon Dutch incursions as a routine affair. The seigneurs of the castles to the north slept on their arms for seven exciting years and each day's record was carved with a sword or branded with fire. The fighting came to an end with an armistice between the United Provinces of the Netherlands and Archduke Albert after fifty years of continuous civil warfare.

In the last year of the truce Albert died childless and the Netherlands reverted to Spain. Civil strife had been raging in Germany for three years between the Catholic and Protestant coalitions fostered by Charles V. The torch was alight and presently all Europe was aflame.

The Swedes, the Danes, and the Dutch swept down from the North. The Swedes were drawn into the vortex

THE LAND OF HAUNTED CASTLES

of the fight by Sigismund of Poland in a controversy over the Swedish succession, but presently became the Protestant bulwark under the able leadership of Gustavus Adolphus, father of artillery tactics.

The Elector of Treves, fearing an attack by the Swedes, placed himself under the protection of Louis XIII, King of France. Cardinal Richelieu, the real government of France, despatched French troops to Treves and to numerous other points along the Luxemburg frontier, menacing the great fortress, then as ever the object of France's covetousness.

Count Embden, governor of the duchy, struck a sudden blow at Treves and captured the elector, whom he turned over to Philip IV of Spain. Then Richelieu declared war on Spain and Europe became a sanguinary inferno from one end to the other. In 1635 a French army entered Belgium and joined with the Dutch commanded by Frederic Henry of Nassau, son of William the Silent. A counter-blow was speedily delivered by an imperial army under Piccolomini which set out to aid the Spaniards by invading France. It showed no favoritism, this army: in its march across Luxemburg, a friendly country, it sacked Igel, Wasserbillig, and Grevenmacher and burned Wormeldange, Canach, and Remich.

So had the Huns come down into France. So did the imperial troops of Germany drive across through what is now the Argonne. And, like the hordes of Alaric and hordes of a later date, they finished at the Marne.

They had been terrible in advance. They were more frightful than a plague in their forced retreat.

Herchen says of this period:

"It is impossible to describe the sufferings with which our ancestors were visited. The armies of that period were nothing more than mobs without morals, without restraint, without discipline gathered from the Low Countries, France, Italy, Poland, Hungary, Scotland and Ireland, willing to serve any one who would pay them. They lived by rapine and plunder. The Poles of Colloredo and the Croats of Isolani, who made their winter quarters in the villages of our country, distinguished themselves particularly by their cruelty. The terror in which they were held was such that at their approach the peasants fled to the woods or to the ramparts of the fortresses. The fields lay fallow during 1636 and 1637 and a terrible famine was the inevitable result. If a report made by three states of the duchy to the Council of State at Brussels is to be believed, the people subsisted upon a bread made from the bones of corpses which were disinterred in the cemeteries, and that soon, mothers crazed by hunger killed their children and devoured them. Presently pestilence came to add to the terrors of hunger and war."

A combination of these terrors wiped out completely one hundred and forty villages in the duchy and reduced numerous others to the vanishing-point.

Even the Peace of Westphalia, which ended the Thirty Years' War in 1648, did not bring relief. Spain and France continued to fight for eleven more bloody years.

One stirring incident lends a high light to these dark days. Louis XIV had succeeded Louis XIII and was already engaged in his work of giving France a place in the sun. In person he led twenty thousand men to an attack on Montmedy, where he found himself opposed by six hundred young Luxemburgers commanded by Jean d'Allamont, a youth of Malandry. Mortally wounded by the explosion of a bomb, d'Allamont sent to Louis his handkerchief stained with blood as a sign of his loyalty to Luxemburg even in death. The town surrendered as soon as d'Allamont died, but Louis refused to enter.

His explanation was an unforgetable tribute to heroism:

"The one whom I would wish to see and redeem from death even at the price of the lives of two thousand French soldiers is no more."

The Peace of the Pyrenees (1659) ended the struggle between France and Spain and brought about the first mutilation of the duchy. By the terms of the settlement, France received Thionville, Montmedy, Damvilliers, Chavancy, and Marville. Still the Grand Monarch was not satisfied. He realized that the towns and districts which he had been ceded were unimportant outposts, menaced so long as the great rock on the Alzette remained in alien hands.

He found an excuse for an attack in 1679, through an interpretation of the treaty of the Pyrenees which provided that the "dependencies" of the Luxemburg districts ceded to him should be conveyed with the cities. It was evidently meant that the "dependencies" referred to were those in existence at the date of the treaty, but Louis decided otherwise. He set a commission to investigating the historical connections of his lately acquired territories and discovered, despite the protests of the Spaniards, that Montmedy, Thionville, etc., had brought him as fiefs virtually all the other cities in Luxemburg.

Luxemburg was not progressing under the rule of Charles II of Spain. The greasy mercenaries of a dozen countries were still quartered in the capital and surrounding towns. The province was a Vesuvius of rapine and anarchy, its people were hunted animals who looked upon death as a welcome relief.

Louis prepared well for his climacteric attack on Siegfroid's rock.

He despatched that excellent devotee of arson Marshal Boufflers upon a long campaign of artillery sharpshooting against the storied castles of the Alzette, the Mamer, the Esch, and the Sure. Boufflers left trails across the duchy that centuries have not begun to efface. They probably will be there when Boufflers is called from his tomb by Gabriel. The castles that Rome had founded and succeeding generations had built into seemingly impregnable refuges heard their doom in the blast of massed batteries.

Boufflers's work was painstaking and thorough. He

THE LAND OF HAUNTED CASTLES

moved his guns in a leisurely fashion from one door to another, bounced cannon-balls against great towers and proud battlements, assiduously avoided melted lead and boiling pitch and similar ammunition of feudal defense, and in the end chased the little garrisons from their wrecked shelters and applied the torch to whatever the artillery had spared.

He was not opposed by any large number of fighting-men during his cycle of destruction. The seigneurs of Luxemburg were at the capital, preparing for the assault that every one knew was in prospect. Boufflers's campaign was designed to draw them away from the fortress to their own castles.

And the ruse succeeded. Louis's main army marched to the attack and for six weeks rained iron and lead upon the citadel. During that period the French lost eight thousand men and the defending garrison was reduced from four thousand to four hundred.

The capital surrendered to Marshal Créqui on June 4, 1684, and the Spanish garrison was allowed to march out with all the honors of war.

The burghers welcomed Louis as they would have welcomed any one who gave them a promise of order and peace. It was no difficult task to feel grateful toward an enemy whose presence insured their supply of food and freedom from pillage, and to feel reconciled to the loss

SWORD AND TORCH

of "friendly" soldiery whose régime had been notable principally for bestial cruelties.

But still the red kaleidoscope ground out its changing patterns. Louis, during his reign of thirteen years, brought considerable French atmosphere into the duchy through his importation of settlers to repopulate the districts over which fire, famine, sword, and pestilence had passed so frequently. The purely French names and much of the pro-French feeling of the grand duchy of to-day may be traced directly to this period.

Under Louis the duchy felt for the first time the hand of an absolute monarch. The last ember of feudalism was in ashes among the cinders of the castles that had represented it. Louis was a prince with a firm hand and supreme self-confidence and had seen the effects of a system in which too many vassals were stronger than the masters they served.

The efficiency with which he operated in Luxemburg is evidenced by the fact that of fifty-seven counts, barons, and seigneurs enrolled at the time of Boufflers's flaming expedition, not one name remains alive to-day.

Louis speedily found himself in trouble. He was opposed by England, Germany, Spain, and Holland, fought for nine years, and came to the finish of his greatness with the Peace of Ryswick. By the terms of this pact Luxemburg was taken away from him and restored to Spain.

THE LAND OF HAUNTED CASTLES

And yet the wars and rumors of war were unceasing. Charles II of Spain died and the royal houses of France and Austria mustered thousands of men to whom the matter was no great concern, to settle the rights of the Spanish succession. It was while this necessary carnage was in progress that England took possession of Gibraltar. A Dutch army invested Luxemburg.

Ambition flares up suddenly in narrow breasts and amateur Napoleons are products of no particular sort of soil. While France and Austria were engaged in their debate concerning the laws of inheritance, Maximilian Emanuel, Elector of Bavaria, completed an arrangement whereby he would support the claims of the Duke of Anjou to the throne of Spain in exchange for the French claims to the Netherlands.

It so happened that the Dutch garrison at Luxemburg had been conducting some experiments with Moselle wine, and Maximilian at the head of twelve thousand men scaled the ramparts and entered the city before any one in the vicinity had learned that he was to be considered a factor in the struggle.

Maximilian retained possession for three years while the larger contestants were too busy to think about him. The Peace of Utrecht, 1713, however, gave the Spanish Netherlands to the house of Hapsburg and the elector withdrew as gracefully as possible.

Charles VI of Austria started the country upon the

THE LOWER CITY
A bit of ancient fortification and the chapel where the bones of John the Blind halted momentarily in their wanderings

THE SUBURB OF THE GRUND, THE UPPER TOWN
To the right the ancient bridge leading to the Bock where the Fairy Melusine is imprisoned
LUXEMBURG CITY

SWORD AND TORCH

first era of peace that it had known for generations. He regulated everything, from Sunday closing and "moonshining" to postal service, passports, and money-lending. He removed the traditional ban against commerce as a means of livelihood for barons destined by tradition and inclination to carry on the more gentlemanly pursuits of highway robbery. It was this latter ruling, merely incidental to a great program of reform, that eventually gave the duchy its place in the sun. Luxemburg is an iron country and the indigent nobles, granted permission to earn an honest living, installed a number of blast-furnaces, some of which were on the sites of to-day's great manufacturing plants.

Charles died and Maria Theresa, queen of kindness, took the throne by right of pragmatic sanction. Her reign added prosperity to the restful peace of the Moselle province. She simplified the processes of justice and reduced clerical and baronial privilege. She was tactful, intelligent, and strong, a fairy queen who was withal very human.

Joseph II, her son, who shouldered the problems of empire at her death, was a sort of Haroun al Raschid with a wealth of untried schemes for the betterment of the world and a supreme egotism.

The brotherhood of man became the subject-matter of all his political preachments. But his attitude seems to have been that the human being who was his brother was also his child, without a mind of his own. "Liberty, equality, fraternity" were combined in Joseph's policies under a broad cloak of paternalism.

He visited Luxemburg city incognito a year after his succession to the throne, took up his lodgings at a hotel instead of in one of the several chateaux which he owned in the district, walked about among the burghers as a private citizen, and generally maintained the democratic airs of his disguised self, while making no bones about his knowledge that his identity had been discovered.

He undertook to eliminate a number of minor religious orders, combining their membership in one or two strong organizations. His plans did not arouse much comment in Luxemburg, where they affected only a few houses. But they aroused the hatred of the Belgian clergy and generally prepared the way for the overthrow of the Hapsburgs in the Netherlands.

His lack of understanding of the people he patronized reached a climax when he undertook to disregard provincial charters in the estates of Brabant, including that of "the joyous entrance." This charter, taking its name from the fact that Wenceslaus, son of John the Blind, upon entering Brussels with his young wife the Duchess of Brabant, agreed to recognize all existing privileges. Among the privileges later incorporated in the official charter which bore the title La Joyeuse Entrée was that of deposing a sovereign who failed to maintain it.

SWORD AND TORCH

In 1787 he suppressed the permanent deputations of the estates of Brabant and overturned the established judiciary system. In October, 1789, came the result. Belgium arose in a general revolt and drove the Austrian troops east of the Meuse. Of the Spanish Netherlands, so called, Luxemburg alone remained faithful to the rule of Austria. Joseph, who saw his reforms overthrown and his kindnesses misinterpreted by these people whom he had determined to make his "brothers" willy-nilly, died of a broken heart.

His epitaph best tells his history:

> Here lies a prince whose intentions were pure but who had the misfortune to witness the wrecking of all his enterprises.

The Belgic provinces decided to return to Austria after overtures by Leopold II, brother of Joseph II. But the pacification had only brief results. Leopold had scarcely been laid in his grave, in 1792, when the French Revolution was detonated. The Republican Government stated that Francis II, son of Leopold, and his Prussian ally Frederick William II, were harboring French refugees as a menace to the revolutionary movement, and declared war against them. Thus began another twenty years of bloodshed. The Prussians started successfully, taking Longwy and Verdun. The road to Paris was open before them, but they were stopped by an audacious manœuver on the part of Dumouriez—mark the place—in the fated passages of the Argonne.

THE LAND OF HAUNTED CASTLES

The Germans fought to a draw at Valmy and retreated through Luxemburg. The retreat did to the army what French artillery and bayonets had failed to do. The advance of the Republican troops toward the Rhine found the duchy virtually without a protector.

In 1794 they laid siege to the Great Rock and there ensued the most terrible period in the history of the fort since Siegfroid and Mélusine had laid its foundations. After seven months, the Austrian garrison and Luxemburg volunteers were reduced to the point of starvation and the unburied dead in the streets of the capital gave potent promise of another pestilence of the sort that is war's best ally.

Field-Marshal Bender capitulated in June, 1795, and Luxemburg was annexed to the republic under the terms of "the National Convention of the Ninth Vendémiaire, the Year IV," and called "The Department of Forests."

A tax of a million and a half francs was immediately assessed against the city of eight thousand inhabitants, whose pitiful fortunes had been further reduced by war. A large sum of silver found in the house of a French refugee, however, lessened this burden by reducing the pro rata. Nine commissioners were appointed to see that the taxes were promptly and cheerfully paid.

War had been hell for the Luxemburgers during a thousand years or more of distinct national existence.

SWORD AND TORCH

Peace under the French Republic was its culminating fury.

Spared the hatreds fostered by doctrinal wrangling in the wake of the revolution, strongly religious and firmly Catholic despite the reformation on one side and the materialistic revolution on the other, they were plunged without warning into the midst of intolerance masquerading under the guise of liberty. They saw their churches put to use as granaries and storehouses, all that they held sacred desecrated, their traditions targeted by a murderous crew of aliens.

Luxemburg must have felt the Terror more than did the loyalists of France. For the Luxemburgers had not the remotest conception of what it stood for. They were told that they were being liberated, and liberty meant nothing to them thenceforward but the assassination of nuns and priests, the wrecking of cherished ideals, and the burning of age-old convents.

The transition from feudalism with its ground-rentals to private ownership with its endless taxes may have been a great step forward in the national life of the duchy, but the unfortunates whom it affected did not recognize it as such.

Their sons, conscripted despite all protest or hope of exemption, were sent into foreign lands to give their lives to perpetuate their enemy's conquests. Here was the first fertile field of *Kanonenfutter* and the harvest

THE LAND OF HAUNTED CASTLES

was thorough. Fourteen thousand young men marched forth from the Department of Forests to serve as targets in the cause of "liberty." Five thousand of them came back.

Unarmed, untrained, hopeless, and helpless, the men of Luxemburg arose against their "saviors" with the courage of despair to protest against all of this. The Kloeppelkrieg, or "Peasants' War," is an epic. The revolt, which started shortly after Napoleon's departure for Egypt, was put down in a series of short engagements and prompt massacres.

Then for four years the policy of repression was carried on with a vigor that made previous tyranny seem like a continuous holiday; firearms, powder, and all bells not serving public clocks were seized and taken to Luxemburg city. "It was," said the Curé Bormann, "a four-years' Good Friday."

Paris capitulates. Napoleon goes into exile.

There follow "The Hundred Days." A peasant tells an emperor: "The way to La Haie Sainte is clear." And the flower of the French army rides on to death in the sunken road of Ohain, and a great conqueror loses the Battle of Waterloo.

The Congress of Vienna established the Kingdom of the Netherlands, uniting Holland and Belgium under William I, Prince of Orange-Nassau-Vianden and Grand-duke of Luxemburg. The grand duchy had been ceded to him by Prussia, its principal claimant, in compensation for his loss of territory in Nassau. Europe apparently had been stabilized. But paper kingdoms had been manufactured many times before the convening of the Congress of Vienna and history had shown them to be very flimsy affairs.

The religious differences which had parted Belgium and the northern Netherlands once before remained unchanged. Holland basked in royal favor while the Walloons made desperate efforts to master the Dutch language. Financial tangles that distressed Brabant, and the unwillingness of William to listen to protest brought new resentment. In 1830 armed men were marching once more upon the bloody fields of Flanders, and Belgium had declared its individuality in revolution. During the nine years that followed, the Prussian garrison placed in Luxemburg city by the Congress of Vienna rested on its arms while the representatives of the grand-duke exercised the functions of government for the eastern half of the duchy. The western half was in the hands of the Belgians, who had founded a new provincial capital at Arlon.

The Treaty of London of 1839 fixed the boundaries of the grand duchy in their present form, slicing off the Walloon territory to form the Belgian "Province of Luxemburg."

Little was left of the duchy that Wenceslaus, the first

THE LAND OF HAUNTED CASTLES

duke, had inherited, except the Great Rock, but that was sufficient to bring Europe to the verge of a new war and to foment a new series of hatreds that were in good working-order as late as November 11, 1918.

France was dissatisfied with the maintenance of a Prussian garrison in an impregnable fortress so close to her own frontiers. Louis Napoleon, who reckoned without Bismarck, imagined Germany a negligible quantity in Europe.

Despite the disillusionment on that score that should have come to him after witnessing the speedy termination of the war between Prussia and Austria in 1866 and sensing, though he might not have seen, the Machiavellian hand of the Iron Chancellor molding new destinies for the Central Powers, Louis believed that he held the whip-hand. He naïvely suggested to Bismarck that in view of the fact that France was willing to recognize the gains of the Prussians in their recent conflict with Austria, Germany should make some concessions for mutual benefit. Luxemburg, he pointed out, had been left out of the new German federation, and was no longer a federal fortress. That being the case, it should be given to France to compensate for the new strength of Prussia. The argument had better basis than the stolid Louis could have realized.

Bismarck, while indicating his acquiescence, contrived to get a damaging statement from the French ambassador

SWORD AND TORCH

in Berlin, indicating that Louis was preparing to "violate the neutrality of Belgium,"—prophetic phrase!

He published it at a psychological moment and war between France and Prussia was held in leash by a hair.

The great powers convened in London in 1867 and settled the matter by arbitration. They decided that as neither France nor Germany ought to have the fortress, it had best be destroyed and it was so ordered.

Luxemburg's neutrality was placed under a guaranty similar to that which established the autonomy of Belgium. The Prussian garrison evacuated Luxemburg city and the work of demolition was begun. In 1870 Siegfroid's rock was no longer a menace. Presently France and Prussia were flying at each other's throats for a cause that apparently had nothing to do with Luxemburg. But the denuded rock by the Alzette epitomized the story of the grudges and envies that had made war for any reason a possibility.

After a thousand years of proud, uprearing dignity, the Colossus of Rhodes had fallen down and been sold to the junkmen. A Samson of strength had pushed for ten centuries against the pillars of alien nations and now lay dead amid the ruins.

A million armed men have marched through Luxemburg since that time and the tiny grand duchy is still a nation. A people's spirit is something that remains after ramparts and bastions have been dynamited asunder and outward manifestations of power have been ground under the hob-nailed heel of military necessity.

CHAPTER IX
THE CAPITAL

City of Cloak and Sword

Then sheathes in calm repose the vengeful blade
For gentle peace

—Adams.

CHAPTER IX

THE CAPITAL

AN overhanging gable bulked ominously into the crooked little street. In the flickering glare of an ancient oil lamp at the corner, one caught a vague glimpse of blackened timbers crossed in the stucco surface of the wall, a window with many small bulbous panes, and a slate roof rising almost perpendicularly into the black sky. Over the way a furtive glimmer of light crept through a tightly closed shutter. Somewhere in the depths of the gloom a pair of wooden-soled shoes clicked a diminuendo tattoo. A decrepit cart, drawn by a leisurely Belgian horse, creaked dismally over the cobbles of the age-old pavement.

The Grimms wrote about such a street. The atmosphere of homely mystery that pervaded the German folklore still lingers in the quaint architecture, the odd angles, and the unexpected quirks of this old-world alley. Time has not passed here. A century has lost itself in the mazes of its curves while the town clock has ticked off the important minutes that lie between tallow dips and electric lights, sedan-chairs and street cars, courier and telephone, ox-cart and motor.

A sad-faced gargoyle wept copious tears upon the worn

THE LAND OF HAUNTED CASTLES

flags. A tuneless song, plaintive and quavering, floated up from a near-by rathskeller, accompanied by sundry and divers beery smells. A German police dog stuck a quizzical nose from a doorway in the shadow of a jutting gable and cast a disdainful eye over his surroundings.

Certainly this was a highway of intrigue in a city of the cloak and sword.

In the distance the lights of the capital cast a dull twilight upward, disclosing the ghostly outline of spire and tower and gable. There was a perfume of roses in the air—and a sense of Mélusine's presence.

It was thus that I first saw Luxemburg city.

No capital in the world is quite like Luxemburg city. It has the pose and poise of Gibraltar, the bridge-and-spire profile of Bruges, the flowered beauty of Paris, the historic charm of Brussels, and the mystery of a temple city of the Orient.

Passmore refers to it as a dozen cities in one.

Renwick quotes J. W. Burgon in describing it,—

"A rose-red city, half as old as time."

And both are right. In intangible pattern, age and roses are bright in the memories that one carries away with him.

There is something in this city that all the nations of the world had a hand in forming, which reminds one of

THE CAPITAL

a Chinese lacquer work. Layer by layer the color and groundwork are laid with deft and careful hand, until, after years of patient building, beauty emerges triumphant. Siegfroid and Mélusine put down the first stratum of the present Luxemburg more than a thousand years ago. Part of their handiwork may be seen to-day. And atop the ruins of the city they built one sees the vestiges of other strata: Burgundian, Austrian, Spanish, French, and Prussian. The art and wealth of the world and its conquerors went into this capital and much of the original investment remains.

Gone is the military glory of the great city. It basks in the sun amid its famous roses like a warrior tired of bloodshed. But, though jealous nations have taken away its sword and smashed its armor, the tokens of its power remain where all may see them.

Paper treaties can never change the contour of its grim rocks, nor alter the courses of the deep-running streams that excavated its fosses. As a fortress it is something of a Phœnix. Some fifty years ago the military experts of France and Germany saw the last charge of dynamite detonated in the leveling of its walls and inspected with pleased eyes the emasculated bastions of the Great Rock.

"The fortress is useless," declared the German expert in his report to the Iron Chancellor. "Never again will it be a menace!"

How Mélusine must have laughed at that! Neither

THE LAND OF HAUNTED CASTLES

Germany nor France could foresee the crumpled turrets of Liège, nor the heroic defense of Fort Vaux. They could not know that in five decades the great outer cincture of Paris would be dismantled as useless.

A great war has passed and the idea of strongholds has changed. To-day a few field-guns would make of Luxemburg city another Verdun, perhaps a greater Verdun. Which proves that a city born to be a Titan will never be a pygmy, whatever Iron Chancellors and learned arbitrators may have to say about it.

The Bock, site of the original Lucilinburhuc, juts out into its ravine on the northeast side of the city. At its base the purling Alzette twists like a letter S into the north. At the bottom of the S, the tiny Petrusse pours into the Alzette through another cañon, surrounding three sides of the capital with a moat, the depth of which is accentuated by its narrowness.

Straight across the S-curve of the Alzette the Prince Henri Railroad strikes into the gentle valley that leads to Ettelbruck. In its departure it rattles over the Great Rock through a great graveyard of wrecked wall, tower, and rampart. It gives a fleeting glimpse of the Clausen where Mansfeld built his storied château. Its squeaky whistles echo between crags that once threw back the challenging gun roar of the army of Louis XIV. Its roadbed is laid atop the unmarked graves of forgotten heroes.

Where the Petrusse casts its lot with the Alzette the

CHATEAU BERG
The Grand Ducal country seat

THE CAPITAL

valley widens and on this floor of rocky chaos "The Lower Town" follows the curve of the streams. The Grund, the natives call this place. And while its date of origin is doubtful, it has a look of antiquity equal to that of the pyramids. From the railroad or the cliff highway of the upper city it looks like a great unroofed catacomb.

The course of the long-gone ramparts which supplied protection for the west and northwest sides of the city, may be traced by a great arc of boulevards and rose gardens that swings about from the Petrusse to the Alzette. About twenty per cent. of the town's area is covered by these parks, a long vista of greenery and flowers that gives no hint of the ugly hillocks that once stood here. Whatever opprobrium Luxemburg may heap upon the heads of the London councillors who ordered the fort dismantled and the nation disarmed, should be tempered with thanksgiving. For the work of demolition made possible this work of civic beautification.

Documents and sketches extant in the Luxemburg museum show that this massive wall was a mountain of stone and mortar. It was so high that it hid the spires of the city's seven churches and so forbiddingly square that even rose-vines and ivy could not hide its gaunt menace.

But the park that has succeeded is the work of M. Edouard André, who designed the world-famous gardens of Monte Carlo. The French landscape engineer has zoned the skeleton of medieval militarism with a cincture of rich and varied beauty. Botanical gardens are succeeded by patches of natural grove, and through the entire belt shady pathways curve in lace-patterns up hill and down dale in a journey of never-ending delights.

The casemates of the Bock, sunk into the rock by Marie d'Autriche, sister of Charles V,—in 1765, before Vauban, came to make Luxemburg the greatest inland fortress in Europe,—still may be seen. The engineers of destruction sent there by the world powers after the decision of the Council of London did not consider them important enough to justify a waste of blasting-powder. To-day they are much the same as they were when Marie's sappers constructed them,—a network of vaults eleven feet wide and ten feet high circling the face of the promontory like a cloistered walk. Loopholes sufficient to accommodate twenty-five batteries looked out upon the Pfaffenthal and Grund. From this rocky gun-turret a subterranean passage led down beneath the natural fosse that separated the rock from the plateau upon which the greater portion of the present city of Luxemburg stands.

All of this excavation was accomplished without the aid of modern explosives and remains a monumental tribute to the military zeal and painstaking thoroughness of the woman who planned it and the men who executed it.

And the tangible engineering, rather than the stirring

THE CAPITAL

romances of the rock, has merited for it the name by which it is known to the present generation of Mélusine's descendants. Hollow Tooth (*Huolen Zant*), is the title they give it. And a descriptive appellation it is. The Bock was the fang of Siegfroid's dragon of the Alzette, a fang that buried itself deeply into the throat of many an adversary, and it looks the part.

Aside from the subterranean passage that leads from the casemates to the city proper, this island in the air was connected with the mainland by a double bridge, buttressed and fortified. The tunnel was an emergency exit for the defenders of the Bock in the event that an enemy should destroy the bridges. The causeway has felt the effects of time and powder. Its ramparts have fallen and its protecting towers are obelisks of ruin. But the bridge itself will have to crumble for many a century more before it will be unserviceable.

It is a strange thing that the greatest test of the Bock and its casemates should have been imposed by the United States, a nation that had not come into being at the time of Marie d'Autriche. But it is a truth that any Luxemburger who lived in the capital in war time will attest. During the German retreat it became known to the general headquarters of the American Expeditionary Forces that the German high command was meeting in Luxemburg city and that ammunition, supplies, and troops were clearing through here for Verdun, Sedan, and

THE LAND OF HAUNTED CASTLES

Stenay. As a consequence, although the neutrality of Luxemburg was recognized, bombing-planes were sent over nightly to make as much trouble as possible for the German crown-prince's advisers.

When TNT began to rain into the vale of the Alzette out of the dark sky, the people fled to the Bock as their ancestors, hundreds of years before, had fled for protection against the petards of Louis XIV. A great portion of the city's populace was accommodated either in the ancient gun-vaults or in similar tunnels of Vauban's fort on the plateau. A town which had come down to modernity through a thousand years of defensive policy did not need to look far for effective shelter.

The Bock withstood these bombardments. There were plenty of direct hits on the city and some loss of life. But the rock turned TNT as it had turned the arrows of the Trevirians and the bullets of later foes.

Of recent years the chiseled passages have served as store-rooms for champagne and an arsenal for the gendarmerie. There was little champagne left, however, at the time that the casemates were used as an abri. The company which stored it was French and the Germans had a definite policy regarding the disposal of enemy property.

Across the river from the Huolen Zant on the southern side rises the Rham plateau, where the Romans once had a camp. Wenceslaus fortified it in 1393 and the mili-

THE CAPITAL

tary tinkers who followed after him to pile new stones on Siegfroid's strong point did their best to make it a worthy auxiliary to the Bock. Four towers erected by Wenceslaus still are standing.

From this point one gazes down upon the Grund with its time-torn parish church. This chapel is noteworthy principally as one of the places where the bones of John the Blind found temporary sanctuary.

The body of the perigrinating King of Bohemia lay for a long time in a crypt behind the high altar beneath a monument that has since been removed to the cathedral. John has departed from here, however, wandering in death as he did in life, so the principal relics of the church are less regal than a king's ashes.

Scattered about amid a quantity of queer appointments are a number of handsome wood-carvings. The baptismal fonts are priceless examples of the wood-working art, and the statue of the Black Virgin—"La Sancte Vièrge Noire (or d'Egypte)"—is a revelation to one who would study the sculptures of the Middle Ages.

Northeast of the Bock is the Clausen, a park-like valley below the wooded heights of Parkhohe, Obergrünwald, and Niedergrünwald. It was here that Mansfeld built his palace, but only isolated groups of stone remain to mark the spot where it stood.

To the left of the Clausen, on the heights that rise up from the Pfaffenthal, three towers are emplaced in one of

THE LAND OF HAUNTED CASTLES

André's groves. They are all that is left of Fort Thüngen. The Three Acorns, they are named in local parlance,—*Trois Glands*, a name that conveys nothing of their bloody history. It was in this fort that the rebels of the Kloeppelkrieg were executed by the sansculottes after the French Revolution.

Near the fort on the Rue Vauban of the Pfaffenthal is the Musée Archéologique, where are collected the visible remains of Luxemburg's peculiarly important place in world history.

This museum is the bound volume of the duchy's romance. It contains national archives dating from 803 A. D. and twenty thousand books on subjects allied to the country's history. And if stories may be read in stones, the material is here with which may be reconstructed the lives of the prehistoric races of the Ardennes. Carvings, statuettes, coins, tools, and pottery, left behind by the departing Celts; Druid relics in stone and metal; burial trappings of the Franks; Roman weapons and coins without number; tapestries and furniture from the time of Ermesinde; mosaics, carved inscriptions; cross-bows that saw service at Wœringen; personal belongings of John the Blind; carved cannon from the battle-fields of Louis of France,—these and a thousand other treasures have been gathered here. The accoutrements of war make up a large portion of the exhibits. But that is natural. Luxemburg's history is a long recital of battle and strife.

THE CAPITAL

The Roman collection is the most complete. Perhaps nowhere outside of Italy did Cæsar's legionaries leave such a quantity of personal property. Every one of their camps has proved to be a mine of weapons, armor, and copper coins. Their temples dotted the Ardennes. Their graveyards stretched across the continent. Their villas, buried beneath the wreckage of barbarian conquest but still preserving much of their original beauty, occupied many a nook in the Moselle country. Bit by bit these treasure-troves have come to light and the duchy is fitting them together in a picture of the Roman occupation in its bloody beginnings, the flower of its greatness, and its decline.

True Romance does not die though the page on which it be written be burned and the ashes cast to the winds.

At the end of the bridge leading from the Bock is the ancient Marche au Poissons, which marked the boundary of Siegfroid's nascent city at the time when Mélusine disappeared. It was in this vicinity that Jean Beck, come back from the wars to be governor, found the wife that he had deserted. Not far away was the famous Puit Rouge, the well sunk by the Austrians. The neighborhood still bears the marks of a strangely isolated community, a city within a city.

The Letzeburgers inhabited this section. It is not difficult to trace their name to "Lutzelbourg," the first corruption of the city's ancient designation "Lucilinburhuc." But while the rest of the capital was making "Luxemburg" out of "Lutzelbourg," the group of market-folk who lived near the Marche de Poissons were twisting their tongues to different pronunciations.

I asked a young woman of Gosseldange one time just who, what, and why the "Letzeburgers" were.

She replied, proud of her ability to tell me in English:

"They are people who live in the Stadt Luxemburg. They have been there long time. Always, I think. Their women dress like their grandmothers dressed. And they speak a language that is very *difficile* to understand. It is not French. It is not German. It is not Luxemburg. It is Letzeburg."

There is much of Luxemburg in this neighborhood that is not French, nor German, nor Luxemburg. Turn southward in the Rue du Gouvernement. It is a winding way, cobbled and sloping and hemmed in closely with shops. A few brief paces, and it leads out of Letzeburg into the era of the Spanish renaissance. To the left, without garden, walk, or terrace to embellish it, stands the Palais Grand Ducal,—the Hôtel de Ville of Mansfeld's time,—a building that holds a unique place in contrast to its surroundings if not in its own worth as an example of Spanish architecture.

This building is old enough to have its legends,—probably has enough of them if one would take time to un-

THE CAPITAL

earth them from the mass of documents in the museum, —but it was only a year or two ago that it figured in a story which the grandchildren of the present generation will some day hear coupled with the myth of Mélusine. In the *Krummerweg* on which it faces there arose a revolution, an opera-bouffe sort of affair in which no one was killed and few hurt, and after the tumult and the shouting had died, a beautiful princess went into exile.

Luxemburg's status after the war was a matter which occupied much of the conversation of the populace, who, however much they might be interested, would have nothing to do with settling it. The capital's politics suddenly developed a number of factions. One group—a rather unthinking group—believed that Luxemburg should remain in the German customs federation and take pot-luck with Germany. Another faction wished coalition with France, another favored a treaty with Belgium, a fourth was openly advocating the establishment of a republic.

Marie Adelaide, a girl about twenty-four years old, was grand-duchess, and for all that she was the ideal princess of medieval romance in a modern setting,—beautiful, intelligent, and accomplished,—she was not particularly popular. The Germans had lost the war. And it was noised abroad that Marie had been over-friendly toward the Germans. It does not pay, even in Luxemburg, to back a losing horse.

THE LAND OF HAUNTED CASTLES

Storm-clouds began to gather immediately after the signing of the armistice, although Marie did much to retrieve her reputation as a diplomatist by inviting the Americans to occupy the grand duchy. This manœuver, which placed Luxemburg before the world in the light of a neutral looking to the conqueror of its invaders for the protection and restoration of its nationality, did much to prevent an annexation to France along with the Alsace and Lorraine of which it was once a part. Also, it insured payment for all damage that might be done by the troops of occupation.

The Thirty-third and the Fifth divisions of the American Expeditionary Forces were moved forward from the Meuse into the grand duchy and internal disorder on any large scale became impossible. But a disgruntled people pay little attention to bayonets. Secret agitation continued in Luxemburg city until January 16, 1919, when all of the factions decided simultaneously upon action.

An American captain, in the city on leave of absence when the uprising came, has given an eye-witness account of it:

> The city was going on about its business of building villainous waffles for the American trade and spending in sedate luxury the wealth extracted from the Germans during the invasion. The street cars clattered along on their quaint little square wheels. The town belles in their plaid coats that until recently had been American horse covers, took the air on the outer boulevard. The motor-

THE CAPITAL

ists wrangled for petrol at a municipal filling station on the Arlon road. The atmosphere was cold and clear. The capital bent upon minding its own affairs gave no hint of what was in the air.

So might Pompeii have been just before the zero hour on Vesuvius.

But the city knew what was going on. Toward noon groups of anxious citizens of the variety and occupation commonly seen in front of American baseball score boards began to assemble before the brown gates of the ducal palace.

The soldiers of the palace guard were a colorful bit in a dull, drab picture—youths in glittering accoutrements of patent leather, cerise, green, gold braid, silver buckles, and cockades. They kept a firm grip upon Erfurt rifles to which bayonets of an approved German pattern had been fixed.

As for the revolutionists, they were as remarkable a collection of radicals as ever assembled to overturn a government. . . . A grocer's boy with a round cheese under his arm, stolid burghers with sharp pointed mustaches, a few old men armed with crutches and canes, and a bespectacled school teacher with an umbrella were in the foreground.

The stage was set for comic opera. It remained only for some one to set the characters in motion. This task fell to the prima donna herself. The Grand Duchess, Marie Adelaide . . . stepped out upon a little iron balcony and raised her hand. The mob ceased its murmuring.

There followed, according to this witness's account of the proceedings, a review of the situation by the beautiful Marie, a brief effectiveness, and then tumult.

The lame, the halt, and the blind gathered there in the Rue du Gouvernement had come for violence and suddenly decided against any argument that the grand-duchess might advance. There were roars for blood, in which the republicans were loudest, a sudden movement toward the startled sentries,—all of the usual indications of mob spirit in the ascendant.

The turmoil was increased by the anguished shouts of the sentries. An officer commanded that the machine-guns be mounted. Presently came the tremulous report of a subaltern that the machine-guns were not to be found, that both of them had been stolen.

"The *verdammte* Americans!" shouted the officer, leaping quickly to conclusions. "They must have stolen them from our soldiers."

All of this would have been ludicrous had not the life of a princess and the destinies of a nation hung in the balance.

The crisis was at hand and Marie—ever the leader, ever the princess—met it. She announced in an imperious tone that she had abdicated in favor of her sister Charlotte. While the thick wits of the populace were working with this unexpected development she left the balcony and started into exile.

There was a sudden movement in the throng shortly after that. But the abdication of Marie and the accession of Charlotte had nothing to do with that. A platoon of American military police had rounded the corner out of the Place Guillaume and had begun, with business-like speed, to clear the street.

THE CAPITAL

The burghers went home. The teacher journeyed onward to his school. The grocer's boy remembered that he had been sent to deliver a cheese.

So ended the revolution.

Marie Adelaide went north to Berg, remained there a few days, and crossed into Germany. A year later she entered an Italian convent.

Two spidery bridges lead from the old city to the newer suburb in which the railroad station is the most important building. One of these, the Pont Adolphe, finished in 1903, is a white stone masterpiece that spans the Petrusse in a single arch of feather grace. Beyond it are several hotels and some questionable cabarets.

Near the Gare Centrale stands a champagne warehouse on the site of an old fortress tower. It is said that a tunnel led from this spot to the Bock. At any rate, a network of subterranean passages have been discovered striking down toward the level of the valley. Like parts of the Bock itself, they have been put to excellent use as winecellars.

Within the next thousand years there can never be another Luxemburg. Yonder a sad-faced gargoyle that has seen "towns burned and murder done and great kings turned to a little bitter mold," weeps rusty tears upon the worn flags; a tuneless song, plaintive and quavering, floats up from a near-by rathskeller. Time has not passed

THE LAND OF HAUNTED CASTLES

this city. A century has lost itself in the mazes of its crooked alleys. Certainly it is the city of the cloak and sword, an eternal mystery in which night is an accomplice.

> Disparting towers
> Trembling all precipitate down dashed,
> Rattling around, loud thundering to the moon.

CHAPTER X
ANSEMBOURG

The Lady of the Spinning Wheel

Love is strong as death;
—The Song of Solomon, viii, 6.

CHAPTER X

ANSEMBOURG

THE white mists were clinging to the rocky hilltops and a fine spring rain was beating into the valley, stirring the turbulent little Mamer to iridescent froth and releasing from the groves and gardens the scent of fresh verdure mixed with pine. Ansembourg's straggling little street was washed white and was deserted save for an ancient dame plodding along in the wake of an irresponsible cow.

The firs on the cliff sides seemed gray-blue and luminous, and the red escarpments gleamed like polished granite under the cascading rivulets from the heights. The dozen houses of the village that cluster at the bottom of the western crag were plumed with smoke that flattened under the rain and spread out in a cirrus cloud as reluctant to leave the earth as the wraiths that have haunted this district since the days of the first crusade. The pounding of the forge, Ansembourg's chief excuse for a modern existence, combined distantly with the murmur of rushing waters in the ditches beside the white road. In a dim overtone blended the clatter of dishes and the voices of women and children.

THE LAND OF HAUNTED CASTLES

On its rock high over the town bulked the battlemented ruin of the great castle,—grim, formidable, overwhelming, even with tower and wall and buttress softened to shadows by the veils of the rain.

There are other castles in Luxemburg as large as Ansembourg, many of them stronger if preservation be an indication of strength, but none placed on a more inaccessible vantage-point or more imposing at first view.

Perspective plays weird tricks with this battered schloss and its feudal town. For all of its distance upon the steep cliff and its loss of height through the influences of enemy artillery and the wasting ages, it easily dominates the landscape, greater to the eye than village or forest or natural escarpment. There is an instant impression of size that lingers even after the proportions of the view adjust themselves and one sees that the eagle's nest on the crag is a bit over bold in advancing its claims to attention.

The seigneurs who built Ansembourg back in the hazy centuries where their history is lost paid little attention to roads. A meager path cuts up from the village through the cliff woods at a heart-catching angle, probably along a trail that was once a bridle-path for the horsemen of the castle. For the greater portion of its twisting course it is squarely beneath the ramparts within easy aim for the wielders of tar-pot and lead-ladle who once paced those battlements, watchers in the castle's defense.

ANSEMBOURG

A last quick turn and steep gradient brings one to the plateau and a turnip-patch beneath the ivy-covered turrets of the outer wall.

The schloss seen from close at hand exhibits greater beauties than might be suspected in a view from the town below.

The great piles of masonry sweep up to undreamed-of vastnesses, damaged only slightly by the marksmanship of Boufflers, yielding only partially to the destructive hands of wind and weather. An iron-studded door, as solid to-day as it was eight or nine hundred years ago, swings on a ponderous hinge below an arched gateway. A black pup perhaps a year old guards the crumbling threshold with an air of confident proprietorship.

Pull the wire loop at the right of the door and at the left of the dog. A bell with a tone like that of a buoy on a dismal reef clangs somewhere in an echoing corridor. There come the clatter of wooden shoes and the thudding of several great bolts being pulled from their niches in the stone arch of the doorway. The great oaken barrier swings back and a boy twelve years old smiles a welcome which he translates in his native patois and French.

Visitors are not frequent at Ansembourg. The tortuous unpleasantness of the upward climb devised to discourage the enemies of the graf now serves a similar purpose in the fending off of tourists. The casual sight-seer is quick to fortify himself with the belief that one castle is like every other castle and to promise himself that in making one exploration that will do for all he will find a ruin easier to get to and closer to a large town. The few who do brave the precipice consequently find a guide who considers them guests and chatters a volume of local gossip as different from the set speech of the usual castle guardian as a boy's quick confidence differs from grown-up avarice.

"Come in," invited this unexpected sentry.

I followed into a wide courtyard beyond which was a second wall, and felt that I had stepped back eons.

A great mass of crumbling stone stables and ancient barrack-rooms crowded the inner side of the wall through which we had just come. Some of the buildings still were sufficiently in repair to provide shelter for farming-implements. Others presented an inferno of tumbling buttress and shattered roof.

Back toward the west where the enceinte turned to follow the wall of the schloss a new stable had been built with the rocks and timbers of the old. In it two great Belgian horses were munching their hay, apparently oblivious of the ghostly steeds that crowded them,—accoutred war-horses back from the crusades, beasts of the marvelous stock of "Bayard" whom legend will keep alive forever.

A brass-bound door led into a dark, narrow passage-

ANSEMBOURG

way that smelled of musty hay. It gave into a second court, much smaller than the first, which probably before the era of Boufflers and his fifteen-pound notices of eviction had been a covered anteroom in the main portion of the castle. To the right of it stood the chapel, three sides of it well preserved, the fourth open but protected from the weather by the rest of the building which towered above it. The altar still was recognizable as such, dingy but intact, as were a number of carved saints in niches about the walls. As for the rest—ruin.

Plows, manure-forks, shovels, the rusted and out-worn accumulations of abandoned farm paraphernalia leaned against splintered prie-dieu and crumbling altar rail. A gray light filtered through cobwebs that seemed to be as old as the castle and added to the depressing influence of the reflection that a peasant's carelessness of a wonderful heritage works greater havoc than the cannon-balls of a Boufflers.

The court was bridged by a great arch that at one time had supported part of the central donjon. The ivy was on it, glistening with the rain. At each end of it was a pot of red geraniums, proof that a woman was part of the latest garrison of old Ansembourg. A red bird in a wicker cage ruffled its wings near the doorway. I could not help thinking that in this instance if in no other the cannoneers of Louis XIV had been artists. Their guns had made a peaceful garden out of what once was probably a very uncomfortable set of living-quarters. That ivy-covered arch was worth two towers.

One could not see the valley from this point. The outer wall of the fortifications was considerably more than head-high, and blind.

The boy led to a narrow door across the court. We wiped our feet on a rag rug and entered the ancient salle des chevaliers. Here was a real surprise. The tiled floor with its mosaic in the arms of Ansembourg at the threshold was whole, though worn a bit. Pillar and arch and carven fireplace had not suffered during the ages. But the impression of grandeur was gone. The stone walls had been plastered and whitewashed. A wooden sink stretched across the stone seats at the tall window on the valley side.

A queer little stove, that looked like nothing so much as a diminutive bath-tub on stilts, stood before the hearth of the knights and stuck a curving stovepipe through a sheet-iron screen that covered the front of the fireplace. Over the chiseled arms of the ancient house at one end of the mantelpiece stood a brass crucifix. At the other end—*sic transit gloria mundi!*—clattered an American alarm-clock. Where the mailed knights had mulled their wine a pot-au-feu bubbled a message of approaching dinner. Where pewter steins had clanked on a long oak table, a baby beat lustily upon the front of her high chair with a spoon.

ANSEMBOURG

The boy opened a door at the left of the fireplace and we proceeded up through a tower in a spiraling ascent. At the second floor the guide halted.

"It was here," he declared impressively, "that Graf Philip of Ansembourg quarreled with his wife. He stabbed her, sir, drove a knife into her heart, and she tumbled all the way to the bottom of these stairs.

"When my great-great-great-grandfather bought the castle, two hundred years ago, the stains were still on the stairs. My grandmother told me that in her day they used to come back every time trouble threatened the inmates of the house. But of that I know nothing. I used to look carefully every day, but I never saw them.

"Graf Philip was very remorseful after the deed. He stabbed himself also and fell at her feet. And the church refused to bury him in holy ground and there was quite a row about it."

Passmore has described Old Ansembourg as a haunt of satyrs, and viewed from the vantage-point of the curving stone stairs it merits the description. There was something blood-curdling in the boy's simple recital of a murder and suicide of hundreds of years ago, though it differed not at all from the gruesome events that one could read about on the front pages of the newspapers in any nation. It seemed, somehow, more atrocious as a crime with a medieval setting.

THE LAND OF HAUNTED CASTLES

There came a flash of white and unconsciously I gasped.

But it was not the ghost of the *Gräfin* that whitened the wall. It was the sudden light from an upper room into which the boy had opened the tower door.

There was little medieval or romantic about the arrangement of the floor across which our course next led. It was a dry, dusty place, odorous of grain and resin, used partly as a storehouse for oats and wheat and partly as family sleeping-quarters. The partitions were rough pine planks. The floor, although evidently laid across the seasoned rafters of the ancient schloss, was thin and poorly fastened and had an exciting way of sagging under one's feet. The boy escorted me through the partition toward a spot where a rickety ladder pursued a crooked course to a hatchway in the roof—shades of Siegfroid! a thatched roof. Then suddenly he stopped.

"Do you hear the spinning-wheel?" he asked.

I listened.

The house was quiet. The rain had stopped, apparently, for there was no patter on the roof. From a very great distance came the sound of a man's voice,—so soft that the words were not distinguishable.

And then, from a farther distance still, came a methodical creek and whir, intangible, indescribable. It took no great stretch of the imagination to identify it as the sound of a spinning-wheel, and my credulity had not yet

Where the "Lady of the Spinning Wheel" wove the wedding garment that was her shroud

From the Spinning Wheel Lady's Window. View from the corner tower of Old Ansembourg

OLD ANSEMBOURG

ANSEMBOURG

been placed on its guard. I had not yet heard the legend of the Spinning-wheel Lady.

"It sounds like a spinning-wheel," I admitted. "What is it?"

"A spinning-wheel," replied the boy in a matter-of-fact tone. "The sound of it has always been here in the building and always will be."

Then he told me the tragic story of the lady and her fateful spinning.

She was a prisoner brought from Burgundy or France to the ancient eagle's nest by a latter-day caveman with whom a show of force and expressions of love were synonymous terms. He adored her and proved it by killing a number of men in accomplishing her abduction.

But she appears to have been a haughty lady. She did not take kindly to her captivity, nor to her captor, and gave him to understand it in no equivocal words.

The love-sick graf then proposed marriage—evidently something of a concession—and sought to have the nuptials celebrated as soon as he had safely installed her in the castle. She appeared to be resigned to her lot. But she begged of him the boon of a delay.

She said that ill luck would certainly follow her and all connected with her unless she be allowed to spin and weave the material for a wedding-garment of the sort prescribed by the traditions of her people.

The superstitious graf granted her request, and night

and day the castle was filled with the squeak of the pedal and the whir of the wheel.

After a long time the graf came to her and demanded that she make an end to the spinning-business. She asked for two more days.

At midnight of the second night the graf came to her again.

"Is the wedding-garment finished?" he inquired roughly. He did not notice that she had moved close to a window overlooking the valley.

She peered out, searching in vain among the trees for a sign of the rescue party for which she had been waiting. At the castle gates should have been her lover from France, fulfilling the promise he had made to her just before her capture. But he was n't there. She turned back to the graf.

"No, sir," she said quietly. "My wedding-garment is not finished, but my shroud is."

She threw the mantle about her shoulders and leaped before he could reach her.

And her body fell on the soft moss of the hillside two hundred feet below, almost across the saddle of a French warrior leading his retainers to storm the castle. Her lover had come too late.

I listened attentively when the boy had done speaking. As before, the creak and whir trickled out of dusty space; there was no tracing the sound.

ANSEMBOURG

An air current under a loose board? Perhaps. An unfastened door in a subterranean passage long since forgotten? Possibly. A squeak is a squeak and a whir is a whir, no matter what causes them. But I felt with my guide that an investigation would be a waste of time. It was much more satisfactory to feel the presence of the Lady of the Spinning-wheel, to fancy her standing in her garments of star-dust where the window had opened out over the ramparts.

The sun had come out when we emerged through the roof to the top of a wall that led forward to the arch across the inner court. There was warmth in the air and the vigor of spring. Hundreds of feet below the valley was smiling with a new whiteness and men and women were astir in the streets of the village. Across the promontory to the left could be seen the spires of the new Château Ansembourg, a brief glimpse through the trees of its chapel and crypt.

Almost directly below was the forge, pounding as energetically to-day as it pounded when Rollingen founded it there.

There is a legend about the forge,—an oft-told legend that has displaced the Lady of the Spinning-wheel in narratives of many a traveler. The noise of the forge disturbed the sleep of the graf of Ansembourg. He sent a retainer down the hill one day to demand that it be closed.

"Tell your master," advised the keeper of the forge, "that this iron shall hammer at his castle gates."

And the prophecy was fulfilled.

Rollingen had connections which the graf of Ansembourg did not dare to overlook and the time-honored recourse of the noble to sword and torch was denied him because of the absence of his men-at-arms on sundry expeditions in the Rhineland. Before he had an opportunity to force the issue death overtook him.

His castle on the rock, and the great estates tributary to it, passed into the hands of his only child, a daughter. Here as always the hands of a woman weave the strands of the Ansembourg legend. She was beautiful. The smith was strong. They were married. Rank has ever seemed a feeble barrier to love. And he became a count in his own right.

The irritable graf lies somewhere on the hill, in a forgotten grave. The smith and his beautiful lady sleep their last sleep side by side in the Ansembourg crypt across the ravine. The grim castle crumbles as peasants ply their homely arts in what is left of its grandeur. And in the valley below, the forge rings out its Wagnerian symphony in excusable pride of triumph.

The other château in the valley below the town is a modern affair,—"modern," in the Luxemburg vernacular, meaning anything less than five hundred years old,—with terraced grounds, private burial vaults, and a wealth of

ANSEMBOURG

heroic sculpturings. It sits quietly among its blue-green fir-trees and continues to be the play-house of nobility.

The new château dates from the sixteenth century. Between the pillars of the arcade at its entrance sit four immense stone figures, "The Corners of the World"—male types of the principal races of Europe, Asia, Africa, and America. The originals of the group were carried off by Louis and placed in the Louvre. They were duplicated at the behest of a graf of Ansembourg several centuries later when the ancient house was rebuilt.

Roman and Greek gods and goddesses keep the great stone figures company along a cloistered walk on the first terrace. A few steps lower, a garden stretches down to the edge of a cress-grown mountain stream, ending in an arbor suggestive of medieval maidens in conical caps, listening to tales of love from the lips of knights in armor.

A scene, this, for a Viennese operetta, with tinkling waltzes, a Dresden-china doll chorus, a prince in disguise, and a princess in love.

Across the stream rise another precipitous hill and another toy forest of pines. Wherever one turns in the castle grounds the prospect is the same,—overhanging hills and stately trees.

The château and its garden are separated from the castle park by a high iron fence. The carriage gate is a carved arch of stone, bearing the shields of the house of Ansembourg, the House of Hollenfels, and numerous other heraldic devices significant of the marriages that united the principal families of Luxemburg when the grafs abandoned petty enmities to fight shoulder to shoulder in the defense of a common country.

The park is cut out of the side of the hill at the front of the château. Through a grove of mossy firs and beeches a staircase of stone and timber extends upward, two hundred and fifty steps, to the door of a chapel. The effect is that of a long tunnel in cool, shimmering, living green, ending in a vista of creamy marble, iridescent in the sunlight, a picture from the Arabian Nights.

Behind the chapel is a burial vault, containing the tomb and effigy of some crusading Ansembourg in full armor. He is worthy of note in that he is the only dead noble for miles around to whom no spectacular legend has yet been attached. He seems perfectly satisfied with his peaceful resting-place at the head of the long stairs and, so far as can be learned, has left the country-side to deal unhampered with the interesting ghosts of the upper castle.

CHAPTER XI
HOLLENFELS

The Hollow Rock and its Dream of Fair Women

> Curse away!
> And let me tell thee, Beausant, a wise proverb
> The Arabs have—"Curses are like young chickens,
> And still come home to roost."
> —Lytton.

WINDOWS OF THE CHAPEL

LOOKING FROM THE RAMPART
Still well preserved, into the roofless, floorless room that was the graf's bed chamber

HOLLENFELS

CHAPTER XI

HOLLENFELS

THE proper way in which to see Hollenfels is to circle the rocky precipice that juts out above Marienthal, to humor the tortuous whimsies of the mountain road, to rest beneath the cool shade of the pines that line the way, and to come suddenly to the edge of the moraine beyond which the spear point of the castle throws itself into the sky with an awe-inspiring grandeur. To see it thus is to realize little of the wasting forces that have made it a ruin. For its massive exterior has taken little cognizance of the sands that run through the hour-glass and the leaves that fall from the calendar.

It is one of the best-preserved castles in the duchy. Its roof is gone and rains and frosts have cracked away much of the masonry of its ramparts, but ages of neglect have not damaged it so that a few hundred dollars would not make it habitable. Hence, when one comes suddenly upon it from below, it strikes the senses not so much as a ruined monument in the graveyard of the past as the living type of a revivified feudalism. It breathes realism into the vague memories of chivalry and carries forward a dim and legendary age into the tangible present.

For continuity's sake, however, it may be best to walk

THE LAND OF HAUNTED CASTLES

up the long steps from the new Ansembourg, past the chevalier asleep in his grotto behind the chapel, and skirt the escarpment of the Ansembourg ravine to the high plateau beyond. From there to Hollenfels is a distance of about two kilometers, most of the way by good wagon road.

In the days when the houses of Hollenfels and Ansembourg first merged, country-side rumor has it, there was a tunnel all the way from one of the castles to the other. In view of the fact that erosion by underground waters has produced many caves and grottoes in this vicinity, the tunnel does not appear to have been so stupendous an engineering feat or so far from the realm of probability. Another rumor links Hollenfels with Schoenfels, which lies a greater distance away. But whether such subways ever existed or not, they have vanished now.

Hollenfels at its busiest is a sleepy place, most of it a frightened little town of white and buff buildings clustered in a single street that ends at the castle gate. There are a few isolated farm dwellings, but they have a discouraged look. Like French towns, the villages of Luxemburg are built with their houses elbow to elbow, in accordance, probably, with a custom that originated in the feudal days when space within the protecting walls was limited.

The sun that was breaking through the rain at Ansembourg brings a steam from the moist street. A venerable

HOLLENFELS

dame drives a remarkable equipage to the café in the middle of the town and dismounts.

Whatever the proud castle may offer to attract the sight-seer must wait for a closer view of this peculiar turnout. It consists of a wagon a bit larger than an American baby-carriage drawn by a donkey which differs from a St. Bernard dog principally in the demure expression of his face. Certainly he is no larger than a dog and no less shaggy.

Madame of the cart is a peddler. Her wagon is stocked with ironstone china of a durable if inelegant variety. Apparently she has had a successful day.

She walks into the café and sits down at a table near the door where she can watch her china and address an occasional word to her impatient steed. She informs the donkey in many words of gurgling Luxembourgeois that he is to remain in the center of the road until she returns.

But the donkey has ideas of his own. The sun is warm and the journey has been long. An odor of Diekirch beer wafts out from the cool recesses of the café. The donkey turns squarely about and follows his mistress into the big room, wagon, china and all. He is promptly insulted; but apparently he is used to scoldings, for he blinks once or twice, then brays a melodious defiance.

"There is only one way to silence him," declares the old dame. "He is thirsty. Bring a bucket."

THE LAND OF HAUNTED CASTLES

The bucket is brought and the water thoughtfully provided by the mistress of the bar is thrown into the street by the mistress of the donkey. It is then filled with a generous helping of foaming beer and set where the little beast can bury his nose in the suds.

The modern château of Hollenfels, a house of sixty rooms, was destroyed by the French torch-bearers. But the flames made slight inroads against the sturdy rock construction of the seventh-century towers.

Hollenfels caps a rocky promontory jutting out into the valley of the Eisch. On three sides of it the precipice drops down sheer to the river level. On the fourth an artificial moat was cut to a depth of more than a hundred feet. A drawbridge gave access to the castle.

Beyond the moat was the outer defense, a straight wall across the cliff with all the conveniences required by ancient warfare,—fireplaces for the brewing of hot tar and molten lead, and overhanging parapets for the dropping of tokens upon the heads of unwelcome visitors.

The roof and fifth floor of the castle have crumbled away, but the remainder of the place is much as it was eight centuries ago. The path of the guards about the upper parapet is intact. It is reached without difficulty by a remarkable spiral staircase of stone in a corner of the square tower. The kitchens on the main floor are filled with age-old rubbish, but the guard-room above is in excellent repair. Much of the mud plaster, applied over laths of thin spruce branches, clings to the walls, and the ornamental carvings of the huge fireplace are clear-cut and legible. The huge oaken beams of the ceiling are still black with the stains of smoke that rolled from the log fire as the retainers of the graf sat at their long table, dicing for the proceeds of their latest raid.

On the floor above is the salle des chevaliers, gathering-place of the elect, a high vaulted chamber, the ceiling of which is supported by beautifully carved Gothic arches. There are three steps leading to stone window-seats on each side of an ornate fireplace where the ladies of this little court knitted chain-mail sweaters for their menfolk in the graf's army, or fluttered handkerchiefs, signaling to watchers in the valley their hope of a speedy and effectual release from a captivity that was quite often the lot of a woman who chanced to be beautiful.

Above the salle des chevaliers is the chapel, now roofed by the skies. The remnants of a Corinthian column, a weather-beaten mantel, and a little altar set in the recess of a Gothic window are all that remain of its ancient grandeur.

The fifth floor was given over to sleeping-chambers, the sanctum of the lord of the house and his family. A fireplace, covered with armorial carvings, clings despairingly to the wall above the broken beams that mark the line of the departed floor.

The artillery of Louis XIV was called in in the mili-

THE LAND OF HAUNTED CASTLES

tary operations against this castle, attacking from the plateau beyond the moat. Because heavy guns were lacking in the defenses, Marshal Boufflers was able to bring his batteries up to within two hundred yards of the outer wall. From this point he bombarded the tower with carefree abandon, and, judging from the marks on the stone walls, the flight of the round cannon-balls as they bounced off the battlements and mowed down trees for hundreds of meters around must have been a wonderful sight to see.

Their effect on the castle was terrific. They put two dents in the wall above the second-floor windows, smashed off a cornice, and knocked down four feet of plaster on the inside of the parapet. It is not hard to imagine the sturdy defenders, stunned at this havoc, manning their tar-pots and lead-ladles with the bravery of desperation.

One of the cannon-balls embedded itself in a soft part of the south wall and is there yet.

To this day the crashing of the artillery about the castle can be heard if one's ear be properly attuned to the preternatural. Through the centuries the Grand Monarch has kept his phantom guns in action beyond the moat, continuing his attack upon the one bit of military architecture that his cannoneers were unable to alter with solid shot.

The castle capitulated after the bombardment, probably because the noise of the guns prevented the garrison from getting any sleep. The more modern portion was burned and the outer wall dismantled. But tradition has it that the knights who poured the hot lead got away unscathed. They fled from the place via the legendary tunnel that ended secretly in a deep well and curved down through the mountain to Schoenfels, three or four kilometers distant.

This mysterious tunnel, rather than the phantom artillery of the discomfited Boufflers, is the favorite topic of discussion in Hollenfels. There is a curse on the tunnel, say the natives. Several times men have gone down into the well to search for the secret opening of the long passageway and have died in the attempt. That carbon monoxid might have had something to do with the operation of the curse is, of course, unlikely. A good curse has no need of chemical assistance.

"Hollenfels in the old days was noted for the beautiful women of the castle," said the guide as we stood gazing across the empty hall of the knights.

I could well believe that. It would have been true concerning nearly any of the old castles. For in the days of the robber barons female beauty went farther than noble birth and the man who was strongest on the battlefield got the fairest wife. It would have been more remarkable if the women of Hollenfels had not been beautiful.

THE LAND OF HAUNTED CASTLES

"There is a story connected with that," observed the keeper of the keys.

And here, embellished only by the local color which the battered shell of the castle itself supplies, is the story he told:

Up out of the valley rode a hundred knights in gleaming mail, the sun dancing in myriad lights from casque and shield and breastplate and uplifted lance. Iron chains and copper headstalls clanked a symphony of triumph as the wiry Ardennes horses, tried in a dozen battles and a hundred skirmishes, tossed their proud heads and strained at the bit to reach the shelter that they knew would be waiting for them above.

> They rode right out of the morning sun,
> A glimmering, glittering cavalcade
> Of knights and ladies, and every one
> In princely sheen arrayed.

At the head of the column, on a black Westphalian charger that blinked quizzically through the goggle-like eye-loops of a brazen bridle, rode John of Hollenfels, knight of the castle.

The ladies of the shining pageant were three in number,—Griselda, a comely blonde, whose beautiful hair, like spun flax with a glint of copper in it, flowed across graceful shoulders and fluttered in the light breeze, and two maids, obviously domestics of her personal retinue, who rode Spanish mules by her side.

HOLLENFELS

Griselda appeared to be unhappy, but her head was held up with pride as she blinked to keep back the tears. She gazed unmoved upon the heights of Hollenfels and spoke scarcely a word to the resplendent chevalier who commanded the troop. He was kind enough to her, soft-spoken in his conversation and sharp in the orders he issued to his vassals, for her comfort. The light of love was in his eyes, the lightning flash of disdain in hers.

Love is eternal. It was born into the world with Adam and probably will continue through the spheres after Gabriel blows his trump. But it has varying aspects.

In those days love was not necessarily a mutual affair. Parents arranged marriages to suit their own convenience and children usually arranged their loves to suit their weddings,—not always but usually.

So with Griselda. Her father, proprietor of a sad little schloss over near Treves, had grown old with glory but little personal cash. His fields for the "taxing of Jewish peddlers," as this sort of plunder was euphemistically called, had been narrowed as the underpaid men-at-arms had betaken themselves and their two-handed swords to other masters. He had been unable to resist when the trained killers in the retinue of Hollenfels rode up to his gate and thundered a demand for his surrender.

Hollenfels announced that he had come to pay a friendly call. He asked for the hand of Griselda in marriage, and forthwith received it. Griselda's father knew

THE LAND OF HAUNTED CASTLES

the meaning of such a request. And so the beautiful blonde, the most coveted prize in a dozen counties, found herself on a splendid palfrey, riding toward the setting sun where the crags of the Ardennes succeeded the gentler slopes of the Moselle.

As the cavalcade advanced along the ascending trail, a trumpeter wound his horn in a blast that echoed like cathedral bells among the rocks. From the castle parapet arose a shout of welcome. Banners of a dozen tints floated from the loopholes of the archers, and the ramparts were crowded with women-folk in gala attire.

The halberdiers at the gates pulled the deer's foot attached to the bell-cord and the rumbling of gears and weights mingled with the barking of dogs, the joyous shrieks of women, the screams of children, and the deep-chested roar of the fighting-men. Out swung the gates of the exterior cincture. Down fell the drawbridge across the dizzy fosse. In rode the cavalcade in triumph, across the bridge and into the keep itself, where the tired horsemen dismounted, keen upon the scent of roasting pig and spiced wine that swept up from the great kitchens below.

John of Hollenfels, his personal lieutenant, and a page, left the men to their ribald jesting with wives and sweethearts, while they escorted Griselda and her maids up the winding stairs to the hall of the knights.

The tiles of the floor were new and highly polished.

HOLLENFELS

Curtains of the finest of German tapestries covered the walls.

A soft, warm breeze stirred the hangings at the narrow windows and carried a breath of flowers across the room. Against the wall opposite the fireplace a long oaken table, with a stretched leather covering tacked at the sides with brass studs, was being set for dinner.

Griselda sank into a Spanish-leather chair and took off the little silver cap that had bound her hair. She gazed about her apathetically as a cowled priest entered the room, and listened without comment as she heard her virtues recounted by the kidnapper whose bride she was to be.

She did not take the trouble to resent the attentions of her admirer. She had been schooled in the customs of her times and was reconciled. After all, one might do worse than marry the lord of so mighty a house.

There came a betrothal-feast at which the wines of the Moselle and the sparkling nectars of Rheims were blended in profusion. Hollenfels, his bride-to-be, neighbors from Simmern, Ansembourg, Schoenfels, and Mersch, and other notables feasted in the salle des chevaliers.

In the squad-room below, the men-at-arms engaged in a similar celebration and their echoing mirth went down through the ravine to Marienthal, where the superioress crossed herself, convinced that some new devilment was afoot.

All day the festivities continued and far into the night. Long before the last of the noble drinkers had fallen beneath the table Griselda had retired.

A chamber on the top floor of the castle, a bit bleak to be the dwelling-place of one so honored, was placed at her disposal. Hangings similar to those of the salle des chevaliers hid the chiseled walls save where two finely carved panels flanked the fireplace. The hearth, too, bore a resemblance to that of the knights' hall. It fed the same flue and hence was in the same relative position at the side of the room. Its mantelpiece also bore the Hollenfels-Ansembourg arms in which the Lion of Luxemburg cavorted formally. A short bed of elaborately carved oak stood in one corner of the chamber. Its "springs" were laced thongs of deer-hide, its mattress a homespun tick filled with feathers.

In the center of the room were two Spanish-leather chairs and a table upon which a candle guttered in a heavy bronze candlestick.

Griselda sighed as her maid came in to attend her. This was all very comfortable, far more so than the decaying manor of her father; and for all his roughness, she was beginning to realize, John of Hollenfels was a fine figure of a man.

So they were married the next day in the little chapel

on the fourth floor. John of Hollenfels did not believe in long engagements and his affianced bride had long since resigned herself to the inevitable. There was a grand celebration that lasted two days.

Love blessed their union, a love no less enduring because of somewhat tardy development. Love is a very peculiar thing.

Griselda, for all that she was a great lady, found plenty to keep her from boredom in the affairs of the serfs whose stone cottages clustered in the sun-baked street before the castle gate. It is somehow a very remarkable fact about serfdom that although feudalism brought caste to the highest development that it has known in Europe, it brought less snobbery. A serf might not amount to much and no lord of a castle would have worried about stringing one to the ramparts, but pending some such violent finish the retainer seems to have been fairly treated.

In Griselda's case, as in that of many another of her time, had she insisted upon consorting only with her own class she would have passed most of her days in silent meditation for distances between the homes of the aristocracy were tedious if not long. And the babies that played in the dust outside the castle gate were very human. In a few weeks every mother in the community looked upon Griselda as an angel and Griselda could have given a detailed inventory of the furniture in any

THE LAND OF HAUNTED CASTLES

given cottage. The Lady of Hollenfels was very happy.

Then one day a messenger rode to the gate,—a lean sunburned man in light armor whose horse was foam-flecked and nearly spent. Within an hour the trumpets were sounding assembly. Godfrey of Bouillon was riding to a crusade and the clans of chivalry were gathering.

The women wept about it as women have always wept when the sword is girded. The men swung to horse without hesitation. The business of the age was war. Everything else must be considered subordinate to it. Agriculture was no calling for a broad-backed, low-browed horseman who had heard the clang of battle-ax and shield. Home life was a passing dissipation to one used to the rough routine of the campaign; and, if the truth be told, family ties represented the period's strongest discipline; there was no discipline in the field.

The Graf of Hollenfels smoothed Griselda's beautiful hair as he kissed her in parting. With his own hands he locked about her waist the iron "belt of fidelity."

Pleasant garments were these belts of fidelity. They may be seen in nearly any museum to-day, a curious commentary upon the skeptical attitude of the medieval warrior toward the virtue of his wife. They weighed almost as much as a well-made coat of chain-mail and had less resiliency than a modern strait-jacket. The woman who wore one carried her own prison.

But Griselda made no objection to this obnoxious iron

zone, probably because she did not know that it was obnoxious. She knew that other wives wore such belts and she was too much concerned over the count's departure to worry about personal discomfort still in the future.

"I shall be true to you always," she vowed.

The count kissed her passionately.

"Remember the belt," he warned. "If you take it off, my curse be on you, though I love you more than life itself."

"I shall wear it in fond remembrance of you," she declared. Hollenfels was too much in earnest to see any humor in that. All atremble he rushed down the winding stairs and mounted his black steed. The "glimmering, glittering cavalcade" clattered out over the pontlevis and down the stony trail. The count's last sight of the castle was hallowed by the vision of Griselda on the ramparts, throwing kisses to him by way of farewell.

A pretty picture this, albeit sad. But Griselda could see none of its prettiness and she soon forgot her sorrow. The plague of the belt was on her. Sleeping or waking it bore down upon her hips, chafed her flesh, and tortured her beyond endurance. There was no relief from it. The horrible iron harness was locked in place and her crusading husband carried the key.

In vain her waiting-women attempted to console her.

"It is a device from hell," she declared. "It is stiffer

than the whalebone corsets of Germany, heavier than a bronze breastplate, and sharp as a sword."

"But, my lady," her maid reminded her, "it is the custom." Whereupon—we hate to say it, but legend holds it the truth—the fair Griselda, angel of the village, became angry.

"Why is it the custom?" she demanded. "Always I have been true to my husband in thought, word, and deed. Always I have been a good woman. Why should I wear this token when he wears none? Is his chastity less to be questioned than mine?"

And that was a point well taken. It has been woman's just plaint for many an age.

The serving-woman remained silent and Griselda, groaning under the weight of the iron belt, pursued her painful course to her own chamber.

Two days later she summoned an aged armorer whose rheumatism had prevented his going to the wars.

"I want this belt taken off," she told him.

He gazed at her in amazement.

"But, my lady," he protested, "it is bad luck and my life should be forfeit. I pray you do not think of such a thing."

"My life will be forfeit if I leave it on," she countered petulantly. "As for the bad luck, it would be a change for the better."

In the end the old man gave in. He brought a file and

ALTAR—HOLLENFELS CHAPEL
The jutting stones above the arch supported the top floor of the castle, the bed chambers of the graf and his family

SALLE DES CHEVALIERS
This was the main room of the castle—still a beautiful chamber with high vaulted ceiling and carved masonry, despite the marks of decay that the centuries have set upon it

HOLLENFELS

HOLLENFELS

presently the belt of fidelity fell on the flags at her feet. Her face shone with the beatific ecstasy of one who has come through insufferable torments into an undreamed-of repose. The old man departed, shaking his head.

"I fear no good will come of it," he declared. But Griselda did not hear him.

In Hollenfels to-day one can see a medieval novelty in the way of plumbing. On each side of the windows in the hall of the knights and similarly placed on the upper floors are little closets, one jutting out over the other like the side of an inverted pyramid. These contain stone sinks with openings directly over the precipice. They were wash-rooms that never were to know running water, it is true, but still something of a concession to cleanliness and sanitation in a period when castle-dwellers had little time to think of such things. In one of these little rooms opening out of her own chamber Griselda found a convenient hiding-place for the accursed belt. It was a place her women would have no occasion to enter.

Griselda hung the belt on a hook above the sink and promptly forgot about it. Her days were very full, what with visits to Schoenfels and Ansembourg and Mersch and the spinning and weaving of wool and linen. Household arts were fashionable then. There was no other form of amusement.

So autumn burned into winter and the snows of the hills washed down into the valley and then sprouted the

THE LAND OF HAUNTED CASTLES

dog roses of a new spring. Still the warriors were hammering at the gates of Islam. And still the curse that the departing husband had made contingent upon the wearing of the iron belt was held in abeyance. The harness still swung from its peg over the sink in the tower room. Griselda, full of the joy of living, had forgotten the shadow that hung over her, just as she had forgotten the emblem of doubt that caused it.

One day, alone, she left the castle gates and wandered down the trail toward the valley, picking the wild flowers that grew in the rocks of the great precipice. A scarlet rose attracted her,—the favorite flower of that husband who might even now be lying dead upon a sun-bleached slope in Palestine.

She felt the surge of love and tender memory and stooped to pick it.

In the castle above, one of the tirewomen had entered the *Gräfin's* chamber. A needle was missing and she looked for it everywhere, even in the little closet near the window. A sudden draft slammed the door and she turned to go. But the slamming had jarred the iron belt from its hook.

It fell to the sink and then through the waste-hole at the end,—a deadly missile that dropped straight and true.

Griselda was found at the base of the castle steeps, a streak of red in her flaxen hair where the weight of the

HOLLENFELS

curse had fallen. She had died without knowing what had happened to her.

To this day the wild roses grow on the spot where she fell.

"Do you believe that story?" I asked the guide.

He took his feathered fedora from his brown hair and smiled as he scratched his head.

"No, Monsieur," he declared. "Few people do. We have seen these belts and we know that the ladies of the castles were forced to wear them. But they were cruel and I do not think that the bon Dieu would allow a jealous husband's curse to destroy a wife guilty only of so excusable a disobedience.

"Now, as for the bombardment of the castle by the French cannon, Monsieur, that is a thing believable and logical.

"Many times the bombardment has been heard and will be heard until the castle falls down."

The sun was shining through the bare rafters of the departed roof and striking through the narrow windows of Griselda's room. The varied tragedies of Hollenfels seemed very real and recent.

CHAPTER XII
MARIENTHAL

The Flying Horseman

Safe in the hallowed quiets of the past.
—Lowell.

CHAPTER XII

MARIENTHAL

DOWN from Hollenfels the road winds around a rocky promontory into Marienthal, vale of eternal peace. A narrow plane of lush meadow is Marienthal, flanked by gently sloping wooded hills,—a harbor of rest beyond a grim coast of battlemented stone. Through the grasses meanders the Eisch, a placid stream with barely a ripple on its surface, quite different in disposition from its brother the Mamer, which flows parallel to it in its journey to join the Alzette. And by the river bank, a vista of red roofs, white walls, vines, and flowers, nestles the Marienthal abbey, home of the White Fathers of Africa.

There is the murmur of insects in the air, the drowsy plaint of the humming-bird, a low vague chant from the chapel. There is age here as obviously as in the ruins of Ansembourg and Hollenfels, but it is of a different variety. It is the antiquity of yellowing ivory and lavender-scented laces, where that of the castles is the antiquity of rusting iron and disintegrating bones. Hollenfels is the typification of swashbuckling history checked in the midst of an interesting and sensational

THE LAND OF HAUNTED CASTLES

chapter. Marienthal is a stately present immersed in the rose perfumes of a continuing past.

The grandeur of Marienthal is gone. The original convent, established by the Princess Ermesinde,—who seems to have founded nearly all the religious houses in the duchy,—was burned by the French revolutionaries.

The buildings that remain are not remarkable for their architecture, intrinsic value, or mode of construction. But the beauty of Mary's Vale, the calm, intangible loveliness of it, is a thing apart from piles of mortar and stone. It will linger forever.

There are never gray days in this valley. In the sunlight it is a scintillant gem. In the rain it is a blend of green and blue and white, and luminous as if through some quality of its own.

The priory of Marienthal is a self-contained village set in a walled park one side of which is bounded by slowly disintegrating ruins. The superior judges them to have been a part of Ermesinde's convent. Peasants of the neighborhood declare them to be another of Julius Cæsar's innumerable relics, part of a Roman camp. Perhaps both are right, for in these parts the cross was the eagle's natural successor.

I stopped at a gate reminiscent of the old California missions and pulled the bell-cord. Through the iron bars could be glimpsed the main street of the abbey, a group of white stone buildings immaculately clean, with a well-

MARIENTHAL

kept garden beyond, carefully cut hedges, trimmed pine trees in orderly rows with benches in their inviting shade.

Presently came a figure that seemed to be an integral part of the picture,—a sun-browned, black-bearded priest in a white cassock and scarlet fez. The peculiarity of such a costume on a churchman anywhere else in Europe might have seemed surprising. But not at Marienthal. In such a spot nothing could be commonplace and nothing could be startling.

He smilingly opened the gates and voiced a welcome in high French, low German, and middle English.

"You would see Marienthal?" he inquired. "I am glad. We seldom see visitors here and new faces gladden the day."

He babbled cheerfully of America, the war, and the chaos that had come from the remaking of the world. He seemed singularly well informed for the occupant of an isolated abbey in a dreamy valley.

"I have been in Africa," he said by way of explanation. "That is where the priests of my order have their work. We do not see many religious there,—French soldiers, many of them, and traders and natives. It is a very busy and interesting life. When we get to the rectory I shall show you some of the relics of our work in Africa."

He told of the eventful history of the Marienthal priory from the date of its founding by Ermesinde as a convent for the daughters of the county's nobility,—how

THE LAND OF HAUNTED CASTLES

Yolande the Beautiful, of Vianden, had fled there for refuge when her parents would have exercised their ancient prerogative of picking her husband; how Joseph II had suppressed it; how the regicides of the Terror had put it to the torch.

Some of the most noble names of Europe must have been on its rolls in those early days, for it was fashionable. To be admitted to Marienthal was to be marked as a woman of blood with a noble lineage traceable back for at least fourteen generations. To be rejected by Marienthal was to take back into the world an impaired social standing.

Who were the prioresses of the convent at the time of its importance is not mentioned in profane history. But whoever they were, they were worthy of more than passing comment. The preservation of discipline in a house where rank and worldly honors were considered prerequisite to a vocation must have required a keen intelligence and an iron hand.

The White Fathers of Africa have come into possession of the place only recently, but the convent has been shaped to fit their individuality so that it is hard to imagine that it ever belonged to any one else. A red-fezzed priest reads his breviary on a vine-covered balcony overlooking the brook. Two ugly dogs rove under the trees. A number of old men who do not wear the garb of the order are at work in the gardens or unloading

MARIENTHAL

building-materials at a flour-mill west of the gate. This is a bachelor's paradise. Women have no place in it.

The dormitories of the priests and lay brothers flank the little chapel, fronting upon a formal terrace ablaze with flowers. Weather-beaten little saints—prominent among them St. Hubert of the Ardennes—gaze down, with a calmness that centuries have not altered, from carven niches about the door.

The interior of the church is a bijou of German mural decoration with royal blue the predominating color. It has none of the clashing tints that might be expected in a place where a Munich artist has been allowed to wield his impressionistic brush. The blue of the predominating tone is strengthened by the blue of the windows fading into blackness where Gothic arches of fumed oak cross in the high vaulted ceiling. Little iron panels here and there mark the spots where the daughters of the men who remodeled world history with mace and pike lie in their last sleep. Here if any place in the world they can find peace.

Leave the chapel by a narrow passageway to a reception-room in the rectory and step into Timbuktu.

Marienthal is the last place on earth where one would expect to breathe the atmosphere of Africa. But it boasts one of the finest collections of African war materials and household implements in Europe. Cannibals' cooking-utensils, nose-rings, battle-clubs, savages' hair ornaments, clam-shell money,—a wealth of oddities from a land that American colloquialism readily concedes to be the hinterland of Nowhere, makes this room alone worth a visit to Mary's Vale. The White Father is proud of the collection and explains in detail the personal history of each ebon-skinned man-eater who contributed to it. He is less verbose concerning the bleaching bones of White Fathers who lie in the hot shadows of the ancient clay walls of Timbuktu. They were soldiers, he says. And they died on their battle-field.

The White Father led me out into the garden and we sat for a while on one of the benches under the toy-shop pines. Gossamer hung in the air—"threads from the veil of the Virgin," he called them—and a light, motionless mist that banked against the grove above which could be seen the towers of the new Ansembourg.

He pointed to the cliffs that rose sheer some two hundred feet at the rear of the priory gardens.

"There is a pretty legend about that cliff, Monsieur," he said.

"In one of the many wars that have swept this country, much of the fighting centered about Mersch. The holy women of the convent here spent day and night in prayer while a few kilometers away towns were ablaze and men were hacking at one another in hatred. I think that it must have been during one of the Dutch invasions, for

MARIENTHAL

the battle line seems to have run east and west, one army in the North, another in the South.

"There were many French with the army of the South,—chevaliers related to the seigneurs of Luxemburg and the like.

"One day the army of the North made a flanking movement and there was a crisis. A party of Frenchmen, said to have been among the best horsemen in Europe, were cut off from their friends and driven upon that plateau. They fought desperately but were crushed by numbers. One by one they were killed, leaving a sorry trail across the fertile fields up there. By the time the fighting reached the edge of the cliffs only one of the Frenchmen was left.

"He must have been brave, Monsieur. Many of the good nuns who were here then saw him turn about, set his face to the enemy, and kill the leader of the pursuing squadron. Hand to hand, cut and slash, he gave battle to every one who approached him. Then suddenly his blade broke across the metal casque of one of his antagonists.

"That should have finished him. But he was a man of wit as well as bravery. Like a lightning flash he swung his horse about and turned toward the cliff again. His foes stopped a moment, amazed at his audacity. Before they could recover, he had gathered his horse. In a second he had shot into the air far out over the brink.

THE LAND OF HAUNTED CASTLES

"The good nuns closed their eyes, fearful of seeing him crushed to death on the rocks at the foot of the precipice. They opened them again to breathe a prayer to God.

"He was not killed, Monsieur. He was not hurt. Horse and man landed together in the green meadow without a scratch."

"He was a brave man," I commented.

"He was a man favored by God," returned the priest, gravely. "The country people hereabouts say that he weighed together with his horse only five ounces. They judge from the tradition that the iron shoes of his mount barely made an impression in the meadow."

"How do you account for it?"

"*Je ne sais pas.* A miracle, perhaps. After all, Monsieur, the bon Dieu who hangs the stars in their heavens would have found little task in aiding a horse and rider down from the heights of Marienthal. It is very remarkable but not hard to believe."

And, somehow, I felt that he was right. It is not hard to believe fairy tales in fairy-land.

The same legend with surprising variations is found in other parts of the Mersch district.

Near Schoenfels is a chapel said to have been erected by a *Gräfin* in honor of the Guardian Angel as a thank-offering for the rescue of her little son from a violent death.

The boy and his mother are said to have been gathering

MARIENTHAL

wild flowers when they became separated. The boy wandered to the edge of the cliff and fell over.

His distracted mother found him seated among the rocks at the base of the steep descent, unhurt.

"A man in white robes caught me and carried me down," was his explanation.

The connection between the Flying Horseman and the legend of the Gräfin's son is not difficult to see.

The priest sank into a reverie and so did I. One does not wish to leave Marienthal, especially after one has seen the blight of war upon the country-side roundabout.

I have seen the valley white with snow in winter, yellow-green with new foliage in spring, and red with roses, poppies, and hollyhocks in summer. But in one respect it remained the same,—calm as the summer sea, peaceful as paradise.

CHAPTER XIII
SCHOENFELS

The Little People

What mysteries do lie beyond thy dust,
Could man outlook that mark!
—Vaughan

CHAPTER XIII

SCHOENFELS

THE castle at Schoenfels is a type distinct from the other castles in the neighborhood. It is built in the valley within the looping of the tiny Mamer,—a great tower that relied upon the mightiness of its own walls and garrison to resist attacks.

The rocks on each side of the valley would seem to have offered innumerable sites better adapted to castle-building than the open marsh on the river bank. But the early knights of Schindels, as the place is called in the local vernacular, apparently knew what they were about. The impregnable fortresses that seem never to have been able to keep an enemy out or turn the tide of a battle, are masses of disintegrating rock inhabited only by wild animals. Schoenfels, embellished by a number of modern improvements, including a cement covering and slate roof, thrusts its tower into the sky and houses a Dutch baron in regal style. It has more of the picture-book appearance than any of the other ancient châteaux, probably because it is intact and tenanted.

Four turrets crown its central donjon, increasing the militaristic impression of its slim windows. But the runways where once were mobilized the wielders of tar-

THE LAND OF HAUNTED CASTLES

pot and lead-ladle have been made over into a simple coping, and a weathercock arrow at the apex is the castle's last reminder of the vanished archers who once upheld its glory.

Schoenfels is east of Marienthal, immediately across the plateau from which the Flying Horseman made his famous leap. It is separated from the valley of the Alzette by still another ridge which narrows to a point as the Eisch, Alzette, and Mamer flow northward to merge at Mersch.

The soft beauty of Marienthal is absent here,—perhaps because of the grim shadows of the castle, perhaps because of the turbulence of the surrounding scenery. But it is not without its potent spell. If Marienthal is the natural abode of fairies, this must be the haunt of elves and gnomes.

In novelty of legend it is the most noteworthy spot in all the grand duchy.

Above the castle, accessible by a difficult trail, is an opening in the Beautiful Rocks,—the entrance to a mysterious cavern. Here dwelt in the ancient days the Little People. Of their early history little or nothing is known. It is generally believed that they were the predecessors of the Celts in the Ardennes, cavemen who had degenerated in stature as they had improved in morals in comparison with their club-wielding ancestors.

Part of this series of grottoes seems to be natural, but

SCHOENFELS
From the rocks of the Little People

SCHOENFELS

the eternal rock bears chisel-marks that support the theory that a race of dwarfed artisans once made their home there.

A Belgian electrician, who had fled into Luxemburg when the Germans were bombarding Liège, was my guide to the cavern.

He had an outsider's natural interest in a local wonder and had a fund of information gained from the natives in five years of questioning.

"These Little People are spoken of in legends all over Europe," he said. "There are traces of them along the Meuse, near Dinant and Liège. But this is the first real proof of their existence that I have ever seen."

He moistened his finger and held it at the mouth of the cavern.

"There is a good draft, Monsieur," he observed. "And where there is a draft there is not likely to be any carbon monoxid. But the caves are low and narrow. Be careful."

He led the way on his hands and knees through passages where the candle-flame lighted niches in the walls and raised places still blackened with the smoke of ancient fires. The tunnels crossed and recrossed dizzily and there came wider rooms that probably had seen service as community centers.

In spots where the springs had dripped through the stone roofs there were glistening stalactite formations.

THE LAND OF HAUNTED CASTLES

But these were very small and not nearly so delicately formed as those of the natural caves of the Jura and the Pyrenees.

Except as a basis for ethnological study the caverns were hardly worth the trouble entailed in the exploration. Both of us emerged with bruised knees and torn clothes, no whit the wiser as to how these prehistoric gnomes had lived or died.

"What did these dwarfs do?" I inquired when we had come back into the sunlight again. "How did they make a living?"

"Hunted and fished, I suppose," the electrician answered. "That was what all the savages in this part of the country did. These people could not have been warriors. They were too small.

"There is much legend about them but almost no fact. The people of Schindels say that they were a very generous, kind-hearted race and that they were endowed with supernatural powers. They are always coming back from the dead to help poor people.

"One old woman of Schindels told me how two of the little men had helped her to carry her faggots down from the forest. Another one told me of the gnome that used to sit at her grandmother's fireplace.

"But the people who live higher on the slopes are not so well disposed toward them. They say that the Little People were like the gnomes of the Schwarzwald, lost souls in misshapen bodies, living for evil and cursing at good. They have told me that the Little People warmed themselves in the rocks about fires that burned with a blue light, and the blue light is a signal of trouble. The lights were seen in the summer of 1914 and a short time afterward the Prussians were pouring through here into Belgium and France. They burned for a whole week as the final blasts were being discharged in the destruction of the great fortress at Luxemburg city. I prefer, somehow, to think of the dwarfs as harbingers of evil. It fits in better with the legends of the other districts."

What became of the dwarfs—whether they died off in a pestilence or were exterminated by the sweep of a hardier tribe from Asia—cannot be determined. Some fossilized bones of their species have been dug up in the western Ardennes and some homely personal utensils that may have been theirs may be seen at the Luxemburg museum. But there is no record of their passing. They were a people of mystery and, as is usual in such cases, the puzzle of their existence lived on while they themselves went back to the soil whence they had sprung.

That they once existed would seem evident from the vast fund of folk-lore concerning them, even without the supporting testimony of their abandoned caves. Every nation of Europe has its stories of the Little People. In Germany they are the gnomes of the Black Forest,—some of them pious creatures, others of them past masters of

THE LAND OF HAUNTED CASTLES

the black art, lieutenants of the devil, despoilers of the cradle, harbingers of bad luck. In France they are made to people the Jura and the Pyrenees, a race similar in every respect. In Ireland their equivalent is found in the Good People, the souls of the damned compelled to wander about the Green Isle, plotting mischief until the place set apart for them in hell is made ready.

That the people of Schindels have clothed them with a wholly gratuitous gentleness of character is due rather to the trustfulness of the people than to any precedence in tradition. Whoever they were and whatever they did, the memory of them will be evil so long as the country folk continue to talk of them.

In Gosseldange, a village on the Alzette across the divide from Schoenfels, the Little People came back again a year ago in a new incarnation.

Women huddled about their fireplaces and men scoured rusty firearms and diffidently set themselves against a new menace.

Up in the forests on the top of the ridge an evil was afoot,—an intangible, indescribable thing that made the woods a dangerous mystery by day and an echoing terror by night. A wild man, some called it; an ogre, declared others; a ghost of one of the Little People, perhaps, or an agent of the devil.

For five dreadful days it howled in the woods and children were afraid to cross their door-steps after night-

SCHOENFELS

fall. Then the burghers, despite certain superstitious misgivings, organized a posse and scoured the woods.

They had no success.

The Thing laughed at them as they beat through the brush, flitted to the tree-tops when they thought they had cornered it, howled derisively behind them when crackling twigs had led them to believe it in front. For the greater part of one night they chased it back and forth through the patches of beech and oak and pine. Then —worn out, disheartened, mystified, and a bit afraid— they plodded back to the village, and down the road the Thing came after them, jeering and howling like the fiend that it was.

It is too bad that this tale must end with an anticlimax. As a true, twentieth-century sort of ghost-story, it should end with the laying of the ghost. But it does n't. Gosseldange met over its hot rum about the porcelain stove in the café and evolved many new theories concerning the nature and source of the Terror, but never found out what it really was.

It made the nights hideous for a month or so, until the men who had failed to rout it with shot-guns seriously considered asking the assistance of the clergy with bell, book, and candle. Then one night the spook departed. Since then has been peace. Gosseldange has ceased to worry about it. A single ghost in Luxemburg is like a fleck of foam on an ocean, a matter of no consequence.

CHAPTER XIV
MERSCH AND PETTINGEN

Coffins and Centurions

Grieving, if aught inanimate e'er grieves,
Over the unreturning brave.
—Byron

MERSCH

To the left is the new basilica, in the center the spire of the ancient church that was built upon a foundation of Frankish coffins, to the right the square tower of the old castle

CHAPTER XIV

MERSCH AND PETTINGEN

DOWN from Schoenfels for perhaps two kilometers tumbles the little Mamer, a sprightly bit of white water at the bottom of the deep valley that it carved for itself ages before there were any castles or men to build them.

At Mersch it meets the Alzette, still singing of Luxemburg rock and the captive Mélusine, and the quiet Esch bearing poppy petals from Marienthal. They flow on united to merge presently with the Sure.

It would be remarkable if Mersch, the ancient Marisca, with all this wealth of waters, did not display important relics of its own. While the valley is wide at this point, and the heights more gently sloping than those to the immediate north and south, the confluence of the streams made possible the construction of a river barrier as impassable as the fosses chiseled in the rocky roosts of the crag fortresses. The barons of old Mersch seized upon the natural advantages of their situation with commendable zeal and ingenuity.

It is said that they had the experience of Roman engineers for their guide, for Marisca was a camp of some size when Cæsar led his legions to the Rhine. Pillars of masonry, resting upon bed-rock under the slime of the valley, were there for the taking when the first seigneur of Mersch started work upon his ugly stronghold.

One's first glimpse of Mersch from any point of view is pierced by a Byzantine church steeple suggestive of ancient treasures, peculiar wood-carvings, and the vastness of architecture that characterized the churches of the period which this spire represents. But one comes closer to discover that though the spire is intact the church is gone. A public square occupies the site where it stood, and a tin-hatted fire-department inhabits what is left of the tower.

Legend says that it was being torn down when the Queen Mother of Holland interrupted the proceedings. She pleaded that the peculiar belfry reminded her of the spires in Russia, her native land, and that she wished one bit of her beloved East to remain in Western Europe. So it was allowed to stand.

The wreckers discovered with some surprise that the foundation stones of the great church were unlike any that they had ever seen in Luxemburg. They were immense blocks, carefully chiseled and sometimes ornamented with outlandish characters. An archæologist was called to look at them and discovered them to be Frankish coffins.

The bones of the Franks who had inhabited them were dust, as were the warlike trappings of wood and leather

MERSCH AND PETTINGEN

that made up the principal part of the funeral equipment. A few stone and metal weapons were found, however, and the foundations of the Mersch basilica proved to be one of the most fertile sources of archæological information in the grand duchy.

It would appear logical that Mersch should be haunted by the ghosts of the countless Franks whose cemeteries were ravished to provide a basement for the old church. But there is where the ghosts failed to utilize a golden opportunity. In all the folk-lore of the neighborhood there is no mention of the Franks. Local history has given them no place.

The hills of the immediate vicinity, however, abound in antiquities. There is a miraculous spring at Helperknap. It now comes under the patronage of a Christian saint, but it was flowing as it does to-day when the horsemen of Cæsar stopped there to water their mounts and declared it sacred.

Hundreds of persons come there on the first Monday in May each year for a noisy celebration. They have been doing so for so long a time that every one has forgotten why the event came to be observed in such an out-of-the-way hamlet. The very name "Helperknap Fair" has come to be a term synonymous with antiquity.

Mersch itself is a modern town; there is the new community's sameness about most of its streets. It presents little novelty of architecture or color and claims distinc-

THE LAND OF HAUNTED CASTLES

tion from any farm village in Luxemburg only in size and the crookedness of its alleys. The ancient château is still standing and still habitable. Its moat is filled and its walls crumbling. Here, one would think, is the touch of the old needed to lessen the crudities of the new. But the strong old building has been painted an eye-paining red—American silo color—and adds less to the beauty of the landscape than would any square, squat, ugly factory.

For the rest, Mersch is business-like. One steps from the modest brick railway station into a cobbled square from which one road leads north to zigzag across the Alzette to Beringen, then north again between stately fir-trees. A second road is straight ahead past modest stone cottages and iron-railed mansion grounds, peculiar little shops that may be reached only by mounting two or three steps, cafés and restaurants, bakeries, livery-stables, implement yards, and garages. There is trade aplenty in Mersch, for the reason that most of the villages of the surrounding valleys have no stores of their own. But bulk of business has not made the shops any vast improvement over those of rural France.

As in France, a *librairie* is usually a place where it is impossible to buy books. There is no shop in Mersch in which one can buy books. Every one in Luxemburg can read. The duchy's educational system in many respects is a little model. But literature apparently has a small part in the affairs of the people.

MERSCH AND PETTINGEN

It is almost impossible to classify the grocery stores. One sort of shop sells canned goods, flour, cheese, notions, novelties, and carbide. Another sells dry goods with a side line of vegetables. A few doors farther down the street will be discovered a dingy shop where one may purchase tobacco of an *ersatz* variety, coffee,—Kathreiner's Malzkaffee, usually,—sugar, salt, flour, beans, lentils, potatoes, sandpaper, harness, and carbide.

Some of the hardware stores sell furniture, reaping-machine parts, bolts, nuts, tools, and carbide. Others show a stock of pots and pans, queen's-ware, cement, tools, cloth, candy of a strange variety, and carbide.

Luxemburg's stores have taken a leap from the "unit" idea of German and French shops. But in what a strange chaos they have landed! They are not quite equal to an American cross-roads general store and are a bit more puzzling than if they distributed only one class of produce and advertised that class. The variety of stock in any class of shop seems to depend entirely upon the whim of the proprietor. It would be hard to imagine an American store, for example, dealing in sandpaper, hemp rope, picture-frames, farm necessities, and hot waffles. But I have seen such a shop in Luxemburg. The only point of agreement seems to be the carbide.

Before the war cheap German lanterns somewhat resembling a three-inch shell with a hook for a handle were dumped in large quantities in the duchy. The

THE LAND OF HAUNTED CASTLES

farmers soon learned that despite their rather dangerous open flame they gave a better light than oil lanterns and were more economical of fuel. So the acrid odor of calcium carbide overcame the perfume of the ever-present roses as the national scent of the duchy.

There are many excellent restaurants in Mersch, none of them very pretentious but generally modest in price as well as in appearance and remarkable for the quality and variety of their menus.

They are operated generally on the French plan, with the woman of the household part owner, general manager, and chef; and, as in France, it must be admitted the women are born cooks.

Railroads and electric lights have not spoiled the charm of the inns. One sits down to his meal in a banjo-backed chair of age-blackened oak, before a table kept white from generation to generation with endless scrubbing. He eats from blue-edged chinaware in the center of which German comic pictures are etched in black. The pretty daughter of the madame serves him, a shy-eyed, rosy-cheeked damosel in a starched gingham apron, short skirt, and wooden-soled shoes. And when the meal is finished she presents him his check, the "score" in vogue in the inns of Rip Van Winkle's time,—a slate upon which the *addition* has been inscribed in white chalk.

The inns have plenty of room should one choose to stay the night. The beds, as elsewhere, are about a foot

MERSCH AND PETTINGEN

too short, but the soft mattress and the feather-stuffed coverlet compensate. For some reason the coverlets are always crimson. Flaming red seems to be a necessary factor in their manufacture. There is no carpet on the floor; carpet would hide it, Monsieur. Why should one have carpet when there is an oaken floor in the house and a streak of cleanliness in the housewife? The wood is smooth as ivory and as white, which means that it is scrubbed every day. Two rush-bottomed chairs, a washstand, and a great armoire of black walnut—an heirloom of ancient lineage—complete the furnishings.

Little enough of splendor even for a country inn, but a homely comfort, a contagious feeling of good-will that is indescribable.

That is what constitutes the attractiveness of Mersch,—its atmosphere, which apparently has nothing to do with the elements that combine to give it a place on the map as one of the duchy's important towns.

Its newness—even the somewhat modern flat-building nearing completion on the west side of the town after six years' delay in construction, because of the war and subsequent high prices of materials—is laid over a foundation of antiquity, like the red paint on the château. One who learns to know Mersch comes to see in it an amusing picture of a dear old lady in search of her youth but unable to forget that she is a dear old lady.

In detail the little city is a disappointment because it

THE LAND OF HAUNTED CASTLES

promises so much and shows so little. But if the visitor possesses sufficient imagination to repopulate it with the interesting ghosts that made its history, it is worth a visit and extended exploration. At any rate, it is the gateway to the sprite-haunted vales of the Alzette, Mamer, and Eisch and a landmark of great adventure.

North from Mersch rather more than a kilometer, nestling in a little nook between the Alzette and the row of hills to the left of the river, sleeps Pettingen, a tiny town situated amid evidences of a vanished greatness.

Here are ruined watch-towers, vestiges of the Roman occupation of the first and second centuries, more pretentious ruins that once were fortress walls, and a mighty pile that was a robbers' roost of unconventional lines. Schloss Pettingen, home of the wandering Centurion, is remarkable for the several ways in which it violates the accepted styles of early architecture and construction.

No one but Julius Cæsar himself, or the general to whom he directly delegated the task of establishing the army of occupation in Luxemburg, could explain why Pettingen-on-the-Alzette should have been chosen for the building of a strong point. Unlike other walled châteaux of the district, it is not built upon a hill. It is close to the river level in a spot that could have been of no great importance strategically. The standing ruins show it to have been an unbeautiful structure of considerable size, U-shaped, with squat round towers at the outer corners.

MERSCH AND PETTINGEN

It was surrounded with a massive wall, sixteen feet thick at the bottom, and a moat perhaps twenty feet deep, connected with the river by a short canal. The walls of the main building were from eight to ten feet thick, which accounts for their state of preservation after some fourteen hundred years. The foundations and remarkable system of dungeons cut out of the rock below the castle are said to date from the first century.

Two towers and one wing of the structure remain virtually intact. The rest has collapsed, filling the moat with tons of rock. The dungeons, however, are still in good condition, as damp and evil-smelling as they were when the Centurion was buried alive in them.

He is said to have been a politician with an ax to grind at Rome, who attempted to lead a rebellion in Pettingen Castle, intending to assault and capture another camp at Marisca. He was betrayed and was thrown into the dungeon by the military governor.

He was a persistent creature, however, and he thought he understood the construction of the castle well enough to carve a tunnel out to the river. Had it not been for one slight miscalculation he would have succeeded. In cutting through the wall he chose a point behind a buttress. The masonry in that place was about forty feet thick. He had dug in twenty feet when the vile diseases of the prison killed him. Had he started to burrow five

THE LAND OF HAUNTED CASTLES

feet to the right, he would have got through the barrier to freedom.

And now, say the oldest inhabitants, he comes back to survey his work and wail over his error,—a useless occupation, one would judge, considering that whether he had succeeded in getting out or not the result would make little difference to him after all these years.

But ghosts were never logical creatures.

Northward the Alzette winds to Colmar-Berg, the grand-ducal country estate.

The wagging tongues of Luxemburg have not dealt fairly with Berg. They have given it no literature of its own. It has no legends.

If it had, they would be thrilling stories of flying rocking-horses, talking dolls, Puss in Boots, Jack the Giant-killer, Cinderella, and the Little Lame Prince. Berg is that sort of palace.

It is an artist's supreme conception of a building-block house on an immense scale, a place of curving gables, spear-pointed turrets, and rococo decorations,—a great white building with striking splashes of color. It is covered with funny little diamond-shaped lattices, odds and ends of flower boxes, carved balconies of a highly decorative order,—lavish magnificence but a bit too lavish.

Local tradition has it that there have always been castles at Berg. This one was a medieval affair, badly

MERSCH AND PETTINGEN

Boufflered in the days of the Grand Monarch but rebuilt out of its own wreckage. In the hands of counts who apparently had plenty of money to spend upon architectural achievement, each succeeding generation saw it "improved" with no direct reference to the work of the preceding generation.

When it became the country residence of the Prince of Orange after the signing of the Treaty of Vienna of 1815, a German architect was called in to complete the improvement. In justice to him it must be said that he accomplished something in making a coördinate whole out of a number of wings, turrets, and donjons that hitherto had maintained a strictly independent part in the picture.

The bare rocks have been covered with stucco, and a uniform trimming has been added to the eighth-century tower, tenth-century gate, sixteenth-century façade, and eighteenth-century cornice. The result is gingerbread, but fascinating gingerbread. A toy palace certainly should not seem out of place in a toy country.

The inside of the building is in Spanish renaissance, and as tasteful, beautifully furnished, and restful as the exterior is jarring.

From here a beautiful young princess rode into exile. That in itself will furnish the basis for a legend sometime in the future. It has been lost in the great mass of more important news incident to world readjustment.

CHAPTER XV
ETTELBRUCK

The Bahnhof and a Cinemadventure

> Nor yet within the common soil
> Lay down the wreck of power to rest,
> Where man can boast that he has trod
> On him that was "the scourge of God."
> —Everett: *"Alaric the Visigoth."*

CHAPTER XV

ETTELBRUCK

A SETTING, this, for the second act of a Strauss opera,—color flashing under the flickering lamps, a wealth of type, a wealth of costuming. The end of the platform is held by a group of men of the grand-duchess's guard,—a dozen soldiers of the palace garrison, a dozen uniforms unlike any others in the world. Here is the red-topped cap of the semi-conical shape familiar throughout the duchy; immediately next to it is another of black patent-leather, reflecting pools of light. A cerise band distinguishes this cap. A collar of the same hue, peering above a greenish cape, marks the owner at once for a man of rank. One catches the glint of golden epaulets and silver ones, of saber knots and lavish ornamentation in gleaming braid. A functionary struts past, seemingly conscious of his own importance as indicated by an edging of silver on his collar. So might a daisy seek attention in a crimson poppy-field.

Farther down the platform a group of French soldiers in faded horizon blue are vainly questioning a railroad official who persists in answering them in German. They are typical poilus, abulge with haversacks and bundles.

A little French sentry at the entrance to the *Wartraum*

THE LAND OF HAUNTED CASTLES

comes to a present-arms and drops his gun to the order once more with a double click on the pavement. His head barely reaches the level of the front sight, let alone that of the slim bayonet.

There is a smell of carbide in the air; a can of it is leaking somewhere.

A station porter has unloaded a grindstone from a flat-car on a siding. He looks at it for a moment in half-witted perplexity, then smiles a wily smile, turns it on its side, and trundles it off like a wheelbarrow, the stone serving as a wheel.

Two portly men in well-tailored clothes and furry hats glare with regularity and precision at the French soldiers.

On an opposite track the Echternach shuttle has just come in. It is bustling with all the importance that an unimporant little busybody usually displays, its squeaky engine moving in a smoke screen, its worn coaches rattling in every joint.

There are streaks in the cinder paths between the tracks where the dim light of the quivering electric lamps is reflected by wet spots. Across the yards in the lee of the hill is a bonfire. The smoke drifts lazily over the platform.

Is plotting an art or a science, an amusement or an occupation, a pièce de resistance or dessert?

There is a question that writers of tea-pot-tempestuous

ETTELBRUCK

fiction have neglected to answer in all the pages that lie between the Prisoner of Zenda and the Sultan of Sulu.

The readers of tabloid romance may have followed the adventurous career of the inevitable American hero through a variety of toy kingdoms and puzzled their brains and strained their sentiments over morganatic marriages, loveless but patriotic engagements, entangling treaties, national bankruptcy, petty wars, and all the other tricks in the bag; but the most avid consumer of the Zenda brand of literature doesn't know how much Rupert paid for his beer at the inn, what a seven counted in the national interpretation of a dice game, where the peasantry got the wood for the "pleasant fire" that was always blazing on the "broad hearth," what the attitude of the general public was toward the toughest café in town, what kind of brass helmets the firemen wore, and what constituted the country's bathing-facilities, if there were any.

The personal history of Graystork, Transylvania, Moravia, Belgravia, Ehrenstein, and the other storied realms of latter-day fiction, is shrouded in baffling mystery. All the Graystorkians ever did for amusement was plot and counterplot. Conspiracy was their national game. They reveled in it. And when they were n't making an assault upon a throne, they dropped out of the narrative. Let the reader guess about their home life. After all, it was a matter of no moment to the

THE LAND OF HAUNTED CASTLES

beautiful princess who presently would have to marry the King of Hasenpfeffer.

True, these fabled countries always had the opera. The daily existence of the people might go on in a vague, uncertain sort of literary way, having nothing to do with the plot, but the opera was a thing quite concrete, and definitely mentioned. The élite of both sides of the customary conspiracy always attended it. Evil designs upon the autonomy of the country sprang into being while the royal orchestra played Strauss waltzes. The opera has come to be an indispensable adjunct to the international romance, indeed.

And in a way it is logical that people who live in fairyland should have tastes above those of the sordid mortals across the frontier. The folk of the mountain-tops should live with their heads in the clouds.

A perfect country ought to produce a perfect race. It should work out that way.

But it does n't!

Emile Meerschaart, the Belgian electrician, and I have been through Graystork from preface to finis. We have seen it all,—beautiful princesses, revolutionists, American heroes, men of mystery,—the whole cast right on its native heath. We know what Graystork has to eat and how it goes about evading governmental food regulations to get it. We have been told how much a steam-heated flat in the capital would cost if there were any steam

ETTELBRUCK

heat. We know how much the captain of the palace guard paid for his uniform. We have learned what are the ornamental distinctions between the traffic policeman at the end of the Pont Adolphe and the chief of the royal artillery. And, what's more, we have discovered where the folks next door go after the dishes are washed or left in the sink.

They don't go to the opera.

Luxemburg has no opera.

They go to the cinema!

Luxemburg is by history and environment a cinema in itself,—in the midst of natural grandeur is the omnipresent conspiracy of the story-books.

The larger powers play for a great stake and the existence of this tiny duchy is tolerated for purely strategic reasons. A war is waged and a great army sweeps over it—confident of victory—and back, inglorious in defeat. A charming duchess plays politics and loses. Strangers sit in conference in a strange land and calmly determine the fate of her abandoned throne. The while petty conspirators plan revolutions, installing new governments, reinstating old, vacillating betwixt republic and monarchy, immensely proud of themselves and all unmindful of the exterior forces that work their ruin.

Had the novelists designed this country to suit themselves they could have done no better.

THE LAND OF HAUNTED CASTLES

A gendarme—or was it a general?—surveyed all comers with a critical eye from a point of vantage in the shelter of a high battlemented building. There was snow in his cerise plume and frost upon the shoulders of his green overcoat that robbed his silver epaulets of their effect. But in his serene dignity he stood as Ajax might have stood in his celebrated dispute with the lightning.

He was impressive enough to have spoiled the business of many a European moving-picture house and brilliant enough to have attracted great quantities of dimes to the cinema palaces of the United States.

One had only to see the disdainful glance which he bestowed upon the Luxembourgeoise questing the joys of the film to see that he disapproved of such idle pursuits. The grown-ups passed him with haughty antagonism. The children hurried by with sidelong glances as if fearful that this splendid figure might interpose himself between them and the doorway behind which flickered the delectable movies.

Once one had braved the guardian at the gate, the way led up three little stone steps to a door common enough in American cottages of twenty years ago,—three panels of wood, a pane of glass, and a wealth of iron grating.

It did n't look much like the entrance to a theater, but, for that matter, nothing in Graystork looks like what it 's supposed to be. The house was a narrow, three-story stone affair with slim windows and green shutters. A

ETTELBRUCK

sign over the door proclaimed it to be a café. A second sign, obviously a generation or two younger, conveyed the added information that the cinema might be found here and that English was spoken.

I pushed down on the brass lever—there are no doorknobs in Luxemburg—and stepped in out of the blizzard.

There was an instant impression of bar glass, electric lights, tables, straight-backed chairs, and warmth, with an all-pervading atmosphere of hot rum. Some civilians in velour hats and tight-fitting overcoats looked up from their steaming drinks as we added ourselves to the party.

The *Kellner*, whose memory of Americans hadn't been entirely obliterated by the long hiatus in the tourist business, came running over from the cage-like bar to bid us welcome.

But we hadn't come to study the liquid nourishment of Ettelbruck. A book may be written on that particular subject some day, if some brave soul manages to live through the dangers of personal research. Meerschaart instantly removed Herr Kellner's doubts concerning the cause of our visit with a question:

"*Ou est la cinema?*"

Herr Kellner looked shocked, then turned to me.

"You will find the moving pictures," he said in a good brand of Minnesota English, "at the end of the hallway through that little door." He indicated a door behind the bar, and added graciously as we started to follow his directions:

"For ten years I lived in the United States."

We walked behind the bar, and a narrow squeeze it was between the porcelain counter and the shelf of glassware. With the venturesome air that befitted the circumstances, I opened the door and crossed the threshold into a cold corridor.

Here was a foyer unique in the world of theatricals. Meerschaart may have been prepared for it—for, after all, his country and this are half-sisters—but nothing in my experience had given me warning. Women's clothes, some very intimate articles of wearing-apparel, hung upon a row of hooks along one side of the hall. I hesitated a moment.

"We're breaking into somebody's bedroom," I declared.

"Maybe that's where they have the cinema," returned the Belgian, in a matter-of-fact tone. "Either there or in the kitchen."

The atmosphere of the corridor, redolent of garlic and boiled cabbage, seemed to give assurance that supper was to be served somewhere soon, but as yet we had no right to leap at conclusions. Anything might happen before we came to the exit.

Beyond the clothes-hooks was another door. We passed through it into a big bare room with plain white

ETTELBRUCK

walls hung with ancient champagne advertisements. On the side opposite the entrance was a double doorway curtained with red chenille hangings, and at one side of it was a table where a woman, probably the owner of the clothes in the hallway, sold tickets.

The entrance fee was three francs apiece. The original cost, however, was the only expense that had to be figured in the afternoon's entertainment. No tip was expected by the "usherette" inasmuch as there was no "usherette," and there was no charge for the program, that being salvaged from the floor in the vicinity of one's seat.

A reel of post-war comedy showing the triumph of President Wilson over a caricature of the kaiser—an animated cartoon of the French school—was just flickering to a close as we entered. The spectators, whom we could not see in the gloom, were dutifully applauding. How much of this frantic enthusiasm was due to inward faith and how much to public policy it would be difficult to say.

National ideas in a country like Luxemburg are bound to change as conditions which affect the national existence are altered. Tastes in moving pictures as in governments are likely to be decided by artillery duels a hundred miles across the frontier.

The lights flashed up and we got a glimpse of what our three francs had brought us to.

We were standing in a sort of low balcony along one

THE LAND OF HAUNTED CASTLES

side of a rectangular room. The screen was stretched across the corner opposite the door. On the main floor the seating-facilities consisted of two benches and perhaps fifty straight-backed wooden chairs. A bar with china fixtures, similar to the one in the room through which we had passed, occupied one end of the room, leading one to suspect that this place had not always been a temple of the cinema.

It is not altogether correct to infer that all of this was immediately visible. For all the brilliance of perhaps a dozen incandescent lamps, we had been in the place some minutes before the salient features of it began to impress themselves upon us. The atmosphere was a vast, well-nigh impenetrable cloud of tobacco smoke.

We found some seats on a bench at the edge of the balcony and disposed ourselves as best we could. The seats in the pit were occupied mostly by children, little girls about ten years old predominating, with a scattering representation of adults. There was an incessant chattering among the youthful patrons, but no functionary in brass buttons came to interrupt them. There seemed to be any number of little black velvet bonnets in the house, some of them trimmed with pink ribbons, some with blue. A minority of small boys in the round cap of the French-marine type assisted in the manufacture of the din, making one notable contribution in the way of a fist fight before we had been in the place five minutes.

ETTELBRUCK

This city was called for the "Scourge of God," "Attila's Bridge." It is a "new town" without great interest on its own account, but for the meeting of the valleys in which lie the castles

ETTELBRUCK

I took advantage of the wait between pictures to look at the red program.

The information conveyed in three assorted languages was little short of astonishing. I learned from the English part of it that there would be:

MOVING PICTURES
at Sunday
In the Afternoon at 3 o'Clock
at night 8 o'clock
at SATURDAY and MONDAY
at Evening at 8 o'clock

ECLAIR JOURNAL
The Kaiser and President Wilson

Sherlock Holmes
the greatest american detektiv in:

ON THE LINE
OF THE FOUR

In 2 Parts

Casimir and the Fireman
Humorist in 1 act

THE BLACK CAP'TAIN
Far West Drama

---

and
Flottes Orchester
1 Platz, 3 Fr.; 2 Platz, 2 Fr.; 3 Platz, 1.50 Fr.

THE LAND OF HAUNTED CASTLES

And there were further words in German to the effect that children would be admitted to matinée performances at half-price.

It was in the French part of the bill of fare, however, that the true eloquence of the cinema management showed itself. To begin with, the pedigree of the films was presented to the attention of the public. To a stranger in the land, an itinerant who might be interested in the English program, a film would be merely a film. It was in the nature of the tourist to take what one gave him and pay well for the privilege. The native sons, however, must be advised of the quality of the product that they were asked to purchase. Hence they were told without preliminary waste of space upon the topics of the pictures that the films were from Paris. To cinema-fanciers who for four long years had gazed upon flickerings from Prussia, the name Paris probably carried a magic appeal.

The kaiser and President Wilson, on this side of the dictionary, were passed over in small type. So was Sherlock Holmes, "the greatest american detektiv." But Le Capitaine Noir came in for a great deal of publicity of the circus-poster variety.

This feature was billed as "A great drama of adventure in four acts and a prologue,—a number of sensational scenes: Chases on the Plains; the Ambush; The Mark of Fire; The Escape; The Burning Granary." One would be a sensation-seeker indeed who could wish for more excitement for his three francs.

I suspected from the first that "On the Line of the Four," however much it might promise as a war picture, was very likely our old friend and neighbor "The Sign of the Four," and so it was.

The original nationality of the piece was a doubtful matter. There was hardly enough of it left to give one a consecutive idea of the plot, and the French captions were so worn that little was to be gained from them. It may have been an American film of that era when there were no stars. At any rate, no latter-day favorites appeared in it. It may have been English. Certain elements in the "locations" suggested England forcibly. But whatever its pedigree, its days of usefulness were nearly done.

The Anglo Saxons in the house, to whom the name Sherlock Holmes was a sufficient guaranty of story action and plot, could not get very far with the titles in French. Those who had mastered enough of the language to surmount this difficulty were certain to become hopelessly muddled in the aimless mixing of scenes that seemed to be the result of many years of "cut and patch."

The children, however, enjoyed the piece just as young America used to enjoy pictures of fleeting express-trains and dashing fire-engines. The doings of the "greatest american detektiv" as marvels of mental acrobatics appealed to them not a whit. But the doings of the East Indian murderer with his shiny black hide, his wicked eye, and his deadly poisoned dart, were truly delightful.

"*Der Schwarze,*" as they nicknamed him, could not so much as twist a finger from the moment of his first entrance into the drama until the last ghostly glimmer of Dr. Watson's romance, without arousing an excited hum throughout the house.

The children wildly applauded his capture and cast upon him any number of maledictions in German and French. They commented volubly upon the flashes supposed to show the theft of the rajah's jewels in India, and stood up in their seats and yelled when the Black was shown in the act of shooting the fatal dart.

They may have gathered something from the torn film to give them an inkling of the motive of revenge that underlay the murderer's desire to kill. But from their point of view the motives were immaterial. This Indian person was downright murderous. They had seen him in his deadly but interesting pastime of shooting poisoned arrows,—truly a reprobate. And he was chased and caught and turned over to the gendarmes. Served him right! A very excellent picture!

We learned, too, that the burghers are a romantic people, as befits their surroundings and traditions. They sighed with sympathy when Dr. Watson breathed words of love into the ear of Mary Marston. They murmured

ETTELBRUCK

approbation when he put his protecting arm about her in that tense moment just before the discovery of the murder; and they howled with startling intensity, adults and infants alike, when the film snapped off short before the climacteric embrace.

The *flottes Orchester* was the greatest disappointment in the show. It failed to arrive. A small boy with a typical toy harmonica attempted to remedy the deficiency with plaintive notes that filtered unpleasantly through the other noises.

Between films we got another glimpse of our surroundings.

On the wall near the entrance there were yellowing posters of past feature pictures. They were uniformly German and slipshod, the type one used to see before the nickelodeons of a decade ago. One bore the title "*Schwer Geprüft*," and showed a Prussian villain staring through a brick wall at a blonde girl playing a piano. Another was a sketch in black and white advertising "*Der Gestreifte Domino*." The domino was a doleful-looking person whose activities in the film were not described.

In a far corner was a French advertisement for "*Deux Ames de Poupée*," played by a "notable cast of three" from some theater in Paris. None of these posters looked new, though the theater undoubtedly had been in use during the German occupation. This led us to believe that any films shown in Luxemburg since the autumn of 1914

THE LAND OF HAUNTED CASTLES

must have been worn-out stock, hastily salvaged from the waste-heaps to struggle through four years more of life. The conviction remained with us even after the proprietor had assured us that a Copenhagen distributor had given him a choice of first-run productions during the entire period in which the French supply was unavailable.

The adventures of the Black Captain started inauspiciously. The picture was improperly framed during the first few seconds and the lower half appeared on top and the upper half below, as is the universal custom with unframed cinema.

Immediately the ensemble of spectators yelled out, "*Hoch!*" with a unanimity that shook the ancient rafters. The film presently slid into its proper groove, and, save for the normal clatter of the children and their parents, quiet was restored. To a visitor the incident was worthy of note as something odd in the system of communication between the house and the management.

It has its points of superiority over the good old American custom of kicking chair backs, whistling, and foot-stamping, as any one will admit. It is no easier on the ears, perhaps, but its effect is quicker. No operator, not even a German operator, can stand the concerted shrieking of half a hundred excited youngsters.

The prologue of this "adventurous picture"—the words are those of the opening caption—extended through about a reel and a half of the total four. Whether out of deference to an artistic color scheme or not we cannot say, but Monsieur Violet, a French actor, was cast in the rôle of Capitaine Black. The girl in the piece, whose name we have forgotten, and the deep-dyed villain who stole her love, were the only important figures in the story aside from the colorful captain. The lady appeared to be at least as old as the film, which was old enough, and had a sharp nose a trifle too long for her own good. But she suited the spectators in the seventy-five centime seats, and from that time forward we knew that the picture was going to be well received.

Monsieur Violet, as the Duke of Chablis, is in love with Miss Arabella, a circus rider. He marries her, much to the grief of his best friend,—another duke whom, for the purpose of identification, we shall call the Duke of Ornans.

After the inevitable elopement of Lady Arabella with the Duke of Ornans, Monsieur Violet meets the wrecker of his home and kills him in a duel. The two former friends become reconciled in the death scene and the wrecker, after the fashion of wreckers, warns the wronged husband to beware of the woman who is "the cause of it all."

The husband encounters the faithless wife as he is carrying the body of the betrayer into the château whither the erring couple have fled. It is a strong scene in many

THE LAND OF HAUNTED CASTLES

ways, about as well acted as it is original, with many flashes of raised fists and kneeling supplication. Here the prologue ends in a hysterical burst of recrimination and anathema.

None of this was in keeping with the moral code of Luxemburg, where marriages are pretty sure to be permanent. But it was romantic, passionate, bombastic, and was applauded with shouts.

The next scene showed the arrival in America of the Lady Arabella, who had journeyed into the Far West to claim an estate left her by the traitorous friend.

And it was truly a wonderful America in which she found herself.

An official with a uniform like that of a milkman carried her suit-cases from an unfamiliar railway platform to a stage-coach. The coach was a long, slim thing like the French army's "Fourgon, Mlle. 1887." It was drawn by three horses and greatly resembled the American vehicle it was supposed to represent in that both of them had wheels.

In the meantime the Duke of Chablis had become the chief of a band of Mexican outlaws, and, under the name of the Black Captain, was spreading terror along the borders of the United States,—a splendid revenge for a husband whose home had been wrecked, but a bit hard on Texas or New Mexico.

The Luxemburgers could not understand this idea of

BOURSCHEID

About these walls rode the ghost of a crusader in battered armor. He ceased his vigil when Palestine fell to the British

vengeance. But theirs not to question why. It was action they wanted and action they got.

The bandits attacked the stage-coach.

Artful bandits they were. They kept themselves informed of the movements of the coach by a clever system of espionage. If the girl had only noted the dark figure at the corner of the station platform, what excitement she might have saved herself! She would have recognized him at once for a foe. For he was attired in a fedora hat with a feather in it, and even a timid European knows that the Indians who have for their tribal insignia the fedora hat are the most bloodthirsty of all.

Of course there was a battle. It was n't a very good battle at first, because both sides failed to show any marksmanship until they warmed up to their work. But after about a kilometer of chase things were different. Nearly everybody on both sides dropped dead at once. It was a thrilling climax.

The few passengers left alive clambered out of the coach to permit themselves to be robbed, the Lady Arabella confronting the mysterious Black Captain. And the house actually approached silence. One could have heard an anvil drop, so quiet was that tense moment when he lifted his mask and showed the once trusted but treacherous love, his sneering lips and hate-filled eyes.

He was very deliberate about it,—always the gentleman, the duke, outlaw or not. He was so deliberate that he turned his back upon her momentarily and she escaped.

The outlaws held a brief conference and leaped to horse in pursuit as she sped down the glistening road.

The house had a wild time about it.

American moving-picture men used to hold long newspaper debates concerning the propriety of applauding the silent drama. But I have never yet seen a decision relative to the etiquette of starting a riot at a thrilling moment. The young Luxemburgers stood up in their chairs and howled.

The people of the grand duchy are not so volatile as those of France. Superficially they bear a closer resemblance to their German neighbors. But they stand proved a race apart to one who has ever seen them at the cinema. They feel deeply and express themselves energetically regardless of time or place. They leap from stolidity to intense animation with the quickness of a flash of light.

The girl outdistanced all the bandits save the Black Captain, and this relentless pursuer chased her through a few Italian villas and other little-known parts of Mexico. Just as he caught up with her the film broke and the cheering spectators subsided with a deep sigh.

That gave us a chance to escape without being trampled upon and we made the best of our opportunity.

It was snowing when we reached the street. The braid-

ETTELBRUCK

ed gendarme stood as we had left him, his silver epaulets glistening like diamonds with the frost.

Down the street was another picture. The shops were alight and beautiful furs and gorgeous uniforms were passing in a continuous pageant under the lamps. A bent old woman and an officer of the princess's guard brushed by us and up the stone steps; then came a little girl and a tall bristly-haired burgher who some months before, perhaps, had been a machine-gunner in the crown-prince's army before Verdun.

A brightly costumed functionary stopped beside us to tack a proclamation on a convenient door. Charlotte was issuing another appeal for harmony.

CHAPTER XVI
VIANDEN

The Dice of the Devil

Till the sun grows cold,
And the stars are old,
And the leaves of the Judgment Book unfold
—Bayard Taylor.

CHAPTER XVI

VIANDEN

HERE click eternally the dice of the devil; here rides the White Lady of the Forest, harbinger of death; here Christian voices make echo, among the tombs of vanished Rome, the hymns of Baal; here is a miraculous statue; here is an enchanted wood presided over by a mischievous sprite; here walk the ghosts of a glorious house. This is Vianden.

No region in Europe is richer in legend than this rocky frontier where the grand duchy sticks an impudent little elbow into the ribs of Prussia. Upon the face of no other district has history so visibly set the mark of its passing. Vianden sleeps now, tends its vineyards, presses its wine, hoes its gardens, and markets its produce content to be what it is, but on the hills above it and along the valley of the purling Our crumble the tablets of a past magnificence.

The tales of Vianden range in subject-matter from buried treasure to black art and cover in passing every one of Polti's thirty-six dramatic situations. Vianden has been a world within itself and its traditions run the gamut of human relationship.

The great castle on the mamelon behind the white

THE LAND OF HAUNTED CASTLES

village, from which the lords of Vianden extended an iron-handed rule over thirty seigneurs and fifty-two villages, still preserves a sort of massive integrity even in its ruins. It was rated impregnable, this schloss, and apparently had greater luck with its impregnability than the rock of Luxemburg city, which it rivaled in artificial protection if not in natural strategic position.

One gets, somehow, the impression that the town has changed even less than the massive fortress which dominates it, that the atmosphere of Vianden is virtually that of feudal days. The people, who are citizens first of Vianden and then of the grand duchy, lend verisimilitude to this fancy. It is not to be wondered at that a few wraiths of a thousand years ago still meander aimlessly down the cobbled streets and across the ancient bridge. The remarkable thing is that there are not more of them.

Vianden is set over in the northeast corner of the Ardennes and is reached from Diekirch by a *chemin de fer vicinal* which achieves the acme of vicinality.

The railroad pursues a diffident course through the city from the Diekirch station, shrieking at dull pedestrians, sleepy horses, playing children, and the dozen and one other things that make steam traffic perilous in city streets. Part of the way it follows the line of the old ramparts of the town. For a mile or two it appears to be traveling in areaways between houses, across back yards,

VIANDEN

It defied armies and the elements but succumbed at last to the insidious junk man

VIANDEN

under the drip of overhanging eaves, and within scraping distance of door-steps.

The whistle blows until one hopes that there will be steam enough left to push the little tea-kettle locomotive to the end of its journey, and the bell is kept at a continual clangor. The novelty of Vianden begins with the means of getting there. For a mile after leaving the Sure, the road follows the sparkling Blees, so close to it that at times it seems that the wheels must be turning in water. But the tiny road is a fickle thing. It rattles suddenly through a woods, dives into a tunnel, and emerges on the right bank of the river Our amid a vast setting of mountain scenery and in plain view of Germany.

The international significance of the Our is emphasized by the striped sentry-boxes at either end of the bridges that span it every few miles where roads come unexpectedly out of woods and hills to go journeying toward the Rhine. Formerly there was only one box on a bridge and that usually untenanted, for, although Luxemburg stoutly maintained her independence, she was in the German customs federation and frontier routine was a mere formality. Now that the duchy is allied to France, the polished patent-leather bonnets and creaking boots that gave an authoritative look to the scenery on the southwest border have been moved to a new field of service.

One may alight at Roth, however, and cross into Prussia to follow afoot the romanceful road to Vianden. The

THE LAND OF HAUNTED CASTLES

local authorities are used to such adventuring and are consequently more lax in their handling of passports than elsewhere along the river. Even at the expense of slight inconvenience, however, a halt at Roth is advisable.

There are many things worth seeing in this neighborhood. Roth itself resembles one of those cardboard villages that came out of the Schwarzwald in vast quantities before the toy-makers abandoned hammer, chisel, and paint-brush for bayonet, rifle, and chlorine-sprayer. A little white church that was built sometime prior to the thirteenth century still bears the arms of the Templars and their successors, the Knights of Malta. It was given to the former about 1225 A. D. and remained in their possession a hundred years. Its earlier history is cloudy, but tradition holds that St. Willibrord built it upon some well-preserved ruins; hence the well-substantiated belief of some archæologists that it was once a shrine of Roman gods. The theory is borne out by other marks of the passing of Diana, Venus, Mars, and their fellow claimants to a sorry deity, where the road sweeps on toward the lordly Vianden.

Formerly there stood at Poschet a castle fortress of the Templars and any one in Roth will tell you that a tunnel connected this stronghold with the sanctuary of their little church. To this day an opening into a mysterious passageway may be seen behind the altar. Where the tunnel originally led in its subterranean wanderings none

VIANDEN

can say, for its walls have caved in not far from the entrance and its secret is buried.

"But," declared the curé, who had pointed with pride to the historic treasures of his chapel, "tradition is too certain on that score to be doubted. The Templars had this tunnel as an emergency entrance and exit to their castle.

"It is still told in these parts how they kept their horses there shod backward to deceive the foeman who might study their tracks in the event that they found flight necessary."

I forgot to ask him whether or not these armored knights ever returned with their depolarized horses after the fashion of the dead-and-gone inhabitants of this stamping-ground for sprites and wraiths. But, after all, it makes no difference. They probably do, leaving outbound hoof-prints all over the country-side.

Between Roth and Vianden, where the road drops down from a German hill to a lowland frontier, are three strange carvings in the flanking cliff, *"die drei Jungfrauen,"* whose identity, after centuries of occupancy of their chiseled perch, is a matter of considerable discussion. The age of the original carvings is said to antedate the incursions of Cæsar. At one time the three Norns—past, present, and future—were venerated here. A later era renamed the shapeless damosels as Faith, Hope, and Charity, in honor, it is said, of the three daughters of St.

THE LAND OF HAUNTED CASTLES

Sophia. The French revolutionists, accepting their final titles as authentic and proper, destroyed them. They were subsequently restored and the community has forgotten that they were ever absent.

The ghost of this spot, however, has nothing to do with die drei Jungfrauen. It is the specter of a huge dog with wolfen teeth, glittering eyes, and a jet coat that here comes back from a dog-pound beyond the grave to plague the midnight traveler.

One is struck by the peculiarity of the boundary line over which the road crosses precipitously into Luxemburg. Although European frontiers generally are ragged things, based upon treaties that universally fail to consider topographic conditions, it is apparent at once that the natural marker between the Prussian Rhineland and the Luxemburg Ardennes should be the Our. A sentry-box, glistening with fresh paint, emphasizes the fact that it is not.

The explanation is simple enough. Vianden lies on both sides of the river; its lower faubourg is quite as large as the remnant of the walled city above. To accept the Our as a national dividing line would have been to partition the town between two nations. So the Congress of Vienna, which settled the territorial claims of all that part of Europe, pushed Luxemburg a kilometer or so into Prussia, unknowingly preparing trouble for the border

VIANDEN

patrols which were to be made necessary by a great war then more than a hundred years in the future.

Although Vianden's name—originally Vienna, from the Celtic *vien*, rocky—indicates that some sort of community habitation existed on the present site of the town when the Druid priests were wielding their encrimsoned knives in the sacred groves of the Ardennes, and the castle ruins are atop the foundations of a Roman citadel, the ruling house came into no historical note until the twelfth century. As nearly as can be determined, the castle and the cinctures surrounding the town approached about that period a strength indicative of their future military importance.

The counts of Vianden became yearly more important, rivaling in time the rising house of Luxemburg. Vianden remained an independent county for many a century.

From the semi-savage sovereigns sprang lines of importance in other countries. The lords of the castle owed allegiance to few, gave it, sparingly, to fewer, and boasted blood relationship with makers of empire in the Eastern Empire and in France.

The fortunes of the house became linked with those of Nassau in the fourteenth century, when the male line was extinguished and Otto of Nassau wooed and won Adelaide, the last remaining representative of the direct Vianden lineage. The combination was productive of a stock closely allied with the fortunes of Europe. William the Silent—great-grandfather of the first King of Prussia and of William the third of England, a nation-builder on his own account—came of the Nassau-Vianden blood. Of the same ancestral strain are Charlotte, present Grand-duchess of Luxemburg, and Wilhelmina, Queen of Holland.

The seat of the family was moved from Vianden when intermarriage bound it to the House of Orange. Its decline is traceable from that date.

The chronicle of the town is that of a world in miniature,—an intermixture of glory and horror, which apparently were the twin brothers of medievalism. Fire and famine, the Black Death and Boufflers the ubiquitous, one upon the heels of the other, accomplished much toward wiping Vianden, its walls, its fortress, and its people from the face of the earth.

The climb to the castle is long and tortuous, considerably more difficult than is apparent at first glance. It strikes up through the town to the left of the hill, then turns back upon itself to a terminal under the tower, where once swung a portcullis.

Inside the gate is the undying spell of clanking armor and swishing silks. Outside, the roses bloom and the sun makes a dazzling spectacle of the white buildings in the cozy little town. The hills are abloom with the promise of harvest, but one passes through the gate into the twi-

VIANDEN

light of the great shadowy building and its encircling walls, and one breathes the odors of decaying wood and leather, the indescribable aroma of ruin.

The passage leads up by a gentle gradient to another, larger, gateway in which oaken doors still hang on rusting hinges. A sign in French, totally out of keeping with the spirit of the place, announces that the ruins are the property of the grand duchy and that a fee of a franc is charged for admission.

A pull on the bell-cord clangs a dismal gong, and a bent old woman peeps out through a crack in the gate.

No better guide for a tour of the building than this ancient crone could have been selected. She has the appearance of an age no less than that of the great unroofed gables that rise sturdily into the wind. When she speaks her voice is quavering but authoritative.

The castle ghosts are her familiars. She speaks of them as of intimate friends.

She is willing enough to tell of them, too, their virtues and their foibles, as she leads along to an open space below the chapel where grass and mosses have made a bower of chaos. Against the outer wall at the corner where it overhangs the town is the cottage where the little old guardian of the ruins lives with her husband. Whether this ancient house was once a gate-keeper's lodge in the old Vianden or is a modern addition erected from the rubble hurled down by the tumbling arches, it would be hard to say. The cottage may be twenty years old or half a dozen centuries.

At a table by her door Madame will serve one with Diekirch beer, Rhine wine, or what appears to be a dilute solution of nitric acid known as *Limonade*. One may gaze across his drink and ponder upon the great accomplishments of the clock, that terrible leveler of mundane grandeurs. Man builds and dies, and the sands from the hour-glass cover his work.

Marie Adelaide had planned to restore Vianden as a historical relic, but the work had not yet been begun when a student assassinated an archduke at Sarajevo. What Charlotte may do toward carrying out this project has not yet been announced. In the interim time takes its toll, a brick here, a scrap of mortar there, and bit by bit the castle approaches the rocky earth from which it sprung.

Little of the schloss is left above the first floor save the walls, which still rise to the point where the vast roof arched them. A portico of the Gothic style and an adapted Roman gateway are well preserved, as are the Roman kitchens.

The kitchens are one of the peculiarities of the house. Their wide, low-swung arches show no sign of disintegration and the smoke of fires that were in ashes long before Boufflers came here for his target-practice still blackens them.

If one fancied large-scale cookery by medieval methods

VIANDEN

Outer wall, chapel and gables of the immense Salle des Chevaliers

and had plenty of fire-wood, he might still cook a meal in the ovens here. They were the progenitors of the fireless cooker. The fire was built in them, not around them, and fed carefully until the rocks were red-hot. Then the embers were withdrawn and the food set in to bake. Smaller stoves of the same type are in use to this day in some of the more enlightened parts of the grand duchy.

An immense salle des chevaliers filled the entire length of the main building along the north wall. To the right of it was a Byzantine chamber which, judging from what remains of it, must have been magnificent. The salle des chevaliers was probably the largest room of its sort in seven kingdoms. It would without difficulty accommodate five hundred men for a feast or a council of war.

Above the hall of the knights was an extensive dining-hall where the nobility of the castle foregathered. Its floor is gone, though one of the supporting arches still rides across it, and its huge carven fireplace hangs ludicrously half-way up the side wall. The arms of Nassau —three roses and two figures leaning against a pitcher— are emblazoned on the mantel-stone that crowns the hearth.

From here may be seen what remains of the tower room where Yolande, daughter of Margaret of Vianden, was imprisoned when she developed ideas of her own concerning matrimony.

There is a pretty story here. While Yolande had refused to yield to love in the form of a brilliant wedding, she was no stranger to kindness and the castle retainers idolized her.

One night she made a rope of her bedding and lowered herself from the tower. Thence, with the aid of a man-at-arms, she scaled the protecting walls, stole down through the sleeping village, and was across the river before the guards noticed her absence.

From Vianden she made her way to Marienthal, where the record of her admission to the sisterhood may be seen to-day, inscribed upon stone. Ste. Yolande, she is now, a holy memory in Marienthal where she became abbess, spent a lifetime in deeds of piety and charity among the people, and was able to offer the penitent Margaret a refuge in her last years. Ste. Yolande died in 1283.

The chapel stands at the southeastern end of the building, opposite the tower from which Yolande made her perilous descent. It is a pentagonal wing some thirty feet in diameter, skirted by a cloistered portico that runs roundabout it from a choir-loft to the point where the tenth side coincided with the wall of the dining-hall. Chapel and portico are intact, a gem of thirteenth-century architecture.

The chief feature of the room is its subterranean adjunct, which may be glimpsed through a hexagonal hole in the floor. This lower room, a rough-hewn dungeon, closely follows the symmetrical lines of the chapel above and even without the mysterious opening that connects them would be recognized as an important factor in the religious service of the house.

But this double chapel is a good deal of a riddle. Some authorities hold that it is typical of medievalism in that it provided separate places of worship for the lords and the minions of the castle. But that explanation is not altogether satisfactory. It has been whispered that in the régime of that dread tribunal, the Vehmgericht, a lord of Vianden was one of its chief officers and provided this elaborate setting for its mysterious trials. Whether the Holy Vehme operated here or not is not a matter of accessible record. There is still another explanation,— that Count Frederick II, a crusader, modeled the place after the church of the Holy Sepulcher, setting aside the lower half of a crypt in which his son Henry, also a knight of the cross, was instructed to lay him for his last long sleep.

There is a chapel a great deal like it in the ancient fortress of Brest and it seems hardly likely that a Frenchman from Finistère and a Luxembourgeois from Vianden should both have decided to perpetuate the memory of the crusades in their own homes with models of the church of the Holy Sepulcher. This would cast some doubt upon the authenticity of the motives accredited Frederick II.

THE LAND OF HAUNTED CASTLES

However, it is just as well that the mystery of the chapel is not too easily solved. It adds to the attraction of the ancient and honorable Vianden that it should thus preserve its secrets.

Legends of secret passages innumerable in and about Vianden fall like well-learned responses to a catechism from the lips of the old guide. She has heard them all and remembered them to pass on with countless embellishments from her own experience.

She lighted a stump of a candle and led me into the cellar, most of which was hewn out of the solid rock. She knocked on the walls here and there to produce hollow echoes in support of her theory that the vast engineering-works of the early counts of Vianden was still only half-suspected.

"Once a tunnel ran from here to the tower on the point below, Monsieur," she declared dramatically. "Thence it led to the town and out under the river. Its entrances have been blocked by the falling stone."

She led me to the well almost beneath Yolande's tower and paused impressively to drop a stone into it. Long afterward the faint tinkle of a splash came echoing back and it was easy to believe her when she said that the bottom of the shaft was far below the surface of the Our. The story of the mile-long tunnel seemed more reasonable when one considered the patience and ingenuity of the

VIANDEN

men who had cut this deep hole in the rock without blasting-powder or modern tools.

But the climax of mystery was still to come. We retraced our steps into the lower part of the ruin once more and presently came to the dismal opening of the Hexlach,—the sorcerers' hole, prison-pen for witches.

The old crone suddenly motioned for silence and bent an ear to the yawning crater of the witches' hole.

"Do you hear it?" she queried.

Memories of the Spinning-wheel Lady of Ansembourg came surging back vividly. There was a dramatic picture in the pose of the old woman, her guttering candle above her head, her sharp little eyes wide open, an expression half of fear and half of expectancy about her withered lips. She was like the pagan priestess of an oracle, a votary at a mystic rite.

I listened and felt an indescribable thrill at the drama of the situation. What I was expected to hear I could not guess, but I confess that I did my best to hear it. My eager ears, however, detected nothing ghostly or grisly in the unseen aura of the witches' well. There was the soughing of the pines, the solemn organ tone of the mountain breeze and a faint whistle of an air current somewhere within the great rock pile. But that I had heard before. Vianden could not claim it as an indigenous phenomenon.

"Do I hear what?" I inquired at length, admittedly

THE LAND OF HAUNTED CASTLES

fearful lest my crass stupidity might cause her to leave me without the explanation that the strange ceremonial seemed to merit.

She shielded the candle and turned toward me.

"The rattle of the dice," she answered. "The rattle of the dice upon the marble table-top."

Once more I listened.

An ear properly attuned to Vianden can pick out the clicking of the dice above the dirge of a storm or the shriek of a blizzard. But I had not yet served my apprenticeship of faith.

Siegfroid of Vianden was one of the gay young blades of his period, a gamester for high stakes, a warrior by occupation, and a lover by way of diversion. He was strong of physique, bold, and none too scrupulous, and the knights of the lower Rhine came to know him for his ability to hammer down a castle gate and plunder a treasure-chest. Many a woman knew him to her sorrow. Many a bead of sweat on the brows of serfs in distant lands went to replenish the treasuries that he had depleted.

Constant companion with him in his enterprises of the sword was Henry the Red of Falkenstein, a neighbor whose rockbound perch was scarcely less impregnable than the great Vianden itself. Henry was a hard-drinking, hard-riding, hard-fighting vassal, in every way an

VIANDEN

excellent companion for so noble and energetic a youth as the redoubtable Siegfroid.

In justice to their memories it must be related that these genial young murderers were playful rather than vicious. They felt the exuberance of youth and they knew the license of their times. They saw nothing wrong in torturing a Jew peddler who happened to cross their domains, or in extracting tribute from Christians who did not pay their tolls voluntarily. All of this was written in the etiquette of the age. The Jews were a natural source of revenue and the Christians traveled abroad at their own risk and expense, which must have been considerable.

So thorough was the Graf of Vianden in the placing of imposts on the country-side that his house prospered. Great stacks of gold and the jewels of India poured into iron-bound coffers in the subterranean treasure-chambers of the castle crag. Wealth brought Siegfroid more power Power brought him more vassals. And more vassals gave him opportunity to extend his hunting-grounds. Which proves, perhaps, that virtue is its own reward.

Siegfroid and Henry one day tired of petty quarreling with the burghers of Metz and the bishops of Treves and embarked upon an expedition of greater magnitude. The lord of an unnamed Rhenish castle was known to have brought a saddle-bag full of rubies back to Germany from the Holy Wars as a present for his beautiful daughter.

THE LAND OF HAUNTED CASTLES

It pained Siegfroid to think of all this wealth of red stones and blonde daughter in the possession of a Rhenish overlord who probably was too boorish a person to enjoy the beauty of either of them.

Siegfroid, now, was a lover of beautiful stones and could recognize a pretty face about as far as the next man. He swept down upon the German castle and claimed the tribute that was his due as the best wielder of Toledo steel in the immediate vicinity.

He garnered the rubies by the simple expedient of pinning the graf to a door with a pike and required the fair daughter's promise of marriage after a short wooing, the primary attestation of love consisting of dragging her across the pontlevis by the hair of her head.

In triumph he and his followers rode back to the valley of the Our.

Henry of Falkenstein did not go home. At all times he had preferred Vianden; more especially did he prefer it now that there were spoils to be divided.

The girl was given a room high in the tower. The men-at-arms received their ration of wine and proceeded to become very drunk and disorderly. Siegfroid and Henry retired to the secret treasure-chambers to examine the loot.

Here for the first time in their long acquaintance Henry showed signs of disagreeing with his boyhood friend. He declined to accept a minor portion of the

THE WATCH TOWER
Numerous legends state that tunnels ran from the tower to the castle and from the castle down into the village

UNDERGROUND PASSAGE
In such rooms as this, carved from solid rock, the rival knights play their game with the devil's dice and the rubies of the robber barons lie buried

VIANDEN

rubies as his share in the proceeds of their joint enterprise. He advanced a claim for a larger dividend, recalling long and faithful service and suggesting that the merit of his plea be decided by the dice.

Henry knew, of course, that Siegfroid's cupidity was exceeded by only one other passion, the zest for gambling. One cast of the ivory cubes upon the stone counting-table and Siegfroid had flung himself into the game.

It was noon when they sat down. Far into the night the throwing of the dice continued, until Henry, by far the cooler of the two, and apparently the luckier, had won all the rubies. Siegfroid, laughing at his loss, arose to go.

"No," declared Henry. "We dice for the girl, also. She is worth more than the rubies."

Siegfroid sat down.

"A fair proposition," he conceded. "We dice for the girl and we dice for the rubies and we play until one man has won all and may the devil take the man who quits first."

"Agreed!" shouted Henry.

That vow, heedlessly given and speedily regretted, was the beginning of endless trouble for the two gamblers.

There was a crash of thunder and a sudden puff of sulphur smoke and his Satanic Majesty stood beside the table. He drew up a chair and seated himself comfort-

THE LAND OF HAUNTED CASTLES

ably to watch the dice. And the play has been going on ever since.

The devil made no comment. None was needed. The two players well understood the meaning of his visit and went on as gentlemen should, paying no attention to his supervision. But they dare not quit until Judgment Day. Unless unfortunate chance gives to one of them the entire estate of the other the game will be endless. The devil, of course, might guide the dice with his evil arts and so hasten the climax of the contest, but, knowing the pair from early infancy, he has no choice between their souls and a wait of a few eons means nothing to him.

"No," admitted the little old woman, "one cannot hear very well to-day. But the sounds are there always,—always the clicking of stone and stone. It must go on until one of them quits. And they will never quit."

I was glad to get out of the place into the open air where the pine balsam sweeps across the ruins. If one imagines that there is nothing eerie about an old wife's tale in the mysterious tunnels of a tumble-down castle, let him gaze as I did into the sorcerers' cage and try to avoid the contagion of a native's unwavering belief. One feels the presence of the devil's dicers even though he may not be able to hear the dice.

The dicers are not alone in their ghostly vigil. A spec-

VIANDEN

tral hound makes the rounds of the ramparts every now and then, baying whenever he passes the tunnel openings whence issue the sounds of the eternal gaming but otherwise conducting himself in a decorous manner, as befits a dog of his reputation and attainments.

A picture of the hound as he appeared in the flesh in 1400 is carved in the monument to Marie of Spanheim, in the parish church.

Marie was the daughter of Godfrey III of Vianden, who rode off to the Holy Wars in the hope of assuaging his grief over the death of his wife. Godfrey took naturally to crusading and came home only on rare occasions. In the meantime Marie's affairs were administered by a seneschal whom fallen arches had kept out of the war.

This seneschal at first demonstrated that Godfrey's confidence in him had been well placed. He was scrupulously honest in the handling of taxes, the little customs collections from travelers, etc. And he impressed upon the village something of his own unwavering loyalty in the interests of the house he served.

But while all this was going on Marie was growing into womanhood. The seneschal discovered one day that she was very beautiful, and straightway his vaunted loyalty was forgotten.

Marie was already affianced to the Count of Spanheim, but the amorous seneschal did not let that interfere with his plans. He declared his love to Godfrey's daughter and made it plain that it would be best for her to wed him at once. She indignantly refused and he threw her into a dungeon to starve.

But the seneschal had not included Marie's greyhound in his calculations. Every day the dog stole food for his mistress and took it to the oubliette.

After a time the Count of Spanheim came to see his affianced bride. The seneschal told him that she was dead. Spanheim, shocked and grief-stricken, prepared to start upon the long journey back to his own country.

While he stood in the courtyard awaiting his horse, however, the hound came running from the building and leaped upon him as if greeting an old friend. The dog fawned upon him for a moment, then darted back toward the castle, returning momentarily to repeat the display of affection. Spanheim became suddenly suspicious. It was apparent that the hound wished to lead him back into the building. He waited until the archer on the outer wall and the guard atop the tower had turned their backs, then followed the dog into the castle.

He found the fair Marie, pale and wan but otherwise unharmed by her imprisonment. As soon as he had carried her to her own apartment he sought out the traitorous seneschal, handed him a sword, and met him in fair combat. He broke down the villain's guard at the first onset and crashed his great blade through his helmet at the

VIANDEN

next. Marie and her rescuer were married shortly afterward.

One nameless seigneur of Vianden is said to haunt the ruins seeking the owner of a hat that is never out of his hand. The story of the hat is this:

There was always considerable rivalry between the counts of Vianden and those of Bourscheid. But somehow the feeling never came to the point of open warfare.

The Vianden knight now concerned about the hat did his best to provoke his neighbor into a combat, but his intentions were suspected. The Count of Bourscheid failed to rise to his bait.

After some years of this animosity Vianden announced a change of heart. He declared a truce with Bourscheid and invited his late rival to his castle to be guest of honor at a grand drinking-party. The Count of Bourscheid, who seems to have been an innocent sort of person for his time, accepted this profession of friendship at face-value and rode over to the castle on the Our accompanied by only a few ornamental pages.

During the drinking and feasting, that began as scheduled, one of the Bourscheid pages overheard the varlets of Vianden chuckling over the manner in which Bourscheid had stepped into the trap. The climax of the celebration, they said, was to come with the beheading of the distinguished guest.

The page gave no indication that he had overheard,

but as soon as opportunity offered he saddled two horses and picketed them in a grove just beyond the main gate of the citadel. Then he joined the servants in the dining-hall and succeeded in whispering a warning to his master.

Bourscheid departed from the dinner without waiting for dessert. He got past the drunken guards at the gate without incident. He and the page untethered the horses and in a few seconds were clattering down the hill road into the village with Vianden's yowling pack at their heels. In the descent Bourscheid lost his hat, which was picked up by the Count of Vianden.

The fugitives reached the pontlevis over the Our just as a sleepy sentry began turning the windlass to raise it. Vianden, baffled, called after his departing guest with ironical humor:

"You haven't taken your hat."

Bourscheid's triumphant laugh answered him.

"Better to lose my hat than my head," he declared truthfully.

The ancient guide was reluctant to see me leave the castle. There were many other interesting wraiths of whom she would glady have told me. It seemed that the graveyard of the Vianden nobles was a useless waste of ground. None of the dead knights ever stayed there long enough to get used to their own graves. But the

VIANDEN

shadows of the tall firs were lengthening, the Our was glowing with the gold of the setting sun, and I had no more time to spend in ghostly gossip. I passed down the hill as the milkmaids were ascending it.

Monsieur Theodore Bassing, member of the Historical Institute of Luxemburg, and secretary of the City of Vianden, under whose guidance I next fell, produced a wealth of archives reciting the vicissitudes of the community from its foundation as a Roman camp to the day when the late Professor Bobo Ebhardt came from Berlin to supervise the restoration of the castle walls.

Monsieur Bassing states that Childebert III was known as the Count of Vianden as early as 711, although most historians of Luxemburg mark the beginning of the house with the accession of Frederick I, the first independent count, in the middle of the twelfth century.

Vianden has well-supported claims to a much earlier existence. Roman coins of the first century have been unearthed in various parts of the town. Legends of Scandinavian gods cling to the forests north of the castle. And among the people there exist to-day customs that were old when Phonicia the forgotten was young.

There is the ceremonial of St. Martin's eve.

It is a rite not strictly indigenous to Vianden, this annual parade of the children in honor of the saint. Düsseldorf and other Rhine cities are noted for similar observances. Here, however, it takes on a new and peculiar significance.

The shrine of St. Martin is on Noell Mountain, opposite the castle, a place known variously as Belsberg, Baldur's Mount, or Baal's Mount. The aptness of the names signifying a memorial to pagan deity is striking, for here are the oriented rocks of a Druid altar and other topographical relics that indicate the ancient use of the place as an open-air temple for the worship of the sun-god.

The children of Vianden know little of the Druids and have heard of Baldur only as a creature in a set of engaging fairy tales. But when they set out to do honor to St. Martin the valley of the Our suddenly steps back two thousand years or more.

At twilight they stack fuel about a tall pole on St. Martin's hill. Rhymes in a gibberish that can be only the corruption of a forgotten language are chanted in runic cadence. Then the boys and girls perform a dance about the fire, snatch flaming brands, and run shrieking toward the village in a weird display of atavistic savagery.

The castle of Vianden reached its greatest strength and extension in 1270, at which time the village was a fortified town surrounded by a double wall with five gates and twenty-four towers.

The ancient watch-tower which still stands intact below the castle walls dates from this period. The suburb across the river was also girded with wall and fosse until

INNER COURT—VIANDEN

VIANDEN

it was really a subordinate fortress connected with the principal defenses by a pontlevis stretching from Roman abutments on the site of the present bridge.

Among the documents in Monsieur Bassing's collection is a copy of the franchise won from the overlord of Vianden by the burghers after the International Association of Archers, Lancers, Swordsmen, and Mace-wielders, Vianden Local No. 1, had thrown down its arms collectively and called a strike. A remarkable clause in the resulting agreement guarantees to the people the right to rebel against their ruler in the event that he infringes upon any other of the privileges guaranteed them in the charter.

After that Vianden became a community unlike any other on the face of the earth. It had its own system of weights and measures, a whole retinue of petty municipal officials, and a series of sumptuary laws that must have made the care-free irresponsibility of unchartered feudalism appear like a relief devoutly to be wished.

There was a quarrel between the Templars and the Trinitarians concerning the religious authority in the county. During the wrangle the ruling count was excommunicated, but he was restored to grace by a compromise whereby the Trinitarians took the upper city and the Templars assumed responsibility for the lesser fortress over the river.

It was sometime during this heydey of Vianden's pros-

THE LAND OF HAUNTED CASTLES

perity that St. John Nepomucenus, known locally by the affectionate title of Bommezines, was invoked as the perpetual patron of the bridge and the river. His statue still stands on the bridge.

John, it is said, was thrown into the Moldau in 1380, by order of Wenceslaus, when he refused to violate the seal of the confessional. Now, at midnight on May 16, the anniversary of his martyrdom, the Vianden statue of John Nepomucenus turns thrice on its pedestal. Any one in the town will tell you so.

Vianden's real trial by fire began early in the seventeenth century, when the terribly jumbled hatreds of the Thirty Years' War began to sweep across it from the four points of the compass.

The Black Death and the famine that followed it reduced the population from four thousand to two thousand when peace seemed at hand. The wandering Boufflers appeared with his well-nigh worn-out artillery, in 1678, and treated the terrorized city to a three-day bombardment. He pierced the outer cincture and reached the town proper. But here, for the first time in his barnstorming tour of the duchy he found masonry that was a match for gunpowder. The best he could get out of his noisy pyrotechnics was a truce with the local representative of William Henry of Nassau. He withdrew his mob of wreckers to the south, leaving the castle battered but firm.

VIANDEN

A quarter of a century later a French captain, LaCroix, came with a cavalry troop to begin an occupation that lasted ten years. "Lacroix" is a noun in the Viennese vocabulary to-day,—a term for otherwise indescribable brutality. LaCroix went and the sansculottes came,— five thousand of them who camped in the town ten days and left it looking like a wheat-field after a plague of locusts. It was an unimportant village during the terrible period when the grand duchy was a province of revolutionary France. Napoleon gave it with the rest of the Netherlands to Louis Bonaparte, who later returned it to him. It was then tendered as a present to the Baron de Marbœuf. The baron died in the Russian campaign, leaving no issue, and the castle was on the market once more. The Council of Vienna made it the joint property of Holland and Prussia, but the rise of the Kingdom of Holland in 1815 brought it with the sovereignty of the duchy to William I, Prince of Orange-Nassau-Vianden.

Here is marked the stronghold's ignominious end. The estate had come back to one who by blood and inheritance was entitled to it and should have taken some pride in its possession. But there was little sentiment about William. Vianden the glorious, still mighty and defiant on its crag after a thousand years of battering, was sold for twelve hundred dollars to Wencelas Coster, a junkman, who proceeded to do what Boufflers had despaired of doing. He systematically ripped it apart.

THE LAND OF HAUNTED CASTLES

It is said that the purchase of the schloss was a good business venture. Coster made four hundred per cent. on his investment, in the sale of the brass door-knobs, the great weathered beams, the carved panels, the lead roofing, the bronze chandeliers, the leather wall coverings, and the precious iron nails of the floors. But when he had finished this commercial vandalism, the pride of Vianden had gone down into the dust forever. Thirty years later Prince Henry of the Netherlands repurchased the place, paying a higher price for the ruin than the wily Coster had paid for the building intact.

Many of the scattered treasures of the castle have since been gathered by the rulers of Luxemburg and placed in the old church of the Trinitarians, among them the tombstone of Henry of Nassau.

Vianden's marvels of legend are not confined to the grim bones of the fallen schloss.

In the wood north of the town, an enchanted forest once sacred to Freya the mother of Thor, wanders the shade of Bertha, mother of the first Count of Vianden. She comes back to earth, as a good ghost should, in the habiliments of the grave, but she sometimes brings with her a chariot drawn by four white horses. And, like the banshee of Ireland, she never appears but to summon a member of her family to death.

Not quite so serious is the tenure of another patch of

THE DOUBLE CHAPEL
The chapel in Vianden was built to permit the serfs and prisoners to attend services by assembling at the bottom of an open court while the nobility prayed in an upper gallery. The picture shows the lower portion

REMAINS OF UPPER FLOOR
Fireplace clinging to wrecked wall of Salle des Chevaliers
VIANDEN

magic forest near Bettel by the Lemennchen, a pixy with a zest for practical jokes.

It is the custom of the sprite to lead pedestrians astray in the wood after nightfall, usually guiding them to a gully or a precipice where a sharp fall and bruises convince them of the danger of taking the advice of strangers.

"Step right this way," he sings out. "Here is the road, good sir. Look out for the hole ahead of you. Turn this way."

And woe to the peasant who hears him!

One Vianden farmer whose case is said to be a matter of recent record was coming home from a wedding-party, full of sentiment and *vin du pays*, when he heard the call of the pixy.

"Right this way, sir! Here is the road."

"I know the road as well as you do," retorted the peasant. "Hold your tongue."

By way of answer the sprite leaped out and struck the farmer on the head with his open hand. The poor man was found in the road unconscious the next morning. He recovered. But the mark of the sprite's displeasure was on him to the end of his days,—five bald spots atop his head where the Lemennchen's fingers had touched him.

Students of the black art were once more numerous in Vianden than they are to-day. Proof of their existence may be seen in the sorcerers' hole in the castle dungeons.

THE LAND OF HAUNTED CASTLES

But they fared badly, what with the determination of the suzerains to crush them, and the general knowledge of devices to render their enchantments futile.

A cloth-mill, established in the ancient abbey of the Trinitarians after the suppression of the order by Joseph II, was once one of the most promising factories in the Netherlands. It was rapidly bringing Vianden into commercial prominence when some stray ghosts seized upon it as a haunting-ground.

Looms persisted in dancing about the weaving-rooms, shuttles took to flying out at the windows for no reason at all, the proprietor's dinner refused to remain within his reach at his family table, the fires burned with a cold flame, and the flax in the hands of the spinners burned like fire.

The owner fired a gun, loaded with silver bullets, in the place, but his aim must have been bad, for this failed to lay the ghost. He substituted old horseshoe nails for silver bullets in his fowling-piece—an effective substitute and much cheaper—sprinkled ashes on the floor, and waited.

His vigilance was rewarded. The morning light, shining through the Gothic windows of the old abbey, showed footprints on the ash-strewn floor, leading to an unused clock. He brought his gun close to the clock and fired, shattering the cabinet, most of a loom, and all the pottery on a shelf behind it.

VIANDEN

But through the splinters of the smashed clock fell the nail-riddled body of a man. It was a discharged servant who had invoked the black art by way of revenge.

He was coffined in a dyer's caldron—the best possible casket for a witch—and buried in the Defendeldt marsh, a place where, according to the natives, the devil would not have to come far in search of him.

It is well to record here the ingenuity of a lowly burgher who outwitted the evil one and saved his child from a painful death.

This burgher was a good man but unfortunate. One after another his children fell victims to a demon who rocked them to death as they lay asleep in their cradles. Eleven children died in this fashion, much to the puzzlement of the learned doctors of the town, who tried every known means of driving away the demon, without success.

A twelfth child was born to the burgher and his wife and for two whole nights they sat up trying to devise some means of preventing the babe from succumbing to the fate that had come to his brothers and sisters. Then the good man had a happy inspiration. He sawed off the rockers of the cradle and nailed its square base to the floor.

The demon came, attempted to rock the cradle, failed to move it, howled in chagrin, and fled to the wooded hills. Not once since has any Vianden child been rocked to death.

The lure of buried treasure has brought more than one adventurer to this beauty spot of the Our. Hoary tradition has it that near Hun's rock, some five hundred feet above the river, not far from the spot where Attila camped with his hordes while waiting to strike down into France, is a chest of gold. It was buried by the Austrians during an argument between them and the Netherlands and was placed nine feet deep under the spot which the shadow of a tall lime-tree reached at high noon. Apparently all that one has to do to obtain the treasure is to dig for it. But there is a quick turn to the story: the tree that now crowns the cliff is not the one which guided the Austrians in the burial of their military chest. So the treasure probably will remain far from human hands until some enterprising gold-seeker comes looking for it with a steam-shovel.

North from Vianden, on the Our and well up in the craggy precipice on the Prussian side of the river, is all that Boufflers left to the world of the castle of Falkenstein, whose principal overlord still sits at the dice table in Siegfroid's dungeons.

A proud castle is Falkenstein, standing aloof from the smelly little town at the base of its cliff like a lady holding up her skirts for fear of contamination from the filth about her feet.

VIANDEN

The affairs of Satan and those of the lords of Falkenstein seem to have been eternally intermingling. The memory of the covetous graf and the unending dice game would be sufficient proof of this. But there is another legend a bit more gruesome illustrative of the same dread relationship.

Although it is related in Bivels and Bauler, the twin towns beneath the castle rock,—with all the emphasis usually accorded to a story locally respected,—this narrative of the black art is also accredited in other parts of the Ardennes. With suitable alterations in cast and locale it appears at least four times in the Belgian hills to the west and each narrator will take a solemn oath that his story alone has the merit of authenticity.

In the days when the founders of the house of Vianden were piling new masonry upon the rocky foundations left by the Romans,—so the legend of the Our is told,—the Knights of Falcon's Rock were already ensconced in a strong château. Third of the line was Philip, whose daughter Euphrosine has been rated by local critics the most beautiful woman of all time.

Some of them may know whereof they speak, for Euphrosine, like other ladies of her time, uses her tomb only as a daylight shelter. By nights she wanders among the fir-trees about the ruins, wailing a love-song and staring at her hands, which drip with blood. Her plaintive lyric blends with the clatter of ghostly hoofs upon the stone road.

Euphrosine was born to nurse an inherited hatred for the house of Stolzemburg, whose castle was only a few kilometers to the north. The first Falkenstein had had words with the first Stolzemburg and had beheaded him. Several times afterward other Stolzemburg warriors had sought revenge and so their name became anathema in the family of the knights who dwelt upon the Falcon rock.

Euphrosine grew to womanhood and was espoused to the Count Conon, whom she loved only indifferently. The whole Rhineland made merry at her betrothal-feast.

During the festivities the knights and ladies of the party rode out to a boar-hunt. Euphrosine lost her companions in the dense woods and was seeking her way back to the castle when her horse became unmanageable and dashed toward the cliff that drops down to the Our. Death was very close to her when a stranger rode out of the shrubbery and by a bit of dexterous horsemanship came alongside her just in time to clasp her about the waist as her maddened palfrey leaped over the precipice.

Euphrosine had opportunity to study her rescuer as he escorted her back to the castle and she found that he was the fairy prince of whom she had dreamed while listening apathetically to the love-protestations of Conon. Both knight and maid had become a bit self-conscious as they neared the end of her journey. Youth was calling to youth.

Then, all too late to steel herself against the promptings of her heart, Euphrosine learned the stranger's name. He was Count Robert of the hated house of Stolzemburg, her father's enemy.

The affair had progressed too far, however, to be stopped by this lamentable discovery. Euphrosine met the brave rider many times after that, in the woods between their domains, and sought by every art to delay her marriage with Conon.

But parental will was a law that could not be scorned. After five postponements of the wedding Philip declared that he and his guests would submit to her whims no longer. He set the following day for the ceremony.

So came the wedding eve. Euphrosine, in tears, walked out beyond the drawbridge to take what enjoyment she could out of her last night of freedom. Then suddenly a horseman rode out of the gloom and snatched her up across the saddle before him. She saw the face of Robert and swooned with joy.

Down the cliff road they swept like the wind, but not before the guards at the bridge had noticed the abduction and spread the alarm. Hoof-beats clattered close behind them. Conon was distanced, but one tall figure, sitting his black stallion like a centaur, slowly gained upon them.

THE LAND OF HAUNTED CASTLES

They reached the foot of the precipice and had barely time to embark in a small boat awaiting them at the end of the road, when the pursuing rider leaped from his horse and threw himself upon them.

Robert pressed into the hand of his stolen love a dagger and Euphrosine struck. The moon paled and there was a flash of light and the stunned girl saw the tall man sinking in death with her dagger in his heart. Her father!

The Count of Stolzemburg had shoved off and the boat was in midstream before she could tear her eyes from the horrible sight ashore to look at him. As she did so he laughed at her and seized her in his arms. The face of Robert dissolved and she found herself gazing into the fire-scarred countenance of the All Evil.

"Parricide!" he shrieked. "You have made yourself mine." The boat sank and the waves closed over them.

Remnants of three lordly stone towers are all that remains of Stolzemburg. The spot is worth a visit if only through its connection with the grisly story of Count Robert, but it presents no spectacular features to one who has viewed Vianden.

It is said that the last descendant of the line of Stolzemburg died only recently—a swineherd, tending his pigs in the shadows of the feudal palace that had been the abode of his powerful ancestors.

But why dwell upon that? Wilhelm II chops wood at Amerongen and the last male descendant of the Polish

VIANDEN

kings was recently a member of the San Antonio police force.

Between Bivels and Vianden the pretty little shrine of Bildchen shows a dainty white spire amid masses of greenery on the steep hillside. Seven little altars, each representative of an episode in the life of Christ, mark the way to it and at the top of the winding path a spring with marvelous powers bubbles up out of the rock. Bildchen has a miraculous history.

The story is that centuries ago two boys found a little oaken statue of the Blessed Lady. They threw it unnoticed upon their fire with other billets of wood. But their attention was attracted to it a moment later when they discovered that the flames refused to attack it. The little statue became dazzling white and the boys ran back to Vianden in fright.

The next day they returned with a curé, to discover that the image had disappeared from the ashes of the fire and was back in the branches of the oak-tree where they had first found it. The statue was taken to the Vianden church several times after that, but always would travel back to the oak on the hill. It was allowed to remain there, the object of much veneration until the oak died, after which it was placed in the Bildchen shrine, specially constructed to house it.

The tiny chapel is now the scene of a great pilgrimage once a year. On the Sunday before the Feast of the

THE LAND OF HAUNTED CASTLES

Assumption the miraculous statue is carried to the Vianden church in stately procession. It is kept there until the Sunday within the octave of the feast and is carried back with a ceremonial no less impressive.

The waters of Bildchen have come to be looked upon as a miraculous aid for the blind. Throughout the year pilgrims come here to wash weakened eyes in the spring, which phase of the chapel's popularity is reflected in the tablet of dedication above the door: PROFER LUMEN CÆCIS; PELLE MALA NOSTRA (Grant light to the blind and banish our ills).

Religion is a living thing in Vianden. God walks very close to these children of the hills. They have been tried in the acid of time and found pure gold.

CHAPTER XVII

DAHNEN

The Wise Men of Gotham

> Though thou shouldest bray a fool in a mortar . . . yet will not his foolishness depart from him.
> —Proverbs. xxvii. 22

CHAPTER XVII

DAHNEN

DAHNEN, which lies on the Prussian side of the Our north of Vianden, is worth a visit. Not for any architectural marvels! Nor for ruins. The only thing in ruins in the town is its reputation. As for legends, there are plenty about, but not in Dahnen. Though other villages in the Ardennes may be proudly concerned over an illustrious past, Dahnen would eat of the lotus flower and forget. One can always start the Prussian equivalent of a riot in these parts by asking questions.

As for Dahnen's ghosts, if they ever left their graves at all, they probably lost their way in returning and have crowded into the already over-tenanted tombs of Ettelbruck or Diekirch and are registering complaints about the accommodations.

Yet the town merits notice as the birthplace of a great and peculiar race. As the shrine of intellectual novelty it is without parallel in the duchy. From here came the wise men of Gotham, Clever Elsa, Handy Andy, and all the other sinister-sided heroes and heroines of history.

Do you remember the tale of the man who stored his

treasure in his house as he prepared to start out upon a long journey and then took the door of the building with him so that no one could pick the lock? He came from Dahnen, was probably one of its most respected citizens.

Dahnen supposedly gets its name from the Danes who settled there after some predatory visit to the Ardennes. To say that the ancestry of the inhabitants was responsible for the ancient and honorable reputation of the town might be going a bit too far.

The stories of Dahnen are many and varied and are told principally in Ettelbruck. In justice to the present generation of the Dahnenites, it must be said that they seem to have lost the ancestral knack for making copy. They attend to their farming and live their modest lives much as do the other burghers of the valley. Most of them can make change accurately in the combined German-French-Belgian-Luxembourgeois currency of the community, and no one has recently purchased gold bricks, rescued sick engineers, tried to guess which shell the little pea was under, or otherwise contributed to the gaiety of nations.

In the olden days, however, if Ettelbruck may be credited, life in Dahnen was more complicated.

They tell the story of the farmer whose cow was not thriving on the sun-tanned grasses of the meadow.

The farmer was at a loss for a remedy when he discovered that the milk fountains of the cow were drying up. He realized that she must have green fodder at once, but could find none to give to her. Then he noticed the weeds growing luxuriantly on the inside of the well.

Here, obviously, was a grazing-ground that offered possibilities innumerable. The only thing that made it impracticable as a pasture was the cow's inability to walk up and down the straight sides.

The peasant retired to his cottage door-step and sat down with his pipe, to ponder on the problem. If the cow could be made to sprout wings, he thought, it would be simple enough. Similarly, a house-fly and a cow, if they could be cross-bred, might be expected to produce a new species of cows with adhesive feet. The latter idea appealed to him from a purely scientific point of view. Undoubtedly the results of such experimentation would bring fame, even now, to one who brought it to a satisfactory finish. It would be difficult to imagine a more noble sight than cows climbing up and down walls, browsing on thatched roofs, or nipping rosebuds from the trellises.

There was this difficulty, however: the experiment would take too much time. Before it could be perfected the weeds in the well would have withered and the cow would have gone dry. Some other expedient must be devised.

The poor peasant was at his wits' end when the great idea came to him. He realized that, as natural wall-climbing aids could not be given the cow, artificial means must be employed. And as, after all, simple methods are always the best, he tied a rope around the cow's neck and lowered her into the well.

Such an ingenious plan was certain to succeed. The cow's eyes bulged with astonishment at the wealth of greenery on the walls of the pit. She gurgled gleefully and kicked in ecstasy. Her tongue protruded to its full length and waved up and down like a red flag.

The inventor at the parapet of the well was highly pleased.

"She smells the fresh weeds," he cried. "Already she sticks out her tongue for the banquet."

But the cow deceived him. She steadfastly refused to consume any of the luscious verdure and that night was dressed beef.

Antiquarians will see in this story a relationship to the tale of the man who taught his cow to fast. 'T was a noble plan," he declared. "But when I had her teached and all, she died."

Of little less scientific import than the problem of perpendicular grazing, as faced by the cow-owner, was the mysterious architectural enigma encountered by a Dahnen house-builder of the same period.

This man, a skilled stone-mason, constructed a two-story cottage that was the wonder of the neighborhood. Nowhere else in the Ardennes might be found a building with walls so smooth and square and regular. From

ROMAN OVENS

ROMAN KITCHENS

VIANDEN
"It is said that the foundations of Vianden were built by the Romans in the first century"

DAHNEN

miles around came architectural critics to examine the work and comment upon it. All were pleased with its novelty of line.

The construction of the house took a long time, for the Dahnen mason was a careful soul, and he intended that his home should be able to withstand all the destructive influences of wind and weather. But eventually the last bit of thatch was bound to the roof-tree. The builder cemented the last stone on the edge of the great chimney and scampered down his ladder.

Then came his problem. The house was marvelous in every way, but he couldn't get into it.

He walked around it several times, examined it carefully, and sat down on his work-bench to review step by step the process of building, to determine what might be this unseen barrier to his entrance. The puzzle appeared unsolvable.

In a quandary he called his neighbors to a conference. They too examined the house, and they too sat down and pondered. And for all their pondering they had no better success.

At that time the church in Dahnen was without a pastor, but the spiritual needs of the community were under the administration of a curé in the village to the north. It was known that he was a scholar and a man of considerable practical experience, so it was decided to have him come over and diagnose the ills of the new house.

THE LAND OF HAUNTED CASTLES

Accordingly, a messenger was sent for him. He came to Dahnen and there was displayed forcibly the value of an education. He took one look at the house and turned to the builder.

"I see what the trouble is," he declared with a smile. "It probably can be remedied. You have forgotten to put in a door."

A great many of the Dahnenites saw without difficulty what the trouble was, now that it had been pointed out to them, but there were others who to their dying days could never get clear in their minds why the mason had not been able to walk right into the house that he had just built, door or no door.

The most interesting bit of lore in which the community figures is the story of how the populace enlarged the church.

How it came to be decided that the church was too small is not a matter of record; for it is said there was always plenty of room in the structure for every man, woman, and child in the village. Some one, apparently, had gone abroad and had returned to Dahnen with enlarged ideas. He had been to the cities and had discovered this truism,—that where there are big cathedrals there are big towns. The conclusion was obvious.

The people of Dahnen, with a great show of civic pride, met in the old church to consider ways and means for increasing its capacity.

DAHNEN

"Tear it down and build it larger," suggested Simon Heller, the town fool. He was laughed to scorn.

"Pour water on it and let it swell," suggested Herr Zimmermann, a graybeard and philosopher, whose opinions were highly respected in Dahnen.

His plan, being more sensible, was put to debate, and the argument continued for several hours before it was definitely decided that it would take too long to haul the water.

Herr Molitor was the next to contribute a word of advice. It was his idea that the stretching of the church might be accomplished easily if all the men of the village were to station themselves inside the church and push the walls outward.

The simplicity of this plan was apparent at once. The good men voiced scarcely a single objection but took their places along the walls and pushed.

But for some unaccountable reason this process was n't exactly a success. Either the men were too weak or the walls were too strong, to paraphrase from "Alice in Wonderland." The church did n't seem to expand a bit.

There would have been more discussion and the trial of a new method, had not Herr Molitor risen to the occasion with the genius that gave him first rank among the village sages.

"No wonder the church does not enlarge," he declared. "It is not to be expected that the walls will move when they have nothing to roll on. I thought at first that we might be strong enough to push them out the proper distance without rollers. But that is impossible.

"Now, if each of you will go home and get a sack of peas and spread these peas on cloths about the walls, you will find that the pressure from the inside will bring the desired results quickly and we shall have our fine, large church."

The explanation was so well grounded that even the skeptics of the parish did not dare to advance an argument against it. All the people of Dahnen knew that vehicles with wheels could be pulled more easily than vehicles without wheels. Hence it was apparent that rollers would simplify the task of public improvement now occupying their attention.

So they went home and got the peas.

They had spread them as directed and had retired to the church to resume their pushing, when a farmer from an adjoining village came through Dahnen in a cart. He took one look at the churchyard and stopped his horse in surprise.

"Can my eyes be deceiving me or has it been raining peas!" he exclaimed. "I am right. Heaven is sending manna to Dahnen and the fools are not here to take advantage of their luck."

He was not a man to overlook opportunity. In a very few minutes he had scooped up all the peas in sight, had

DAHNEN

deposited them in his cart, and had vanished over the hill, warbling spring songs in a dolorous voice and a very complicated dialect. He was several kilometers distant when the pushers inside the church decided to step outside to see how the work was progressing.

They had no sooner assembled in the churchyard than they began to berate Herr Molitor.

They pointed in sorrow to the place where the ball-bearing peas had been spread and called upon him to explain whither they had vanished.

His position in the community was precarious for a moment, but his brain saved him. He gave the situation ponderous thought and with an uplifted hand stilled the tumult.

"Be quiet, dunces," he advised. "Can you not see that you have pushed the walls of the church out without noticing it? So great was the ease with which you accomplished this task that you never realized that you were working. The walls have rolled out as I promised they would, and now the peas that you spread here are covered by the church. That is as it should be."

Every one admitted that and apologized to Herr Molitor. A few sacks of peas were a small enough price to pay for the enlarging of the church.

The present generation in Dahnen does not deserve the visitation of the sins of its fathers. The people are

THE LAND OF HAUNTED CASTLES

good-natured and quiet. They support a good school and are trying to live down their Ettelbruck reputation; but the bad name clings. Let even a philosopher don the cap and bells but once and he is damned forever.

CHAPTER XVIII
ECHTERNACH

Where Thousands Dance for the Glory of God

> A motion and a spirit, that impels
> All thinking things . . .
> And rolls through all things.
> —Wordsworth.

CHAPTER XVIII

ECHTERNACH

WHERE the grand-ducal Ardennes tumble in rocky rebellion out of the Little Switzerland and dip down to the Sure, is Echternach, gray little town of haunting memories.

No bleaching bones of château fortresses attract one to Echternach. Its architectural marvels are few and its peaceful scenic setting a bit disappointing after the tumultuous grandeur of the heaving highlands to the west. But Echternach is an enchanted city, medieval still, despite the encroachments of railroads and electric lights, a place of cherished tradition and splendid history.

Here the sainted Willibrord, apostle to the Ardennes, planted his cross and founded a dynasty of religious whose work in the humanization and education of the Rhineland continued for eleven hundred years. The torch which he set ablaze was a beacon light of learning in the valley of the Moselle and the gorges of Luxemburg, while seventy-one abbots succeeded one another "spreading the gospel and teaching agriculture and good manners," as Bertholet put it, and bringing to the Ardennes glories of peaceful accomplishment no less than those that followed the brave banners of the knights back from the crusades.

The light was extinguished by the sansculottes, who took the dust from Willibrord's tomb and scattered it to the four winds. Since that time Echternach has ceased to figure as an outpost of the church. Its abbey has lost the power that accrued to it in the days of its grandeur. Its sacred buildings have been put to utilitarian uses. Its once-famous hospice has dwindled in size and usefulness. All that remains to it is tradition. But what tradition!

The ghosts that walk in Echternach are gentle ghosts, the spirits of martyrs, the wraiths of princes who sacrificed fame and title to aid those serfs upon whose backs their family fortunes had been builded, the souls of philosophers who spread the light of a "liberty, fraternity, and equality" far nobler and more far-reaching in its ultimate effects than the blood-stained democracy of the French Terror.

A strange feudalism of the cross was that of the early Echternach. The district was ceded to Willibrord in 698 by the Princess Irmine, daughter of King Dagobert II of the Franks, and abbess of the convent at Euren near Treves. At that time the town consisted merely of a hospice, the original of an institution later to become famous throughout Europe, and a tiny chapel. Willibrord established the abbey of St. Benedict and later

ECHTERNACH

built a seminary for the instruction of young missionaries. To this, the only seat of learning within hundreds of miles, came young men from Germany, the Netherlands, France, and Lorraine. Families of pious and intelligently ambitious laymen came to build their homes about the famous abbey. Christian culture was taught to semi-savage. The fame of the place went abroad and other men and women came to share in its peaceful prosperity.

The agricultural school which instructed the peasantry in the value of soils and the rotation of crops and the methods of intensive farming still in vogue throughout Europe, maintained experimental gardens in which its theoretical courses were given practical test. This probably was the world's first "technical college" and it disseminated knowledge of an inestimable value.

It was an axiom of the middle ages that peace would bring prosperity but that prosperity would bring war. So it was with Echternach. Without recourse to the baronial system of levying taxes upon travelers through their domain or confiscating the gold of Jewish peddlers for no reason at all, the abbots of Echternach waxed wealthy. The people of the district seem to have shared in the prosperity, for they were better housed, better fed, and of a higher culture than the retainers of the castle seigneurs elsewhere in the duchy, and they never hesitated to take up arms against the invader. Wealth excited the envy of the spendthrift knights of the region and the abbey town of Willibrord—unwalled, virtually unarmed, and without a sky-flung citadel from which to conclude worldly argument with bon mots of molten lead and copper-tipped arrow—was forced time and again to unsheathe the sword and meet the despoiler on his own field.

Not always were the defenders of Echternach successful. War, pestilence, and famine are no respecters of civic righteousness. Armies of friends and foes alike sacked the abbey at various times during its eleven centuries of stirring existence. Its treasures are scattered to-day over the length and breadth of Europe.

The chief charm of Echternach is that it stands unchanged despite the flight of years. In mode of thought and in appearance it remains as it was hundreds of years ago, an interesting picture of life in the middle ages. Automobiles have come, hundreds of them since gasolene and good roads discovered the hidden charms of the Ardennes, but Echternach's streets are still paved with ancient cobble and rough as the seaways of Finisterre. Electric lights produced by the churning waters in the cañons of Little Switzerland have found favor in one or two interloping tourist hotels. But the tallow candle still illuminates the simple kitchen living-room of the little stone cottage. A few sequestered mansions on the outskirts of the town, property of wealthy ironmongers and cloth-makers who realize the charm of its

THE LAND OF HAUNTED CASTLES

peace, are modern enough. But Echternach the ancient disowns them. Old age frowns upon the foibles of youth.

The Sure curves about two sides of the town. Steep cliffs shelter it in a mantle of greenery. On the slopes across the river, in Prussia, hang immense tapestries of orchard and vine and wonderful mosaics of plowed field and dark forest.

"Blue as the sweep of Our Lady's skirt," says Passmore, "the broad river threads the abbey gardens, laps the town and whisks into the woods." The description is apt.

In the nook between the blue water and the railroad that somehow seems to have been placed there by accident, is *le jardin du casino*, a fairy garden where crystal fountains sing an untranslatable song and a rainbow of flowers curves under the gnarled beeches. At the point where the Sure makes its abrupt bend is a pavilion erected by the last of Willibrord's successors,—an observation-post whence one can look out upon the alluvial plain rolling out to the embracing hills, or down upon the buildings of the old abbey and the roofs of the little town beyond.

Across the park below the pavilion one may obtain a detailed view of the abbey buildings, including the Basilica of St. Willibrord and the little square-turreted church of Sts. Peter and Paul on the rising ground behind. The parish church has, an interesting story if one could

ECHTERNACH

go back far enough into the ages to get it. There is plenty of evidence to show that the wooden chapel of which the present peculiar edifice is the successor was erected upon Roman foundations, which in turn were partially formed with the rough altar-stones of a Druid grove. This spot seems to have been consecrated to the worship of deity under one name or another since the adventurous sons of Adam came here out of the cradle of the world.

Of the structures that made up the old abbey, the most important is the basilica, otherwise known as the *église abbatiale* which dates from the eleventh century. Originally it was in the Roman Gothic style, but its architectural purity has been affected by additions and improvements. In the thirteenth century its windows were enlarged and its roof replaced by the one which covers it to-day. During the epoch of "the long Good Friday" it was dismantled by the sansculottes, who, after they had looted it, put it to use as barracks and stables. The other buildings of the great convent suffered a similar fate. Part of them were sold to an earthenware-maker for use as a factory. His kilns were placed in the basilica and it was not until the people of Echternach formed a society and raised funds for the repurchase of the church that its progress toward complete ruin was checked.

Color is lavishly used in the interior decoration of the basilica, reds predominating, but the effect is harmonious and pleasing. Only softened tints find their way to the

THE LAND OF HAUNTED CASTLES

eye between the long rows of alternating round and square pillars.

At the entrance to the choir is a tomb of Carrara marble, last resting-place of a bit of dust overlooked by the French revolutionaries when they scattered the remains of St. Willibrord. These mortal ashes were found in the desecrated crypt and carefully saved until the Terror had passed. They then were removed to the parish church and remained there until 1906, when they were carried back in a solemn procession to the basilica.

The other abbey buildings have suffered various fates since the monks were driven from their principality of prayer by the revolutionary army in 1794. These structures, which comprise twenty-five per cent. of the town, stand in their gardens as they did when the first rumblings in Paris were heard with no great concern. To-day a girls' school occupies one of them. Another serves as a barracks for the gendarmerie. The remainder are tenanted variously by public offices, a dairy, a gymnasium, and an electrical plant.

Not far from the park, where the sixty worn steps of the church of Sts. Peter and Paul start upon their breathtaking ascent, is the famous hospice of St. Willibrord, a queer little group of small stone buildings, odd enough shrine for an age-old idea. Since Irmine decreed that old men should have an asylum here, old men have always found at the hospice a tranquil resting-place in the eve-

ECHTERNACH

ning of their years. A dozen of them live here now. More than that taxed the meager accommodations of the place during the period of profiteering that followed the German invasion.

A sweet-faced mother superior, carrying on the work begun twelve hundred years before her time, willingly displays her little refuge and declaims its history. It is the oldest hospice in Europe save one, the Hôtel Dieu in Paris, she says. And she recalls with a trace of justifiable pride that even the infidels of the Revolution, who reverenced neither king nor God, bowed their respects to the superior in charge and passed on without touching it.

Up the long flight worn down by the feet of suppliants innumerable,—come here to seek spiritual aid and temporal blessing at the shrine of the saint,—the way leads to the Romanesque walls of the ancient church. The chapel of Sts. Peter and Paul is built upon a rocky eminence and is reached by two staircases from north and south. The one from the north is the more important. When the ceremonial for which the town is famous came to its end on this mound, it was from this direction that the Pied Piper procession of pilgrims wound out of the town.

There is little that is beautiful about the old church except purity of architectural line, extreme simplicity of construction, and that ineffable charm that comes with

FROM THE PRECIPICE
Over the edge of which the Flying Horseman took his historic leap

VALE OF ETERNAL TRANQUILLITY
MARIENTHAL

THE LAND OF HAUNTED CASTLES

mellowing age. Its interior is whitewashed, its altar and furnishings carved wood of no great pretensions.

A picture to the right of the choir, said to date from 1554, shows St. Willibrord in a vision bestowing his approval upon the annual pilgrimage. Some of the saint's vestments, his haircloth shirt, and an arrow—supposed to be one of those which killed St. Sebastian,—are among the precious relics displayed in a case beneath the picture. The Roman sarcophagus which contained all that was mortal of St. Willibrord prior to the removal of the dust to the basilica in 1906 is to be seen beneath the high altar.

So much for the glories that were Echternach's. What remains of them can be seen quickly and with small expenditure of effort. There is little use in asking the quiet townsfolk to repeat the legends of the place, or in lingering in the gardens in the hope of meeting a communicative ghost. The traditions of Echternach are too poignantly historical to have been translated into fairy stories. The harmless wraiths that leave their tombs, to roam beneath the beeches, take no mortals into their confidence.

But once a year the abbey town stirs itself from its peaceful sleep. The spirits of the dead monks troop down from the abbey cemetery. The feet of the live burghers slip into the most comfortable shoes available. And there begins a religious ceremony like nothing else

ECHTERNACH

in Europe, a pageant as dignified as it is startling, and as wierdly unnatural as it is hallowed by usage—the famous dance of the *Springprozession*.

Dancing has had its place in the church ritual elsewhere than in Echternach. Traces of it may be seen to-day in the strictly processional marches of acolytes at an impressive mass. A ballet once was part of the cathedral staff in some of the more important Spanish churches. In the mystical rites of the worship in ancient Greece and Rome Terpsichore was a temple goddess.

Hence it is difficult to say when Echternach's procession had its beginning. It is mentioned in records of the eighth century, when pilgrimages to the tomb of St. Willibrord began. But it probably existed centuries before that. It is not hard to see in it a Christianized survival of the springtime rites in honor of Diana, whose priests probably borrowed the dance from a propitiatory pageant of an older cult.

Legend explains its origin in detail, however careless written history may have been about the date. The good burghers of Echternach once came close to dire poverty as the result of a strange illness that attacked their cattle. The picture as presented by the folk-tale lacks only the cat and the fiddle to make it very familiar to the friends of Mother Goose. Though the cows did n't leap over the moon and the music of the cat's fiddling may not have been the cause, they did do a bit more leaping than is

THE LAND OF HAUNTED CASTLES

considered good for cows. Many of them died as the result of their debauch.

They ran out into the fields and danced, stopping neither for food nor water, until their tired hoofs folded beneath them and they expired amid convulsive shivers and piteous moos.

Even the learned doctors of the agricultural college could suggest no remedy for this startling complaint. They suggested a procession of prayer.

How it came about that the march which was to petition a stoppage of the nimble feet of the cows should itself have become a dance, is not clear.

At any rate, the populace of Echternach formed in a sedate line at the river and proceeded to dance through the town to the tomb of the saint, circle the church, and dance out again. And the devil's itch went out of the feet of the cattle.

Each year after that the procession was repeated, growing in importance as greater numbers of pilgrims heard about it. Its original purpose accomplished, it became a "prayer of act" in behalf of humans afflicted with epilepsy and its kindred ills. And it has been held regularly ever since, in rain or shine, in famine or plenty, in war or peace.

Dutiful townspeople who would not venture upon the slightest infraction of church discipline during three hundred and sixty-four days of the year calmly ignored

ECHTERNACH

ecclesiastical censure to join in the dance on Whitsun Tuesday. Civil authority, reverenced in Echternach as nowhere else in the duchy, was equally powerless to halt it or alter it. Attempts to end it were frequent.

Late in the fifteenth century the Archbishop of Treves ordered that the dancing-feature of the service be eliminated. The clergy acquiesced without argument and announced on Whitsunday that the march would be slowed to a sedate walk.

The people listened respectfully and started to walk up the hill from the Sure. But the habit of years was stronger than the pronouncement of a day. They had proceeded scarcely an eighth of a mile when the leaders began to sing the simple air of the dance. In a few minutes thousands of feet were in motion, hundreds of voices had supplied the place of the absent orchestra. The clergy, powerless to stop it, went on to the church as in the years gone by.

Joseph II the great eliminator ordered it suppressed. Had he ordered the people to go without one meal a day for an indefinite period they would have complied without questioning. In feudal Luxemburg the word of Government was an echo of the word of God. But they did not recognize Joseph's right to stop their dance any more than they would have admitted his power to stop the fountain in the abbey garden with an imperial com-

THE LAND OF HAUNTED CASTLES

mand to the rock whence it sprang. Despite the archbishop, despite the emperor, they danced. The French crushed the dance with everything else that savored of religion. But it came back. William I of Holland—an economic genius he must have been—figured out that the time lost by so many people on a workday for such frivolity as a dance represented a tremendous waste. He transferred the festival to a Sunday; and he was ignored as the other meddlers had been.

Only once was the dance stopped,—by whose authority it is not said. On that occasion, though human beings went loyally to their work, the cattle felt an atavistic tingling in their feet and capered out into the hills with scandalous abandon. Many of them died as had the cows afflicted by the dancing-epidemic years before.

The ceremonial of the procession starts at five o'clock in the morning with the celebration of masses at numerous roadside altars scattered through the town.

On the bridge across the Sure and on the Prussian banks of the river opposite Echternach the clans of the dance are gathering,—old and young, sick and well, spry and halt. Wreaths of spring flowers and silken banners embroidered in tarnished gilt are flung from the windows. The morning sun strikes a strange carnival of color and motion.

The streets fill rapidly as men in their high hats and

ECHTERNACH

ceremonial black, women in finery that has been handed down without alteration for years, girls in starched linen and tight braids, boys scrubbed until the outer layer of skin seems to have vanished from their ruddy faces and omnipresent hands, step out into the cobbled street and hurry toward the assembling-point. It is not yet half-past five and the procession does not start until eight, but the hurry of preparation is always a part of the solemn ceremony.

In 1913, it is said, more than twenty-five thousand men, women, and children took part in the dance and countless hundreds more crowded the narrow streets to watch them. During the war, while the Prussian pilgrims were more numerous, Luxemburg's delegations were smaller. In the year after the signing of the armistice Luxemburg journeyed once more to the age-honored shrine. But American guards on the Sure were a bit inquisitive concerning the intentions of the pious Prussians. The dance has not yet regained the proportions of 1913.

Long before the appointed hour a vast host has assembled in the fields across the Sure. The bridge is packed with them,—as strange an assemblage as ever met for the glory of God.

The priests file down to the bridge-head to take up their place at the head of the procession. Before them

THE LAND OF HAUNTED CASTLES

march a cross-bearer, eight banner-bearers, and numerous acolytes with tapers and censers.

For three hours the incense has been burning at a score of shrines and the air is spiced with a blend of aromatics and flowers.

The bell of Maximilian, a present from the emperor to the abbey, sounds a solemn summons. From the moment of its first peal it has a solo part in the symphony of Echternach. The town is so quiet that a spoken word at the bridge would carry to the hill on which stands the parish church. The bell ceases. The clank of censer chains disturbs the muffling stillness. The priests and their escort move out toward the church. The throng on the bridge stirs itself, with a murmur that is like a sigh. There is movement in the crowded battalions across the river. An orchestral choir falls in behind the priests and strikes up a simple melody that becomes barbaric as it is echoed by a weird medley of voices and given a pronounced rhythm in the shuffling of regiments of feet. The first of the marchers enters the town. The dance begins.

"*Sancte Willibrorde, alme pater pauperum ora pro nobis,*" is the chant that sweeps up out of the vale in an awe-inspiring volume; "Saint Willibrord, dear friend of the poor, pray for us."

The dancers move on into the town—three steps for-

ECHTERNACH

ward and two back—with a sureness of foot and a sense of rhythm that sets the ground to vibrating.

Instruments new and old, familiar and strange, in tune and out, blast out their hymn-tune with a savage energy that lends a wild note to the monotonous drum chorus of dancing feet. Bagpipes, flutes, flageolets, reed instruments of a hundred shapes and sizes, battered brass horns take up the air.

Until 1906 it was customary to conclude the dance at the church of Sts. Peter and Paul and the pilgrims stepped their peculiar polka up and down the sixty stairs with as much freshness and energy as they had displayed at the starting-point. This was no small feat, when one considers that the dance usually consumes more than five hours, a period during which all the dancers are in motion. With the removal of St. Willibrord's remains to the basilica, however, the rigors of the ceremonial were lessened. Now the crowds dance into the abbey church, continue their rhythmic glide up the center aisle, separate, dance down the side aisle and out at the door, and their part in the ceremony is over.

No bacchanalian reaction follows the dance of Echternach, which is perhaps the strangest part of it. Many a kermess in the Ardennes nearer the Meuse starts out as auspiciously as this and ends in a carouse that no stretch of imagination could provide with a cloak of religion. In Echternach the end of the dance marks the end of the festival. The tired pilgrims go to their homes, divest themselves of glad raiment, and fall to their dinners with

ECHTERNACH

energy, discussing, most like, the much larger procession of Grandmother's day when everybody danced in wooden shoes and the clatter was too awe-inspiring to permit of description.

CHAPTER XIX

A GARDEN OF THE GODS

The Tale of a Three-Legged Cat

Some say no evil thing that walks by night,
In fog or fire, by lake or moorish fen,
Blue meagre hag, or stubborn unlaid ghost . . .
Hath hurtful power o'er true virginity.
—Milton.

CHAPTER XIX

A GARDEN OF THE GODS

WHAT Willibrord's Echternach may lack in the way of material for the spinning of old gaffers' tales, over the curling flames of a peat fire on a stormy night, is plentifully supplied to the country-side about the old town. In the village rested the bones of the saint. In the hills roamed the devil. And where the Prince of All Evil has set his cloven hoof there is certain to be a wealth of narrative.

High in the rocks above the town may be seen the remains of a grotto which once served as a hermitage for the Holy Cyrillius. At night the candle before his tiny altar shone like a fixed star of hope for the villagers, above a wood through which no layman could be tempted to pass after dark because of the evil spirits that haunted it.

In the Benedictine abbey, outpost as it was of the church militant, courage was one of the chief requirements of him who would consecrate his life to the service of God. Hence tests, as severe in their way as those required for the gaining of knighthood, were as much a

THE LAND OF HAUNTED CASTLES

part of the seminary curriculum as philosophy and theology. It was the custom to send novices on midnight errands through the haunted wood. Only the pure of heart dared to go in the first place, and only the brave came back.

One night the prior called a novice before him and despatched him to visit Cyrillius.

"You will bring back from him," he ordered, "some token to show that you have reached his hermitage. Otherwise you will have to make the journey a second time."

So the novice set out.

He reached the hermitage without mishap, only to find that the holy man was not at home. He sat down to wait but realized after a stay of several hours that the hermit was quite likely to remain away until after daybreak. To wait that long would be to incur the suspicion of the prior, for it was widely known that the evil wraiths of the haunted wood disappeared at the first peep of dawn.

While the novice was pondering upon the problem of conduct, a black cat, long the pet of Cyrillius, rubbed against his leg. At once his course became clear to him. The cat was the only thing save altar furniture in the grotto, hence the cat must furnish him with the token of his visit. Without further ado he cut off one of the creature's forepaws. With the cat's foot in his pocket he went back down the lonely hill to the abbey.

Shortly after his departure Cyrillius returned, to find his pet mewing in pain on the floor. He bound up the wound and might have healed the injury save for the fact that the severed paw had been carried away.

"I can do no more for you," he told the cat. "Go out and find your paw. Bring it back to me and I shall put it back on."

The cat obeyed the command and hurried down to the village, only to find that the gates of the abbey were closed.

From that day to this the cat comes down from the hillside in search of her paw. The prospects of her finding it grow dimmer every year.

Another story of the same three-legged cat ascribes her predicament to an entirely different set of circumstances. According to this account, the hermitage of Cyrillius was once owned by a magician named Kitzele. Theofrid the Learned was abbot of the Benedictines.

Kitzele was supreme in the haunted wood and mobilized his noisome retainers to plague the good people of the town. Theofrid prayed that the community might be freed from these sundry devils, but he neglected to pray for himself. Whereupon the demons went back to their wood and appointed seven of their number to visit upon the abbot all the troubles hitherto distributed about the village.

By various unnamed expedients the abbot succeeded in ridding himself of all of the fiends but one who had taken the form of a black cat. All night long this cat would howl at his window, keeping him from sleep and disturbing his pious meditations.

This persecution went on for several weeks, until one night the good abbot set a trap outside his window. The cat came to howl as usual, stepped into a noose of linen cord, and was speedily snared. Theofrid dragged the spitting, yowling quarry into his cell and chopped off one of its paws.

The cat leaped out at the window, but the abbot threw the paw into the fire and scattered the ashes. By this simple method he had condemned the demon to go through eternity beneath the hide of a cat; for not until the evil creature should be able to reassemble the parts of his enchanted body would he be able to reassume his natural shape.

The magician Kitzele was never seen again, but a three-legged cat still roams the woods, especially on nights when there is no moon.

Across the river from Echternach is Bollendorf, Prussia,—the Roman Bollena,—and in the rocks above it is a garden of the gods. More properly speaking, it is a burying-ground of the gods, for the deities whose

BRANDENBOURG

Here a small garrison made a gallant stand against the torchmen of Louis XIV—and strange things have been happening ever since

A GARDEN OF THE GODS

biographies are written here in a hundred strange relics have passed on.

Baal and El, Sin, Shamus, and Bin, Jupiter, Diana, and Venus, Odin, Thor, and Holda all have walked across this plateau and left their footprints in undying rock. Their sacrificial monuments are strewn across the plateau, interspersed with the fortifications erected by the men who fought for them. If Echternach may be classed as a survival of medievalism, then this strange museum may be said to represent the infancy of man. Age is here,—age so hoary that the mind staggers in the contemplation of it.

The mysteries of the Druid groves are multiplied a hundredfold at Bollendorf. There is a trail, ever so faint but still a trail, connecting these priests and their gluttonous gods with the movement of race. But how the gods of Chaldea came into the North and West, modern man can only guess.

Opposite the abbey town two relics elbow each other in significant rivalry. One is the villa of a Roman proconsul, the other a rock-strewn camp of Attila the Scourge of God. The palace of the patrician is a hotel now. Yesterday it was part of the estate of the Benedictines. Willibrord's escutcheon still is to be seen, carved in the time-stained wood panelings and chiseled in the stone mantelpieces.

All of the calm of Echternach is here, and greater

magnificence. The hotel has never ceased to be a palace. No amount of modern necessity—even the Prussian brand of modern necessity—has been able to replace the array of rare old tapestries, ancient furniture, inlaid flooring, or massive chandeliers. Broad doors give access from one room to another and when all are open the hotel becomes a long hall, mysterious in the half-lights, delightfully cool when the sun is blazing outside, and peaceful as a convent cloister. It passed out of the hands of the Benedictines during the French revolution and was sold to the family of its present owners for a price less than the figure that its fading tapestries would have brought in the open market.

The Garden of the Gods lies at the apex of the hill behind the village of Bollensdorf in a wood that somehow gives a first impression similar to that of an overworked American picnic grove. Undoubtedly this is a famous holiday resort and favored trysting-place. Among the tombs of long-dead conquerors and the altars of dispossessed deity, the youth of the valley comes to dance its heavy-footed dances, sing its throaty songs, and plight its love eternal.

Yonder boy and girl who sit very close together, gazing down with unseeing eyes into the dizzy valley of the Sure, probably are not concerned with the dust of antiquity that a perverse summer breeze sweeps up at their feet. Venus once made this grove her home; what

A GARDEN OF THE GODS

cares the youth who sees her reincarnation in the buxom rosy-cheeked maid at his side? Adonis had his shrine close to the rock on which they sit; what cares the maid for dead Adonis, when living in all his beauty he could not distract her eyes from the love-lighted countenance of the farmer lad who holds her hand? The dead are dead, whether gods or common clay, and life at its fullest makes no compact with them.

The feet of Diana still cling to an altar in the light-spangled shadows of the forest near by, but only her feet. The chiseled image of the chaste huntress lies in scattered and unrecognizable fragments about the base of her pillar.

An inscription, still legible, shows that this shrine was erected by one Q. Postumius as a thank-offering for the granting of an unnamed favor. Who Postumius may have been, and what was his place in the turbulent history of this portion of Gaul, none can say. Passmore remarks concerning this relic that though Postumius may have been the general of Gallienus, savior of Gaul, renowned for his prowess as a tactician and master of men, the record of his splendid achievements is gone and forgotten; there remains to bring back his name to the world only this mark of his lasting piety.

Follow the dim path upward through the rocks, past the cleft where a breath of ice sweeps out of the chill mountain. The Celts built a fortress in this bit of sacred

THE LAND OF HAUNTED CASTLES

wood and gave battle to Cæsar. It is here still, a rocky pile of the sort which fathered the great castles.

South of the fort is the Heidestein (Heathen Stone), a Druid altar, weird in its setting of gaunt rock and whispering beeches. There is a plaintively human note in the organ tone of the wind in the trees, and elfin laughter in the trickling water that plashes over the stones from a near-by spring. Nature itself seems to have conspired with the spirits of the departed mystics to keep their memory alive.

Within sight is a beech-tree which until a century ago was the center of a dancing-park. Where each year the young people of the country-side assembled for a revival of a pagan pageant that their forefathers had celebrated even before the arrival of Cæsar. Gaul and Roman tombstones, markers of the death struggle between savagery and a forceful civilization, are strewn promiscuously in this part of the garden, showing it to have been an important frontier in the march of Progress. Farther on is the Schweigstelle (which Passmore interprets as "Site of Silence"), a drinking-trough of stone into which bubbles a natural fountain. The name of one Artio, who leaves no biography, may be read on the side of it.

Up winds the way to Kruppicht Felsen and the top of the world. The duchy is spread out on a vast table of vari-shaded green, with Thionville and its furnaces marking the rim at one corner and the towers of Arlon

A GARDEN OF THE GODS

peeping up into gray distance at another. Close by is the Fraubillen Kreuz, Bellona's cross, which was uprooted from its peaceful business of being a relic and given practical work in the marking of the boundaries of the County of Vianden.

To the north of the plateau is Wikingerbourg, Viking's Tower, a thrilling sight to one who has seen the ruins of the pre-Columbian structures that once must have been numerous along the Atlantic coast of America. The Scandinavian voyagers did not confine their expeditions to the western seas. Here is their autograph in the hills, a landmark of common import in the destinies of two hemispheres.

It is noon. From the vale comes the tinkling of a distant chime,—three strokes—a pause—three more strokes—a pause. The Angelus!

Other bells take up the anthem. A dozen villages sound the call to prayer. And here, amid the ashes of the gods, one begins to realize the magnitude of the work that Willibrord wrought.

CHAPTER XX
BRANDENBOURG

The Hunted Huntsman

Wandering between two worlds—one dead,
The other powerless to be born.
                    —Matthew Arnold

CHAPTER XX

BRANDENBOURG

FOLLOW the singing river north from the Druid haunts of Diekirch.

The valley is like a furrow thrown up by a giant's plow,—rocky, shadowy, forbidding, suggestive in its tumbling escarpments of the castle ruins it harbors. If ever the stamp of sedate antiquity was set upon a landscape, it is here.

But the Blees, foam-crested where it strikes the rock points in its obstructed course, laughs at the dignity of its surroundings. A noisy river is the Blees, a Lodore of a river, sometimes whispering, sometimes chuckling, sometimes roaring a protest at the intruding feet of the cliffs. But always it is a beautiful river, a mountain stream of crystal water, cold as the springs from which it rises, and swift as the white horse of the phantom Otho.

One passes through Bastendorf, landmark on that invisible frontier between Gutland and the Oesling, between schist and sandstone. Here the Blees, flowing down from the North after a continuous quarrel with Oesling wilderness, strikes the scattering orchard land that fills the valley to Diekirch, and carves an easier path

THE LAND OF HAUNTED CASTLES

through the sandstone of the South, abandoning its chatter of protest for a song of content.

From this point the highroad proceeds up the river into chaos. The valley narrows, the verdure fades, the rocks emerge in frowning nakedness.

Comes presently the Mullenbach, a tiny ribbon of white water cascading into the Blees, an open space, a vista of spear-pointed poplars, a tremendous uplifting rock, and Brandenbourg.

Brandenbourg Castle, forlorn as an outpost of Tartarus, is an excellent example of the military construction of the wild Oesling. Its great pyramid of rock rises higher and provides fewer footholds than those of the South. The soft reddish tint that softened the stone walls of the Gutland strongholds is absent here. Instead, the gray schist of the cliff merges to blackness in the schloss,—a blackness made deeper by the purple-tinged firs that entwine their roots within and without the spectral walls.

A soporific scent of pine and lilacs sweeps down the white road. A crowing rooster and the murmuring waters alone compete with the grand symphony of silence. A woman is washing clothes in the river. Near her a gay and festive goat is chasing a frightened baby. And all of this is like a moving picture that presently will fade out.

On up the road, wreathing the base of the castle prom-

BRANDENBOURG

ontory, choked in by the encroaching cliffs, is the village of Brandenbourg, a sparkling place where the sun, filtering through the pines, strikes moss-covered roofs. Low-hanging cirrus clouds float above the castle and scatter their torn veiling over the hillside.

Something like the peace of a vast cathedral pervades Brandenbourg. Patches of color, like reflections from stained glass, drip from the cliff walls. Colonnades of trees throw up a lacy maze of Gothic arches toward the sky. The road marches on like a wide aisle to the high altar of the castle. The village kneels, a congregation at prayer. The Blees and the Mullerbach sing the responses. And over all is the solemn organ tone of the breeze in the pines.

In such a setting rides the Hunted Huntsman. In such a silence is engendered the ghostly sound of a phantom horn and the eerie baying of the devil's bloodhounds.

Count Otho, one of the first of the Brandenbourg line, was the cause of all this. For a thousand years he has been riding through these shadowy glens and over these stony crests, scarcely an arrow-shot ahead of the hell-hounds that seek his soul. And the wild chase must continue until Judgment Day.

Otho, who lived in the tenth century, was a huntsman of note in the northern highlands. When he was not occupied with the business of war and pillage he threw himself heart and soul into the pleasures of the chase. At

THE LAND OF HAUNTED CASTLES

the gallop he rode until his horses dropped under him, through village gardens, across plowed fields, over budding vineyards. The ribald shouts of his followers, the clatter of hoofs, and the winding of the huntsman's horn, disturbed the inhabitants of the near-by villages at their prayers. But the burghers dared not protest and Otho paid no attention to their unspoken grievances.

One Sunday as the count rode after his hounds he encountered two cavaliers, one in crimson armor, one in white. They gathered their horses as he passed and cantered abreast of him.

Otho had distanced his retainers or he might have spoken the resentment he felt at this uninvited attendance. But both knights looked formidable, so he greeted them gruffly and continued on the trail of the flying dogs.

"Otho," said the white knight in a soft, musical voice, "this is Sunday. You have desecrated the sabbath and have disturbed the prayers of good people who would make their peace with God. You should cease this folly, call off the dogs, and go back to mass."

"I do not need a spiritual director," declared Otho, hotly. "Nor do I need company. You have not been invited to this chase and you are imposing upon good nature."

The red knight laughed. The hills thundered, although the sun was shining brightly.

"Well spoken," commented the rider in the crimson

armor. "Worship is for churls who have nothing else to do with their time. When they go to church they keep out from under the feet of their betters. On with the hunt.—Hallooo!—Hallooo!"

Out of the brush before them suddenly dashed a hart, snow-white and luminous, the most wonderful animal that Count Otho had beheld in all his years as a huntsman.

The count set spurs to his tired horse and gave chase.

The two strangers continued at his side and thus accompanied he dashed over hill and hollow, over meadows and through forests, until presently the quarry made an abrupt turn and fled into a little white chapel that Otho could never remember having seen before.

The count was about to ride across the threshold of this sacred place when an aged hermit arose in the doorway before him.

"This place is holy," said the hermit. "All that comes here has the right of sanctuary. There must be no violence in the House of God."

The white knight listened in silence. The red knight cursed violently. Otho became purple with rage.

"Stand aside!" he commanded. "I am lord of this domain. No greasy, maundering old fool is to cheat me of the finest trophy ever sought by a noble hunting-party."

The hermit made no sign of yielding.

THE LAND OF HAUNTED CASTLES

"Take the idiot's head," suggested the red rider. "It will make a pleasing companion piece to the stag's antlers above your mantel."

Otho, crazy with anger, raised his sword to strike.

The hermit raised his crucifix.

There came a blinding flash and a crash as if the world had opened. The chapel, the white hart, the hermit, and the red knight had vanished. The white knight was dissolving in a lucent mist.

"Otho," came the voice of the white rider. "You have rejected God and listened to the counsel of evil. Henceforth you must pay the penalty. You will ride these hills the quarry of fiends who will give you no rest. Until Judgment Day your plight will be a warning to those who live in this valley."

Count Otho, left alone, heard the blood-curdling cry of the hounds behind him. He set out upon his never-ending flight, not dead but foredoomed, with murderous demons at his heels.

Otho's place in the genealogy of Brandenbourg is not well marked. Godfrey, son of Ferdinand I of Vianden, was the first of the estate's hereditary counts. His descendants were men of power. Not an intrigue, not a battle in the stirring history of the duchy found them absent.

One Count Godfrey fought a successful battle against the Duke of Bergundy, who claimed the castle through

BRANDENBOURG

a deed by Elizabeth of Goerlitz, who never owned it. Brandenbourg could afford to laugh even at the mighty Bergundy in those days of the infancy of gunpowder. Even in its wrack the castle carries a swashbuckling air of defiance to the world. Then, it spread across the craggy top of its promontory like a flat and serviceable helmet rather than a towering and stately plume. Its walls were oversized, its ramparts double, its fosse deep to a point that betokened excess precaution and kept filled with water from the Blees. There were no "dead spaces" along its approaches where the enemy could rest for a breathing-spell in the assault. Brandenbourg stood out in the open, and so did the enemy engaged in the attack.

It is said that Julius Cæsar, when he had completed the fortifications at Besantina (Besançon) declared:

"With twenty men here I could hold off all the armies in the world."

But Cæsar at Besançon had no such natural advantages to work with as Godfrey or whoever it was that laid the corner-stone of Brandenbourg.

Brandenbourg scoffed at attack and poured hot tokens upon the heads of its enemies for many a century, until Boufflers mobilized his batteries for target-practice. Even then the marshal of the Grand Monarch found his task cut out for him. A small garrison in the castle made a brave stand against the torch-men while the bronze cannon were finding the weak spots in the thick walls.

THE LAND OF HAUNTED CASTLES

Since that time, of course, strange things have been happening amid the castle wreckage. It would be strange indeed if Brandenbourg's dead could sleep more peacefully than those of the other battered relics of feudalism.

The schloss now is in the abomination of desolation. Fir-trees have grown thickly in the hall of the knights. Groves hide the arches in chambers where once the fair women of the castle strummed their guitars to the lyrics of love. A wilderness of vegetation fills the courtyard and blocks the gate. And the mountain zephyrs play a "Dies Iræ" in the tree-tops.

CHAPTER XXI
BOURSCHEID

The Restless Crusader

Where e'er we tread, 't is haunted, holy ground
—Byron.

CHAPTER XXI

BOURSCHEID

GRIM and gaunt—frowning structures blending chameleon-like with the frowning landscape— were the castles of the Oesling. In a region of igneous rock, where valleys were narrower and slopes steeper than in the more gentle regions of the Gutland, a chain of strongholds sprang up in the barren hills and made a barrier for the duchy against the tribes of the North,—Vianden, Brandenbourg, Bourscheid, Clervaux, and Esch. And as strong as the strongest of these was Bourscheid.

The ending of its place-name, "scheid," is derived from the old Celtic root meaning "shed" or "divide" and indicates its position in the geography of Luxemburg. Bourscheid was a lighthouse on a coast of wrack. Behind it the wild Oesling casts up its waves of stone. Before it the world drops away in a haze of softened greenery where the crops of the Gutland are growing.

But the shore-line between the Oesling and the Gutland is a variable thing. The schists of the hard-rock region have slipped down along the valley of the Sure almost to the edge of Ettelbruck. One leaves for Bour-

THE LAND OF HAUNTED CASTLES

scheid, to the north, through a valley buttressed with basaltic cliffs of the frontier country, while the banks of the streams are lined with fertile farm lands.

With each mile the roughness of the country increases. Green is glimpsed now as square patches of forest on black hills or irrigated farm land in the bottoms. The trees are gnarled and bent, and covered with mosses that give them strange colors. The air is filled with the perfume of flowers and the tang of balsam. The valley has become a gorge.

Then suddenly, through a cleft in the rock as the train emerges from a tunnel, one catches a glimpse of a castle on a far-flung hill,—a castle from whose cone-roofed turrets the sun drips silver; a master castle that strikes the eye with numbing effect. There is no picture quite like it in Luxemburg.

The road curves, the rock leaps up, the shadow falls, the train strikes straight at an overhanging cliff, and the castle is clipped from view. Then come a tunnel and a burst of sunlight in the midst of an incalculable vastness.

One alights at Michelau to visit Bourscheid. Michelau lies in the valley, a thing apart, neither claimed by nor claiming any portion of the wreck upon the hill. It is quite like any other village except that it is close to Bourscheid and possesses a reflected charm. It is proud of its germane relationship and a bit self-satisfied. This is its picture: A few crooked little white streets, a few

BOURSCHEID

The castle was one of the strongest in the duchy but was dismantled by Louis XIV when he set Vauban to strengthening the works of Luxemburg City, inland Gibraltar.

"It is a fitting spot for romance, weird enough in its aspect to stimulate the imagination of the local story tellers and beautiful enough to tempt even a crusader back from the grave."

BOURSCHEID

cramped little stone houses with pink walls over which rose-vines grow irregularly, a few snarling dogs, a few laughing children, a Minorca rooster, and a number of goats.

Everybody in this village seems to have something to do and to have plenty of time for the doing. The play of the white light and the black shadow, the warmth, and the verdure combine to make Michelau resemble somewhat a Mexican adobe town. The villagers, pleasant but unhurried, do their bit to complete this picture of the land of mañana.

A little bridge lolls across the river, and thence leads a road in a zigzagging maze up the hill.

The natives smile as one starts up the grade. They realize, of course, that the traveler must wish to view the castle. Else he would not take the trouble to mount the hill. But, mon Dieu! what a waste of effort when one can see the castle from the village! Their lack of understanding is evidenced with many a shaking of the head and mutterings in Luxembourgeois.

Passmore has declared the swaggering Bourscheid to be the most remarkable of the duchy's ruins, but neglects to explain why. There are other castles as large in Luxemburg, many as well preserved. And yet one feels that his dictum is well founded.

Certainly one senses the influence of Bourscheid. There is a throat-catching grandeur in the first glimpse of

THE LAND OF HAUNTED CASTLES

it and a remnant of awe in its beauty when one studies its might from closer range.

I believe that the setting of the castle is chiefly responsible for its appeal: below it a vast panorama of bucolic peace, above it the crags as warlike to-day as they were when they supplied spear heads and hammers for the Celts, on one side a zone of dark firs, on the other the turquoise and cobalt of the sun-filled sky. Of course Bourscheid itself is Bourscheid, quite unlike any other schloss in the wilderness of the Ardennes; but had the castle been crudity itself instead of a masterpiece of fortification, it must still have been stupendous by reason of the advantages with which nature surrounded it.

Upward the road curves through forest tunnels. Openings between the bordering firs yield sudden unexpected views of the country-side and an unseen hand turns the little crank on the kaleidoscope. Each curve brings its new point of view; each point of view its own vision; now greensward and meadow marching toward blue distance; now a surf of shrubbery breaking upon a coast of rock; now rock in its own mightiness, and presently the climax of the castle.

The feudal village of Bourscheid is behind the schloss and farther up the slope. It was there, probably, when the sugar-loaf hill first was selected by the original lords of Bourscheid as a likely spot for a robbers' roost. Tradition has it that the Romans had a camp on the crest and

BOURSCHEID

it seems likely that this queer little group of buildings, which appears to be more of a bas-relief than a village, was set on the height because of the home-building advantages afforded by foundations and cut rock already on the scene. The village chose its sleeping-rooms on an upper story. The castle came to spread its protection like that of a watch-dog across the threshold on the main floor.

An ancient crusader in battered armorings is said to guard the destinies of Bourscheid.

The dilapidated ramparts and crumbling towers of the fortress palace make a fitting scene for romance,—a spot weird enough in its aspect to stimulate the fancy of native story-tellers and beautiful enough to tempt even a crusader back from the grave.

The castle, said to be one of the best examples of tenth-century military architecture in the duchy, is triple-walled, guarded by gigantic towers, and balanced against the sky in all the aloofness of the tip of the Matterhorn. It was built prior to the crusades, but its nobles first came into prominence as warriors through their exploits in the fighting for the Holy Sepulcher.

In the sixteenth century the château passed into the possession of the House of Metternich. It escaped the bombardment of the French in 1684, by the strategy of a quick surrender, but failed to bear up under the less spectacular but more insidious attacks of an unsentimental junkman. In 1803 a Vandal metal merchant bought the castle, then in excellent preservation, for a few hundred dollars. Bourscheid's subsequent history is that of Vianden and Esch sur Sure.

When the grim rider of the castle first was seen is no more certain than the exact date of Bourscheid's foundation. But it is an easy matter to find traditions concerning him. Every household in the village has its own version of the story of the armored knight who has kept silent vigil about the castle through the ages. Of late years he has disappeared. Presumably, with the fall of Palestine to the British during the war he felt that his task was accomplished and left his century-old home for more comfortable lodgings.

It is worthy of observation here that there are sepulchral rumblings in the mysterious depths of the hill beneath the castle floor, far more persistent than the clicking of the dice in Vianden or the roaring of the phantom artillery at Hollenfels.

Fitting subject-matter for a legend, but alas! centuries too late to obtain the position in folk-lore that their immensity entitles them to. Regarded from the medieval point of view, they would appear as sounds from hell. The bones of the knights now scattered across this mound must turn over in their graves even now at these terrible vibrant messages from below. But your modern, even the imaginative peasant who tends his goats on the slopes and has little to occupy his mind save thought upon the

BOURSCHEID

incredible details of home-made history, listens to the noise and pays it no attention. He knows that it is caused by the railroad train in the tunnel that runs beneath the long-forgotten castle crypts and dungeons.

A hedged path leads into a grove of Christmas-trees, darts past a little white house that seems to have fallen down from the village above, and stops between two squat towers before a shattered gate. We have come to Ragnarök, the twilight of the gods.

Until Bourscheid's crusaders assemble at the call of Gabriel's horn there probably will be some remnants of the castle outlined against the blue, but one needs only to glance at it to see that in a few hundred years it has fallen far from its high estate. Its turrets are decapitated, its arches are broken, its gables have collapsed, its dungeons are filled with accumulations cast down by fire and weather. And over the grave of its greatness ivy and moss weave a soft covering.

From the disintegrating ramparts one looks down a dizzy distance across Michelau and the rolling valley with its parquet of orchard, vineyard, and truck patch. Through it rides the Sure, a blazing river where the sunlight fires it. Bricks fall one from the other. Masonry crumbles as do the bones of the men who erected it. But the glory of Bourscheid is a thing apart. Schmittbourg the vandal could not tear it to bits and sell it by the pound to other vandals.

CHAPTER XXII

ESCH-SUR-SURE

Ghost Bells in Fairyland

Asleep in lap of legends old.
—Keats

ESCH—sur—SURE

The crusading graf hung a Saracen's head to the ramparts in testimony of his prowess . . . even now can be heard the noises of the men at arms, the clanking of heavy armor and the jingle of chain-mail

CHAPTER XXII

ESCH-SUR-SURE

ESCH-ON-THE-SURE needed no castle. Its stronghold was carved out of solid rock ages before the coming of its first knight. Nature, with one loop of a tiny river, had provided it in advance with an impregnability beyond the dreams of even Siegfroid the castle-builder. Fosses, water-filled and deeper than man could have devised, guarded its approaches from below. Crags with saw-toothed edges, far separated and circled by perilous chasms, made approach to it across the highlands a daring feat even for men unincumbered by armor. But its main strength lay in another direction: only a chosen few knew where to look for it.

For Esch, like Sinbad's valley of the diamonds, was lost to the world in a wilderness that few of the quarrelsome warriors of feudal days had the hardihood to explore.

When Esch was founded no one can guess. It might have existed a century or two before its next-door neighbors became aware of its presence. It probably did exist, gathering riches and therefore power for the hard-fisted knights that first encamped there, while the county of Luxemburg was still considering it as the mythical abode

THE LAND OF HAUNTED CASTLES

of devil-nurtured night-riders. That such a place as this gorge-guarded stronghold on the roof of the Ardennes actually had been built to house a splendid retinue of fighting-men and serfs was only half believed long years after Henry of Esch had ridden forth to the crusades with Godfrey of Bouillon.

In fireside legend throughout the land it took its place as "The Lost City of the Sure," its inhabitants were rated as supermen, and its treasure-troves were exaggerated beyond all measure. Investigative wayfarers reached it after a time, picking a fearsome course across the mountain-tops, but their return served only to give new impetus to tales already in circulation. The secrets of Esch were not common property until centuries afterward.

There was reason enough for all this. The site of the castle is a wide place in a cañon of the Sure where the river in turning has pushed back its own walls and left a promontory of rock jutting out into the gorge. The moraine, before and after reaching Esch, is deep and narrow, with no foothold between the river and the cliffs at the bottom of the abyss.

One who wished to reach the castle rock might have done so by wading the stream, but few ventured that. At first sight it seemed like a useless undertaking. There was nothing to indicate in the narrower parts of the cañon that the Sure would ever widen sufficiently to permit the

ESCH-SUR-SURE

building of a single house, let alone a schloss and a feudal town.

So Esch, designed by Nature as a wonderland, remained as a fairy tale until 1850, when some engineers, constructing a new road from Ettelbruck to Wiltz, cut a hole through the cliff with dynamite. That was the end of Esch's exclusiveness, the prosaic solution of its mysteries. It has ever been thus in the world's history. When pretty legend competes for honors with dynamite, the dynamite wins.

A wide-eyed world came on tiptoe through the tunnel and looked in at the town as if surprised to find it there, despite the fact that by that time it was officially represented on all the government maps. But little was left of the castle when the gaping citizenry of the adjoining hamlets dropped through the hole to look at it. Boufflers had left it untouched. The various other destructive agencies of the same period had passed it by. But no gorge is too deep nor peak too perilous to halt the goat-like flight of the junkman who scents his prey.

Sight-seers had to wait for the construction of a tunnel before they dared penetrate into the rocky heart of Esch, but Walhausen of Arlon had preceded them. The metals of the castle and all its furnishings had been carried over the crest piece by piece and the walls knocked down and sold as building-material. There must always be, it seems, some one willing to end a fairy story by tearing the page from the golden book and using it to light his pipe.

But if a fairy tale had gone when the world looked in upon Esch, an epic was in its place.

The stern towers that crown the bleak rock of Esch could be nothing but monuments to a great house. The race that built them must have been imaginative and resourceful and therefore a race of historical achievement. Might has been sculptured in their designing and the suggestion of a glorious past clings like the ivy to their ruins. There is a bit of the grotesque in their architecture, and a bit of the sublime.

Two masses of weather-beaten rock face each other belligerently across a cleft in the mass beaten out of the cliffs by the anger of the Sure,—one a prism, square and squat, the other a cylinder that carries an impression of greater architectural pretensions. The abyss between them once was spanned by a drawbridge, but the years and Walhausen have made good their separation for all time. The ruins of the old château are behind the square tower, a sort of pen-and-ink background to a Doré painting. They are modern, as modernity goes in the Ardennes, —four or five centuries or so old.

At the base of the rock, following its curve in a horseshoe from cliff wall back to cliff wall, is the village, a straggling town that clutches desperately at cracks in the stone and seems to owe its existence entirely to some

ESCH-SUR-SURE

oversight on the part of Vulcan or whatever mighty smith was the landscape architect of this weird caldron. The uplifting ramparts of the hill slope more gently just before they dip into the river and it is on this lower buttress that the village has obtained its foothold.

Victor Joly writes:

> This district is one of the most wildly beautiful in all the Ardennes country.
>
> Situated at the foot of a deep funnel between two mountain tops, the village is held in by abrupt walls that climb from the Sure to the pinnacle of the rocks where the ruins of its romantic and powerful house are profiled. Nothing could be more austere than these rocks, enormous and somber, nothing more imposing than the majesty of the vast ruins of the countryside.

And here is a word from Passmore, who to a greater degree than any other English writer has caught the spirit of the country:

> I have seen this picture outlined against blue-black vapors when from the valley behind there swept up the purple pageant of the storm, and to see it so or to see it blindingly by the flash of lightning is to shiver. After rain the dark rock is shot with prismatic colors here and there. But when the snow enshrouds all and the river is silent in its rocky channel and the sky rests rayless, a leaden dome upon cold and shallow horizons, then Esch might serve for Niflheim.

To see this picture "outlined against blue-black vapors when from the valley behind there sweeps up the purple pageant of the storm," is to see it in a perfectly natural mood, for Esch's peaks catch many a rain-cloud that would cross other portions of the Ardennes. And its

THE LAND OF HAUNTED CASTLES

wintry aspect of Niflheim remains while other Ardennes towns are plucking the first violets of springtime, for the sun comes sparingly into the rocky moraine. Days are short, twilights long, summers cool, and snows persistent.

Until a few years ago the tumble-down towers of Esch and the refuse-strewn nooks in the walls of the château were inhabited by a race of beggar-folk quite as impossible as their use of feudal bones for shelter. The rough board partitions that they installed in the ruins still may be seen.

They were expelled by the Government a generation ago, but their memory is kept alive in the community by the surnames that they acquired through their life in this exalted ghetto,—the Luxembourgeois equivalent of "Baker" for those who inhabited the ancient ovens, "Hall" for the folk who lived in the debris of the salle des chevaliers, "Tower" for the families that crawled for shelter into the odd pigeonholes of the black cylinder.

These people were true Luxemburgers, living cheek by jowl with ghosts and finding no novelty in the situation. For there were plenty of restless dead on the hilltop, as any one in the village will tell you. "Many a man is now alive" who has heard the clatter of armor and the drumming of unseen tankards upon invisible table-tops as the departed crusaders of Esch hold eerie reunions in their crumbled banquet hall.

Godfrey of Esch is said to have brought back a Sara-

ESCH-SUR-SURE

cen's head from one of his expeditions against the pagan to hang on the ramparts of his castle as proof of his prowess. Though the castle has gone the way of all earthly tenements, the head of the Saracen seems destined to hang to the tower throughout the ages. For it keeps coming back.

St. John Nepomucenus, sentry of the causeway at Vianden, stands guard at a single-span bridge across the river below the round tower. The statue is life size and is said to have been brought to the town in 1759 by the Baron de Warsberg of the Austrian Army, who purchased the estate after the house of Esch died out.

Dare the baleful stare of the protecting John, who seems to signal an unspoken warning, cross the bridge, and follow the path into the awesome ravine beyond. The rocks close in upon one another to a smothering embrace, the abyss becomes cavernous, then like a roofless tunnel in which the dark masonry of nature is made more dark by blue-green coverings of moss and brush.

Up the hill the path leads to a plateau from which a broad cyclorama is suddenly unfolded. Here, hundreds of years ago, there stood amid oaks now vanished a hunting-lodge of the barons of Esch. One of them, lately returned from the foreign wars that seem to have been the ruling passion of the house, discovered one day—when he came upon the body of his cousin, murdered on the door-step—that the place had become suddenly unhealthful.

There was nothing particularly remarkable about the assassination of an Esch. That more of the seigneurs did not die in the same fashion was due to their extreme caution in guarding themselves, rather than to any love on the part of their subjects. But the lord of the castle saw in the fate of his cousin a warning that he could not fail to heed. He turned the château over to an order of monks for use as an abbey.

The monks remained in possession for less than a year. One night when they were gathered in the chapel for midnight offices an incendiary, believed to have been the murderer of the seigneur's cousin, came to the place, turned the bronze key in the lock on the great door, and kindled a fire.

Most of the monks died in the flames before they could reach the windows. Those who leaped from the blazing casements to the ground were promptly killed by a band of fiendish foresters whose identity never was learned.

So far was the lodge from the sleeping village, and so well screened by trees and rocky dikes, that the murderers may have believed the foul story of their evil deed would be read only dimly in the cold ashes of a day to come. But the heat of the rising flames set the chapel bell in motion and the clangor echoed through the valley with terrifying insistence.

The village was aroused and the half-clad burghers rushed up the stony slope to the rescue. They arrived too late. The bodies of the slain monks were scattered about the clearing in which the château had stood and of the abbey only the belfry remained. Then that too fell and the death-toll of the bell ceased.

The villagers buried the martyrs on the scene of the holocaust and retired to their cañon, vowing vengeance upon the evil-doers should they ever be caught. But the band escaped over the mountains to continue its rapine and murder unmolested. The tale lacks an ending. To fit properly in the rich lore of the duchy it should reach its climax in poetic justice with the drawing and quartering of these forest fiends.

But it does n't. The tale never ends. It goes on forever, with the monks singing their tenebræ on the plateau where they died and the simple country-folk reverencing their memory. At midnight, the burghers declare, the dismal clanging of the abbey chimes echoes through the clefts of the Sure as it did on that long-gone night of the tragedy. Ghost songs swell in the woods and ghost bells are their accompaniment.

There is a more practical tale to tell of the chapel of St. Anne on the outskirts of the village.

A statue had stood in a niche in the rock where the

chapel has been erected. How it came there no one knew. Within the memory of man there had never been any explanation for it. The villagers would willingly have provided some sort of protection for it, but Esch had fallen into the clutches of poverty after the death of the last lord of the ruling house, and there was no money for the building of a shrine.

Then an old woman, pious but poor as her neighbors, died and left "all of her estate" to provide the necessary funds. All of her estate proved to be three lean goats worth no great price in the existing market.

The trustees named in her will, however, were men as pious as she had been. They undertook their trust as a holy work. Under their administration of the estate the capital stock of three lean goats was increased to three hundred fat goats. The sale of the herd provided more than enough money to defray the expenses of building the chapel.

In the shadow of the old castle towers is another shrine, a chapel rebuilt in 1906 on the foundations of a little church that was built shortly after the round tower.

The old chapel was closely linked with the destinies of the grafs of the schloss.

Whenever death approached any one of the blood of Esch,—even long years after the relationships with the original house had become so distant that the descendants of the first Henry knew nothing of their kinship with him,

ESCH-SUR-SURE

—the chapel would glow with a miraculous light. Promptly at midnight a bent old priest would ascend the altar and sing a requiem high mass. Unseen voices would chant the responses while the villagers, hearing the strange chanting from afar off, would kneel and pray, as much for themselves as for the doomed Esch.

Esch was once one of the most important weaving-centers in the Netherlands. That glory has departed from it as the grandeurs of the castle departed. But one feels no regret over that. The peace of the village is that of a *vieillard* who has done his work well and retired to spend the twilight of his life in holy solitude.

CHAPTER XXIII
CLERVAUX

Et Get Fir de Glaf!

Strike—for your altars and your fires!
Strike—for the green graves of your sires!
  God, and your native land!
            —Halleck.

CHAPTER XXIII

CLERVAUX

CLERVAUX, north and a little east of Esch, is the duchy's monument to criminal neglect. Vianden, Bourscheid, Esch, and Beaufort combine in a pageant of ruin that might be excused upon the tenuous plea of commercial expediency. No such excuse can be advanced for the slow disintegration of the mighty château where the Sure and the Wiltz unite.

The ancient castle stands intact, a splendid mass of wall and buttress, rampart and turret, crowning a gentle slope in the middle of a peaceful valley, like a living illustration for "The Idylls of the King." But the weather that sweeps through its cracks has played sad havoc with treasures that no one seems to have thought it worth while to remove. Here is a wrack of broken crystal from a massive chandelier, rotting leather, tattered and faded tapestry. Vandals have added their bit to the work of moisture and frost in the slashing of portraits that may have been historic.

The echoing of smashing glass as one walks the ill-kept corridors sounds like the dismal protest of the ancient against the forgetful present. Continual reminders of

THE LAND OF HAUNTED CASTLES

what Clervaux once was and easily might be again make it the most depressing ruin in the duchy.

Beyond the castle is the new château, which looks like nothing so much as a new château. In it lives the Comte de Berlaymont, who, whatever may be said in his favor, is no sentimentalist. Most of the furnishings of the schloss have been given an uncomfortable setting in the electric-lighted, steam-heated mansion. If the ghosts of the illustrious Clervaux seigneurs prefer their old dwelling-place to the new, who can blame them?

Clervaux's name begins to appear on official records early in the history of the County of Luxemburg. At the wedding of Ermesinde a Clervaux battler stood to the forefront in an assemblage of powerful chivalry. Another Clervaux came to the financial aid of the improvident John the Blind in 1340.

Marriage allied the house with Brandenbourg and Mysembourg, whence later it passed by similar chance to the Count Nicholas de Heu. Godefrey of Eltz assumed its leadership and then the Lannoys, under whom it enjoyed an era of renewed prosperity. The Lannoys were famous men-at-arms. One of their knights was commander-in-chief of the armies of Charles V and by conquering Francis I at Pavia made a place for himself in history so long as men shall read of the deeds of men.

The Lannoy blood gave out near the end of the last

CLERVAUX

century and the estate passed as a heritage to the counts of Berlaymont. In that family it remains.

Clervaux's story is not a fairy tale. It is a proud recital of a deed that no peasant imagination can embellish, of brave men who made a supreme sacrifice for a principle and fared forth to be butchered in as forlorn a hope as ever inspired men to battle.

Clervaux was the birthplace of the Kloeppelkrieg, that wild, sublimely useless crusade against the oppression of the trained troops of the French Republicans. Men of steel were bred in these hard hills of the Oesling. They never forgot that they were men.

"Et get fir de glaf! [Here goes for the faith!]" was the slogan on their lips as they armed themselves with cudgels and scythes and axes and swept up this fair valley against the gunpowder and shot of the invader.

They fought as only the despairing can fight, asking no quarter and giving none, compensating for inequality of weapons with a superb disregard for death and pushing back an army too shocked by the ferocity of the peasants' onset to realize its own superiority.

In Clervaux as in other sleepy valleys of Luxemburg one comes upon one of those hinges of history. A few guns, a few handfuls of powder and lead in the hands of these maddened farmer-lads, and the geography of the world would have undergone a new revision. There would have come a turning-point in the success of the

THE LAND OF HAUNTED CASTLES

French Revolution. There might—who knows?—have been no Napoleon.

But the peasants had no powder.

For two hours they cut a bloody path into the ranks of the revolutionists, who company by company fell back only to find relief in the advancing of fresh reserves. For two hours the generals of France considered the problems that they must encounter in a complete withdrawal. Then human muscle and hickory club reached the limit of achievement. French artillery blasted the Kloeppel *Armee* aside. French bayonets came forward in an unwavering line to complete the slaughter that bullets had started. The backbone of the peasants' war was broken at Arzfeld on a field that resembled the floor of an abattoir.

A story is told of one of the unfortunate scythe-men who fled before the Republican advance and took refuge in a hollow tree. He escaped detection but was too weak to drag himself out of the hole. So he remained there until he starved to death. His skeleton and the iron-tipped cudgel that he had carried to the last were found years afterward by a farmer.

His companions in arms who could find no hollow trees in which to hide experienced no easier fate. They were captured, taken to Luxemburg city, and given a mock trial before a military tribunal. Opportunity was

CLERVAUX

given them to escape execution by embracing the cause of their enemies. But to a man they refused.

"We cannot lie," was the answer of their spokesman. "We die as men should die."

And die as men they did,—the few score who had not already died the death of heroes at Arzfeld. They were beheaded in a trench outside the ramparts of the capital.

The shaft erected to their memory is one of Clervaux's most imposing relics. One of the plaques on the monument shows these aroused countrymen clasping their homely weapons as they kneel before the uplifted Host, asking a blessing upon their cause. And beneath this picture is the inscription:

Es ist besser dass wir fallen im Kampfe als dass wir sehen das Ungluck unseres Volkes unt Heiligtumes.

"It is better to fall in battle than to see the woes of our people and the sanctuary."

A second tablet is commemorative of the court martial of the heroes in Luxemburg city. And this bears the legend: *Wir können nicht lügen.*

"We cannot lie!"

From the base of the monument one looks across an outcropping of the grim Oesling, the Thor-sculptured Northland, a scarp of tumbled schist, a black band of pine forest, and one beholds a picture. Clervaux, castle and convent, is set like a luminous bloodstone on a cushion of

THE LAND OF HAUNTED CASTLES

green satin; about the château lies the village of pink and white, in the embrace of a gold-spangled river.

Nowhere in the world is the peace that succeeds the trials of bloodshed better typified than here. Clervaux is a place of whispering quiet, of flowery odors, and of chapel bells that seem always to echo from a musical distance. In such a vale might have walked the Monk Felix to whom a hundred years seemed but a minute as he meditated in the presence of God. Here is the peace "which passeth all understanding." And yet it was only yesterday that Clervaux's sons said hurried good-bys and hastened to Ettelbruck to entrain for the South. It was only yesterday that the growling of the guns at Liège and Namur rumbled through the northern Ardennes.

To-day great-grandsons of the cudgel warriors lie under the poppies in Flanders, with the *cocarde* of France on the crosses at their heads. They died fighting side by side with great-grandsons of the invaders who crushed the Kloeppelkrieg. Motives seem to get all mixed up in a hundred years.

Yet principles are not changed. The battle-cry of these youths who died for France is what would be expected of Clervaux's sons.

"Et get fir de glaf!"

CHAPTER XXIV
BEAUFORT

THE SPLENDID ROMANCE OF JEAN BECK

To enlarge or illustrate this power and effect of love is to set a candle in the sun.
—BURTON.

CHAPTER XXIV

BEAUFORT

FROM Müllerthal in Little Switzerland, where the eternal waters jeer at the ghostly plaint of Griselinde of Heringerburg, the quiet vale of the Hallerbach beckons the wanderer. Plush mosses and ferns as countless as the laces of Brittany carpet its shadowy rocks. Splashes of color, a chiaroscuro of flowery tint, give relief to its green-gray twilight. The Romans are gone, but in such a place as this the nymphs of woodland and brook live on undisturbed by the political cataclysms of the centuries.

Indefinitely the watery guide leads on through a wonderland of shrub and stone that stops the clock and dims one's eyes to landmarks. There is no time. There is no distance.

Then suddenly the veiling flowers and mosses fall away. The rocks of the glen stand huge and gaunt and naked in the sun like Titans dipping into the little river for a bath. The Hallerbach turns to the left. Taupesbach, cascading over its rocks, beckons to a grimmer cañon. The flowers no longer mark the course and no arching greenery hides the sun. Taupesbach strikes deeper into its rocks and becomes silent. And then is heard the murmuring of a mill-wheel.

Out of nowhere comes a white stone bridge to dart across the stream. The walls of the glen close in, only to widen again in unforseen vastness, opening a vista of a quiet lake covered with rushes and pond-lilies, green-cloaked bluffs, a village, and a castle.

This is Beaufort, a schloss of song and story, in a way the most notable example of medieval architecture which Boufflers left to posterity.

Its slender towers and long windows give it a Gothic grace. Its carefully constructed masonry marks it for the stronghold of men of culture who sought a home as well as a tower of strength against their enemies. There is a white cleanness about it that is lacking in other castles. Cleanness of line, cleanness of finish.

Apparently it sacrificed nothing of its endurance to the demands of architectural nicety and interior finish. Smooth as were its walls, delicate as were its towers, it stands better preserved than the more massive Bourscheid and the more inaccessible Brandenbourg.

Adjoining it is a castle of the seventeenth century still habitable, with a slate-roofed tower and a complement of lesser buildings set cloister-like about a wide court. Modern Beaufort has inherited a ghost, the White Lady who walks the hill at the foot of its towers, but without her it would have no lack of legend. The old building

BEAUFORT

is now used in the manufacture of *Kirschengeist* and if any spirit possesses the power of raising less material spirits, it is *Kirsch*.

The family of Beaufort is an offshoot from that of Wiltz. The castle is doubtless of very ancient origin, but the first record of the existence of its knights is found under the date of 1236, when one of the Beaufort (or Befort) seigneurs signed the *charte d'affranchissement* given to the city of Echternach by the Princess Ermesinde.

Another historical mention of the Beaufort family is found in 1593, when Gaspard de Heu, lord of the castle, joined with Vianden in the support of Orange against Philip II. Gaspard was beheaded and the castle was bestowed by Philip upon Mansfeld, his governor at Luxemburg city.

Five decades later Beaufort castle once more became a palace of romance. With its history from that point intertwines the strange story of Jean Beck, the shepherd-boy who rose to power but little short of sovereignty.

It was a woman who started Jean the shepherd on the road to glory, a fruit-seller as humble as himself. But the tale is a bit different from the usual recital of the self-sacrificing inspiration of sweetheart and wife. This girl was as uncultured as she was lowborn. She married Beck only as a means of achieving a great ambition,—to increase her fruit business until she had the largest apple counter in all the duchy.

She was a daughter of the capital at the time of her marriage and despite the importunities of her husband, who saw opportunities farther afield, in Luxemburg city she stayed. For the sake of romance we should overlook one phase of her character which seems to be a bit out of the picture. Mrs. Jean Beck was something of a shrew, and as her temper grew worse so did her appearance. She became noted as a slattern even among the other market-women, who were not exactly models of feminine charm themselves.

Spurred on by this inspiring home life, Jean Beck set out to make a memorable name for himself. One evening when Mrs. Beck had climaxed a stirring argument by striking him on the head with a faggot, Jean heard the call of glory. He packed all his goods in a pocket handkerchief and deserted her.

He joined the Austrian Army and went adventuring. One night he overheard a plot against the emperor. Native shrewdness suggested his course. He promptly ignored all his superior officers, from corporal to field-marshal, sought an audience with His Majesty himself, and laid bare the details of the conspiracy. The would-be assassins were captured and executed and Private Jean Beck was rocketed out of obscurity.

When the flames of the Thirty Years' War had begun

to spread across Europe, Jean was a field-marshal with a natural gift for strategy and mass action that made him a hero. He came back to Luxemburg city as governor of the duchy.

A queer romance, this! The love interest in it seems to be all mixed up. But the story straightens itself out in the end.

Jean Beck the conquering hero rode into the land of his fathers with thousands of fighting-men at his back and cheering multitudes spreading roses in welcome before him. The grand knights of fifty castles were waiting to dip their banners in his honor and lay their swords at his feet in a grand ceremonial in the public square of the city. But suddenly, at the moment of his triumph, he slipped from his dancing war-horse and disappeared.

He moved unnoticed through the throngs that were shouting praises to his name and moved straightway to the market-place.

At her stall next the fish market stood the heroine of his youthful love, still slattern, still bitter of tongue, and withered more than a little by the winters that had passed since his departure.

There was sadness in her eyes and wounded pride in her voice as she talked with the other dames of the market. She had heard the name of the new governor and she did not doubt his identity. She listened sneeringly to the tumult in the square.

THE LAND OF HAUNTED CASTLES

"Jean Beck will sit in his castle," she declared protestingly. "Jean Beck the shepherd will call and the proud ladies of Luxemburg will come to him without shame. And the woman he took to wife will sit here and sell apples and grapes and sleep in a hovel."

"Yes," said the fish-lady, who was a student of the world and something of a philosopher, "so he will. He will forget——"

A quick step and the clank of armor startled them. Both women turned, to see a plumed knight resplendent in trappings of gold and silver. The knight lifted his visor and Jean Beck the shepherd-boy and governor looked into the eyes of his first love.

"Jean Beck does not forget," he stated with great calmness. "Jean Beck will sit in his palace, but only one woman in the world has the right to sit by his side. Marie, will you come back to me?"

Too startled for speech, too overjoyed even to release the tears that welled to her eyes, Marie threw herself into the arms of her knight. Still clad in the humble garments of the market-place she followed him back to the grand square and by his side received the homage of the nobles.

Jean Beck bought Beaufort as a personal estate and erected the modern wing. There he and his wife, now old enough to know the meaning and necessity of mutual

BEAUFORT

The chateau is remarkable chiefly for its excellent masonry. It is one of the duchy's finest examples of mediæval military architecture

BEAUFORT

sacrifice, lived many happy years before the shepherd-boy field-marshal died at Arras.

The castle stood in excellent condition until it was purchased by the Count de Lidekerke-Beaufort, who tore down a portion of it to get materials for the construction of a mill. The villagers followed his lead and it was only when the count died and a more sentimental owner acquired the estate that the vandalism was checked.

The White Lady is a wraith whose identity never has been definitely settled. Why her ghost still flits behind the long windows depends entirely upon the peasant who tells you the story. She is everybody, from a Grafin slain by the artillery of the Grand Monarch to a lady-in-waiting who was betrayed by an unscrupulous seneschal and hanged herself from the battlements.

One explanation makes her Marie the wife of Jean Beck, and ascribes her inability to remain in her grave to remorse for the shrewishness which transformed the simple shepherd-boy into the mighty warrior. But perhaps there is still another way to account for the apparition. Moonlight on white walls has been known to produce visions of "White Ladies" elsewhere than below the bastions of Beaufort.

CHAPTER XXV
HERINGERBURG

The Lady of the Magical Voice

The devil hath not in all his quiver's choice
An arrow for the heart like a sweet voice.
—Byron.

CHAPTER XXV

HERINGERBURG

THERE used to be a castle at Heringerburg—parts of the foundations still may be seen there—where lived Griselinde of the magic voice. A rotund denizen of the Mullerthal told me the story in a basso-profundo that set the Petite Suisse to echoing, punctuating his recital by banging the oaken table with a stein, after the approved fashion of rural entertainers.

"The most marvelous voice in the world, she had," he declared. "I have heard some very good singers in the concerts in Luxemburg city, but none of them could boast of such a voice as Griselinde had. The angels taught her to sing and no mortal has ever sung so well since.

"But she was proud of her accomplishments, with the sort of pride that has very little to do with angels."

He paused to thump the stein with an emphatic gesture.

"By some means she obtained the magical gift of punishing her critics. A word of adverse comment and the unappreciative listener was turned into stone. Perhaps the angels did that. The golden voice was their gift. Perhaps they retained the right to chastise those who spoke ill of their handiwork.

THE LAND OF HAUNTED CASTLES

"At any rate, such was the case, and to this day you may see boulders at the foot of the old Heringerburg rock, said to be the transformed bodies of those who did not like Griselinde's singing. She was beautiful, but she was proud. Oh, very proud."

Bump, bump, bump sounded the great stein.

"Many men loved her!" Bump, bump, bump! "And why not? She was as beautiful as she was musical.

"But although they were as numerous as the liquid notes of Griselinde's song, she declared that they were as one so far as their matrimonial prospects were concerned. She ordered them to go and leave her in peace.

"Then one day came a young graf from Pettingen. He was a handsome youth, straight and strong, with hair as dark as a blackbird's wing. He wore gilded armor and carried a great sword that showed the marks of many battles,—truly, a hero of the sort to appeal to any young woman! He had only one defect: he had no ear for music.

"He loved to hear Griselinde sing, but that was because she was Griselinde and he was in love.

"Her father did not favor him greatly, for the wars with the Saracens had cost him nearly all of his patrimony and the Count of Heringerburg felt a father's natural solicitude over making a good match for his daughter. But even in those days love was superior to the match-making instincts of parents.

HERINGERBURG

"Griselinde succeeded in signifying to the youth from Pettingen that she reciprocated the love which he flashed to her from his dark eyes. At night she would stand in the balcony outside her chamber window and sing to him. Down in the valley he would sit in the shadows and listen, enraptured.

"One night he grew emboldened and decided to go to her in spite of the guards at the gates of the castle. He started to scale the precipice. It was a perilous climb in daylight, for the steep rocks came down in those days as straight as a wall. At night it was close to impossible. But the knight was in love and he lacked nothing in bravery.

"Though forced to feel in the darkness for footholds in the precipice, he crept up and up until the valley was a black nothing below him and the sky above an impenetrable void. He was almost at the top of the castle wall when the beautiful Griselinde came out as usual to sing to him. She did not know that he was only a few meters below her. He had failed to remember that she would appear almost within whispering distance. Her burst of song struck his unattuned ear without warning.

"He shook with sudden shock and then, excited by his climb and the closeness of the castle guards, he called out to her:

" 'Stop that caterwauling or you will be the death of me.'

THE LAND OF HAUNTED CASTLES

"She ceased to sing, but she was the death of him anyway. He felt his fingers stiffen and a sudden chill creep toward his heart. He slid from his precarious roost and plunged out into the black toward the valley. Griselinde hastened down the rocky pathway in front of the schloss, to his side. But she did not need to see the silent stone figure in the river-bed to know that her dream of love had flown forever.

"She went sadly back to her balcony and sang a long chant of farewell.

"Never had Heringerburg heard such a song. It filled the valley and echoed in the hills and the birds wept with the grief of it. When she had finished, men and women and little children sat weeping in their homes, moved beyond all explanation by that wonder-song.

"It was her last song, mein Herr. She died of a broken heart some years later. But until they laid her in a casket her golden voice was hushed.

"Sometimes she comes back, they say. She comes to stand in the ruins of the castle and sing to the black rock that is said to be the remains of the Graf of Pettingen. And when she sings it is a potent sign that some maiden in the village is to have an unhappy marriage."

He rocked the stein meditatively on its broad base and sighed as if in Griselinde and her knight he had known a pair of personal friends whose tragic fate af-

HERINGERBURG

fected him more than words—even the polysyllabic words of Luxemburg—could hope to describe.

There are other creepy stories told of the robber barons of Heringerburg. You can hear them in any hamlet in the vicinity as any toothless crone prepares a draught of *Malzkaffee* on her funny little stove. Most of them concern Konrad, quite the bloodiest old pirate of an encrimsoned house.

Konrad was a past master of pillage, who made his wars close to home and reaped great revenue thereby without having to support an expensive retinue. Everybody in the neighborhood hated him.

But the eternal law of compensation worked as well in the case of Konrad as it seems always to have worked in the shaping of human destinies. Konrad had a daughter who was as virtuous and lovable as he was hateful. She went about doing good in the very districts where his cruelty and rapacity had wrought untold evil.

Every one loved Adelinde, especially the Seigneur Klaus of Mersch, whom she favored above all the others. Everything seemed to indicate that the match would come to the usual happy ending, when Konrad became incensed at Klaus. The Graf of Heringerburg waited until one day when the Seigneur of Mersch came into his district to hunt. Then without warning he waylaid him, carried him to his donjon keep, and buried him in a deep pit.

THE LAND OF HAUNTED CASTLES

For several days Klaus remained there, subsisting on bread and water, while his retainers at Mersch thought that the earth had swallowed him, as indeed it had. One day, however, Adelinde stole down to the dungeons, released the prisoner, took him to a postern-gate, and set him free. So cleverly was the escape effected that Konrad the swashbuckler continued to drink ribald toasts each day to his "prisoner," not suspecting that the dark hole under the castle was empty.

Konrad in the meantime had sounded the call of his clan.

From the valleys of the Eisch, the Alzette, and the Mamer rode hundreds of men-at-arms, splendidly mounted and richly equipped. Tried warriors were these horsemen, hardened by long campaigning against the paynim. Every castle in the deep clefts that joined at Mersch disgorged a troop of them and presently Klaus rode toward the gorge of Kasselbach at the head of as splendid a force as ever set out to do battle in Luxemburg. The knights of Fels were there, and Pettingen, Schoenfels, Hollenfels, Mysembourg. Ansembourg, Beaufort, and Septfontaines,—the finest of the chivalry of the southern Ardennes.

Konrad from his lofty roost watched them defile into the cañon below, a thread of silver and gold where the sun was thrown back from shield and breastplate and lance, a picture wonderful in its beauty and terrible in its

HERINGERBURG

menace. But he gave little thought to the splendor of the sight and his own peril worried him not a bit.

He laughed at the pomposity of these warriors who presently would be sending forward a knight under a white flag to demand that he give up Klaus. His garrison was small and not remarkably well equipped. But so long as he held Klaus he held the whip-hand. At any time that he chose, he told himself, he could end the siege by threatening the death of the hostage he held in the person of the seigneur of Mersch.

He was still chuckling to himself when he went out to the ramparts to get a closer view of the approaching knights. He took only one look, then ran back into the stony corridors, shouting for Adelinde. He had recognized the man who rode at the head of the enemy column and that man was Klaus, whom he had believed to be shut up safely within the bowels of the mountain.

Adelinde paid the penalty for her love. The irate father dragged her to the oubliette where Klaus had been imprisoned, and hurled her into it. Then he went back to the walls to wield the pitch-ladle and encourage his terror-stricken archers.

The battle was of short duration. The Heringerburg garrison was insufficient to man the walls against a force of picked men such as that mustered in the three valleys. Nimble-footed swordsmen scaled the cliff on one side, where attack was least expected, while the main force attacked across the fosse at the main gate.

In the gray light of the dawn they rode to the onslaught, an irresistible cavalcade. The castle archers found themselves suddenly set upon from behind. The lead-ladles dropped from dead hands into the valley below. The drawbridge creaked down across the fosse and a score of torch-men clattered into Heringerburg to set a blaze that was shortly to be visible from one corner of the duchy to the other. Konrad, wounded but still defiant, surrendered as the first wreath of smoke from the lower chambers of his doomed stronghold was wafted up to the parapet where he stood amid his dead bowmen.

"Where is Adelinde?" demanded Klaus of Mersch.

"You should know," replied Konrad.

There was little time for parley between the two knights, for the fire was biting into the dry old rafters of the building. In a very few minutes they had patched up a truce whereby Konrad was given his life in exchange for information concerning the location of his daughter's prison. Klaus rescued Adelinde, allowing her father to ride unscathed through the ranks of the disappointed knights, and remained to complete the destruction of Heringerburg.

Adelinde and Klaus were married that night. Their life was happy and peaceful, as peace was measured in

HERINGERBURG

those days, and they thought no more of the disorderly Graf of Heringerburg until one night a pilgrim came to their gate begging food and a night's lodging. It was Konrad. He had come back from the Holy Wars, footsore and penniless, a sorry wreck of the overlord who once had spread terror through a dozen counties.

Klaus looked at him and was suddenly aware of a bond that few psychologists mention in their ponderous works and none explain,—the tie that exists between men who have engaged in a life-and-death struggle.

"Konrad," boomed Klaus, in surprise.

"Klaus," murmured Konrad, in penitence.

"Come in," invited Klaus. "This house is yours so long as you choose to stay here."

And thus it came about that the bloody Konrad spent the last days of his life telling fairy stories to the children of the village.

A battery of the German crown-prince's field artillery recently established a field kitchen over his grave.

CHAPTER XXVI
LA ROCHETTE

FOUR-AND-TWENTY BLACKBIRDS BAKED IN A PIE

All tenantless save to the crannying wind.
—BYRON.

CHAPTER XXVI

LA ROCHETTE

ONE of the strangest railroads in the world climbs the hills over the ancient trail of the chevaliers from Cruchten to La Rochette. Officially its title is the Chemin de Fer Vicinal Cruchten-Fels; too long a name for so short a railroad. During the American occupation it received a more descriptive if less elegant title: "The Bubble and Squeak."

Its tea-pot locomotive, leaking steam like a peanut-roaster, travels in a cloud of its own manufacture, a fog which on cold days is so dense that the engineer can scarcely see the crooked little rust-streaks ahead of him. The coaches are a bit larger than the cars of a Coney Island roller-coaster and seem older than Vianden. They protest rheumatically every meter of the climb, a plaint that on the curves becomes fearfully like the wail of a death-agony. Somehow they hold together, which might be taken as proof that the fairy Mélusine still watches over the destinies of Luxemburg and that all is right with the world.

The cars were last painted the year before the Roman invasion. But the paint apparently was war-time qual-

THE LAND OF HAUNTED CASTLES

ity, for not enough of it remains to permit a guess as to its original color.

In one respect, at least, The Bubble and Squeak resembles the great railroads of the duchy. Its conductor and engineer are sticklers for the etiquette that governs the purchase and presentation of tickets.

One must always purchase a ticket before entraining. Should he be a bit late in arriving at the terminal, all he has to do is to signal the train crew. They will delay their start any number of minutes until he attends to the fare-paying ceremonial in the station. And woe betide the unfortunate traveler who fails to avail himself of this politeness!

Once I neglected to buy my twenty-five centimes' worth of transportation in advance. The Bubble and Squeak was just whistling its farewell to Cruchten as I ran across the platform. So, instead of halting the departure, I swung aboard the rear platform of the second and last coach and seated myself, complacent in my belief that a cash fare would cover my delinquency.

But I was disillusioned. There came presently a gilt-laced functionary to demand my ticket. I explained that I had none, but that I would pay him the twenty-five centimes with whatever penalty was customary for payment on a mileage basis. And never, though I live to be as ancient as the Bubble and Squeak itself, shall I forget his look of disdain.

LA ROCHETTE

I experienced all the sensations of the felon at the bar of justice; the cowardice of the murderer who stabs from behind; the inexplicable moral collapse of one who spills the soup in the lap of his hostess.

He left me with a Prussian shrug too terrible to contemplate and marched up to the head of the train to tell the engineer the story of this atrocity. For it seems that I had done something more than neglect to buy a ticket. I had deliberately shattered a sacred custom. And beyond that there is no sin of which the human intellect can conceive.

Many times after that I rode the Bubble and Squeak between Fels (La Rochette) and Cruchten. But the general officer in the gold braid never forgave me. He would scrutinize my little paper billet, back and front, as if to assure himself that it was not counterfeit, and then hand it gravely back, showing by every means of unspoken insult that my touch had contaminated it. I might have ridden on the General's railroad every day from that time until now without paying a centime for my passage. And in time I should have become a legend. Mothers would have used my story as a tale with which to discipline their children. Repetition of the yarn through the neighborhood would have endowed me with Satanic powers and my fare-less journeying would have assumed a dire significance. I should have ranked with the headless horseman of Ichabod Crane's experience and

THE LAND OF HAUNTED CASTLES

taken on new romance as "The Mysterious Rider of the Bubble and Squeak." And perhaps some good soul would have bequeathed his entire fortune for the erection of a monument to my memory, in the Square of the Lindens at Fels.

Stranger things than that have happened in Luxemburg.

Only La Rochette could cause one to forget his experiences with the Bubble and Squeak, but La Rochette does that speedily. The town rises from the tiny station in a series of linden-walled terraces, square and strong, toward the encircling rocks upon which the walls of the castle retain their death grip. There is a gabled dike rising out of the trees to the right and a fortress tower to the left. One looks at them for a long time before realizing that they are separated by a cañon in which the village loses itself.

There is in the ruins a touch of the awesome grandeur of Esch-le-Trou and Bourscheid, a suggestion of the capital in the garden of lindens, and a bit of old Echternach in the customs of the people. The world goes by the gate of Fels, but does not pause to enter in. The Angelus rings. The men, women, and children of La Rochette halt where they happen to be and bow their heads in prayer. The simplicity of a Millet painting is in the atmosphere they breathe.

LA ROCHETTE

Sit down to luncheon with the Widow Knaff-Reckinger and she will tell you a story.

It appears that La Rochette was the spot where occurred the events since made famous in that stirring epic "Sing a Song of Sixpence." Mrs. Goose has given no credit to the knights of Fels in her thrilling recital, but legend has insured their glory. The history-making episode of the "Four and twenty blackbirds baked in a pie," occurred long before English nursery rhymes were collected between covers.

Ludwig von Fels is the hero of the piece. He lived in 1782, when Emperor Joseph II ruled the duchy of Luxemburg and the affairs of Austria in the Netherlands were verging upon collapse.

There had been considerable ill-feeling between the personal troops of Ludwig and the Austrians billeted in the duchy, but a spirit of compromise—fostered, perhaps, by the amiable Joseph—ended the controversy. Ludwig arranged to celebrate this armistice with a great feast. The Austrian officers were invited to attend and many splendid culinary specialties were brought to the castle as peace-offerings by the principals in the recent argument.

The feast proceeded with great good fellowship until, at its climax, half a dozen masked waiters came into the dining-hall, bearing upon their shoulders an immense pie. This offering, which Ludwig knew had never come

THE LAND OF HAUNTED CASTLES

from his own kitchens, was vigorously applauded. The host, with a pretty speech of appreciation, signaled that the pie should be placed before him and arose to serve it in person to his guests.

One slice of the big knife lifted the top crust. Whereupon many a guest leaped up from the table without apology. It was discovered that the interior of the pie was stuffed with birds that had been dead too long and not quite long enough.

Ludwig, pale and angry, immediately charged the insult to the colonel of the Austrian Protestant regiment from Kaunitz.

There followed, of course, the inevitable duel in the vaulted salle des chevaliers and Ludwig, who apparently was better at challenging than supporting combat, eventually rolled under his own table with a hole over his heart.

The authenticity of the blackbird incident is solemnly vouched for by any number of Fels's best authorities on local history. That some of the narrators declare the birds in the pie to have been pheasants and the scene of the duel Luxemburg city does not change it so far as Ludwig is concerned.

The remains of the castle are now the center of what one might call a national park. The grand-duke, father of the princess who now rules in Luxemburg city, bought the estate and went to considerable expense restoring

LA ROCHETTE

parts of its walls and making the place safe for sightseers. The rock which in the days of the castle's glory was considered inaccessible, now may be reached without difficulty by a wooden stairway that zigzags up through the clustering firs and pines.

The ruins, even after a bombardment by Boufflers and subsequent centuries of inattention, still present an overwhelming vista of staunch wall and unconquerable donjon.

At the top of the stairway is a barred gate with a bell-pull at the side. A single jerk brings the modern lord of the manor with considerably less speed than would have been shown by his predecessors in this domain at a similar signal had strangers thus shown themselves on the top of the lofty rock. But the guardian has one grace that makes him ideal for his position. He lets one in, closes the gate, and promptly disappears.

The gate has opened into a park, a green bower where sun-sequins dart through the thick clusters of trees. This was the courtyard of the castle, as the encircling ruins proclaim, an ideal place from which to view this great poem of rock and to meditate upon the fate of the men who placed it there.

The house of Fels was a long-lived family, exerting a powerful influence throughout the duchy from the crusades to the French Revolution. Boufflers the batterer looked upon the castle as a strategic point worthy of special attention and if thoroughness of destruction be what it is generally credited with being,—a sign of resistance,—then Fels must have mustered all its available strength in one last stand. Many a cannon-ball and bomb combined to produce this wreckage.

But even Boufflers could not tear it up from its stone-bound roots or crush its uprearing head. To-day its haughty skeleton outlines the vanished halls and the perpetual twilight of the pines fills in the gaps where the walls have fallen.

The beautiful carvings of the ancient chapel still cling to the walls in an inaccessible nook in the donjon tower. The delicacy of the façade has not been lessened by the fact that it is now a false front to nothingness. The tower at the corner remains to-day sturdy and solid, though winds course down out of the north and wandering roots pry into the mortar to cleave apart the age-old masonry. The town of La Rochette sleeps beneath this tottering cliff, serene in the knowledge that its crown of weathered rubble will stay in place, come wind, come storm.

One of the show places of the castle park is a well nearly two hundred feet deep. It was once famous for the purity of its water, but a number of things have happened to it since then. It has become the storehouse not only for the mysteries of the castle, but for the secrets of the entire country-side,—a gloomy bourne whence no dead man comes back to tell any tales.

Things began to collect in the well in the thirteenth century when the castle was besieged by the Templars and a young woman of the house, crazed with the fear of their rumored cruelty, jumped into the black pit. John of Bohemia visited the place on business, at the head of an army. Two knights of Fels refused to admit him and fought with him until starvation had reduced the garrison. Then they followed the example of their virtuous ancestress in a leap over the parapet. There are various legends of lovelorn maidens who in various centuries have gone to keep them company. Once the bones of a child were brought up by the old oaken bucket. The old well has fallen into disuse.

At the bottom of the bore, it is said on excellent authority, the treasures of Fels, to a total that would stagger the imagination of a Monte Cristo, lie hidden in a grotto. But they are guarded by a fearsome object,—a dragon, the last survivor of his interesting race, skilled in the strategy of age-long experience.

Should one go treasure-hunting one's fate is sealed. If the carbon-monoxid gas fails to act, then the dragon promptly blows out the visitors' candle and slays him in the dark.

What effect the windy trickery of the dragon might have upon an electric flash-lamp is not explained by the

THE LAND OF HAUNTED CASTLES

castle guardian. The very mention of electricity somehow seems to spoil the story.

There is probably not a man or a woman in Fels who has not seen the Grand Master of the Templars riding in the ruins with his knights on Maundy Thursday. No ghost or group of ghosts in all the Ardennes comes better recommended. One is a bit awed by the preponderance of evidence in favor of the Grand Master's spiritual existence until one hears of the circumstances that attend his annual parade: he may be seen only by those in the state of grace.

In this story is a quaint suggestion of Hans Christian Andersen's tale of the "King's Garments."

The king, you will remember, had ordered some clothes from a rogue of a tailor who informed him that the completed costume would be one that only the clean of heart could see. His Majesty was unable to see it himself, but dared not say it, for to have done so would have been to admit that something was amiss with his soul.

He announced to his capital that he would lead a great procession so that all might behold his miraculous garments. The entire town turned out to see him and all admired his invisible cloak until a little child piped up that His Gracious Majesty had on no clothes at all. The king then borrowed a coat and went back to the tailor's shop, where he beheaded the deceiving garment-maker with his own fair hand.

It is said that a two-year-old baby of La Rochette was with its mother near the base of the rock one Maundy Thursday when the mother beheld the train of knights. She directed the baby's attention to the sight, but the baby stoutly denied that anything was to be seen. The mother took the child home and spanked it for stubbornness, despite the fact that even in Fels two-year-old babies are seldom steeped in sin. The mother, it appears, had not the sense of the good king who accepted the verdict of an innocent above the plaudits of fawning thousands in the matter of the invisible cloak.

The crevasse between the castle proper and the watch-tower on the opposite cliff is known in local parlance as the Verlorenkost, "the lost dinner."

It acquired its name in this wise:

A wooden bridge once connected the two bluffs. A repair-man was setting some new stones in the masonry of the north pier, walking over from his home in the south part of the village in the morning and returning at night. Each noon his wife brought his dinner to the south end of the bridge and sat with him while he was eating it. One day she was waiting at the customary meeting-place and he had started across the bridge as usual, when the rotted wooden supports in the center of the trestle gave way. The good man plunged to his death and the shocked wife let go of her basket, which dropped over the cliff after him.

Townsfolk who had heard of the crash of the falling bridge came running across the rock and found the woman sitting stupefied. When they asked her what had happened she replied:

"The bridge is gone and the dinner is lost."

And so the name remains to-day, a monument to wifely affection.

In pleasant contrast is the love-story of Margaret of Fels and John of Beaufort, an idyl worthy of the space given it by Passmore in his book on the Ardennes.

The action of the story took place in the thirteenth century when Ludolph was overlord of Fels and Conan ruled at Beaufort. The lives of these two seigneurs were linked by kindred misfortunes. The young wife of Conan had closed her eyes forever when her son was three years old. Margaret of Fels, bride of less than a year, died in giving birth to a daughter.

The two knights became fast friends and their children grew up as brother and sister.

Then the chivalry of Christendom heard the call of Pope Honarius to a holy war and rode forth to do the will of God. The child Margaret was left in the care of Dame Godelinde, under the protection of the esquire Gottfried. The venerable Father Siegfroid, chaplain of Beaufort, undertook the education of the boy.

LAROCHETTE

Above the town on its high rocks sits the castle. Much of the village is built within the line of its dismantled outer circle of defenses

LA ROCHETTE

Throughout the years that followed, while the endless battling of the crusade was in progress about Jerusalem, John and Margaret were constant companions. Only when he was taken to the court of Count Henry, to be armed and knighted with impressive ceremony, did the son of Conan leave the daughter of Ludolph for a single day. For all his honors, John would rather have remained in the vicinity of Fels than be separated from his "little sister." But he respected the orders that his father had left with his preceptor and rode to Luxemburg with as much preparation and regret as if he, too, were departing for a protracted campaign in a far country. But the separation had its use. Margaret and John had been brother and sister so long as they saw each other every day. A week apart made them aware of the promptings of love.

They plighted their troth after John's return from the capital and lived in a continuous dream of happiness until one day clouds of dust in the valleys signaled the return of the crusaders. This home-coming, which should have brought happiness to a climax, proved to be a calamity. Conan and Ludolph had quarreled. The former friends were bitter enemies and a ban went forth from both houses against the union of the lovers.

So it went on for more than a year while the lord of Fels and the lord of Beaufort, scarred though they were with the sacrifices of a holy war, nursed their growing hatred, obdurate, deaf to the warnings of their chaplains, unrepentant, and unshriven.

Shortly before Easter-time in the second year of the quarrel, the Dame Godelinde "began to smell the pine" as premonition of death is described in Luxemburg. She called Ludolph to her bedside and whispered to him a farewell and a warning, then folded her hands across her breast and died. Ludolph, in tears, sought out a priest and acknowledged his fault with true humility. Then he and Margaret set out for Beaufort.

Midway between the two castles they met the lord of Beaufort and his son, for Conan, it appears, had been stricken with remorse precisely at the hour of Godelinde's death. The two warriors embraced and Margaret fled into the arms of John. The Easter bells were sounding in the valley.

Margaret, whispering prayers of thanksgiving, began to weep. And where her tears fell upon the rock a crystal spring arose,—a fountain that trickles down the mountain-side to this day and keeps alive the memory of the lady of La Rochette in its name, "Tears of the Lady Margaret."

CHAPTER XXVII

CHRISTNACH AND MYSEMBOURG

Swanhilde and the Love of Rodoric

> I have builded a monument more lasting than bronze.
> —Horace.

CHAPTER XXVII

CHRISTNACH AND MYSEMBOURG

EAST of La Rochette—between it and the Müllerthal in the heart of Little Switzerland—is Crucenacum or Christnach, with a story worth repetition.

Crucenacum must have been a camp of some importance in the day of the Roman occupation. Save for the Teutonic signs on its houses it might well be a suburb of Rome. Few houses in the Eternal City itself have foundations more ancient.

The present town is said to date from 752. Its name appears in a document of that date, although there is no telling how long it may have been in existence prior to that. The struggle of the Cross with pagan superstition developed one of its minor crises in the village during the sixth century—an incident typical of the great drama that was being enacted at that time throughout the Rhineland, the Moselle district, and the Ardennes, where Christian gleaners were following the Roman reaper.

Rodoricus, a Gallic chief and devotee of Diana, lived at the castle Zorodertsbourg, the first stronghold on the rock of Fels. At Crucenacum lived Swanhilde, the fairest woman in all that wild region. She and her sister Vallida had listened to the preaching of the hermit Wulflaicus and had become Christians. The young women had devoted themselves to acts of piety, but this did not stay the arm of the powerful Rodoricus.

He discovered the charm of Swanhilde and without so much as the formality of a proposal of marriage picked her up and carried her to a dungeon in his castle.

Something in Swanhilde's holy wrath deterred him from further violence. He decided to let the wonder-woman remain underground until a diet of lentils and water had brought her to her senses.

In the meantime Swanhilde occupied herself in prayer, vowing to destroy Diana's sacred forest should she obtain her release from captivity.

Rodoricus grew tired of waiting upon the whim of Swanhilde. Something in her persistent refusal of him, a chief toward whom all the women in three counties had cast luring glances in vain, aroused a resentment approximating hatred. One day he sent an axman down to the dungeon to behead her.

But the execution was not carried out as scheduled. The axman was a Christian who had been forced to conceal his beliefs from his pagan chief. When he came to Swanhilde's prison he promptly released her, led her

CHRISTNACH AND MYSEMBOURG

through a secret passage to the mountain-top, and set her free.

Rodoricus, searching for her body, discovered the trick. He set out after her with all his men-at-arms.

During their hunt through the wild ravines of Little Switzerland they captured a priest. Rodoricus, seeking information concerning the whereabouts of the vanished virgin, quizzed the monk at great length and received in reply a few soft-spoken words on the doctrine of the cross. The warrior chief, impressed, halted the hunt and sat down to listen to further instruction in this strange new faith. Rodoricus the pagan arose from that impromptu conference Rodoric the saint.

He and the beautiful Swanhilde were married shortly after that. She took the name Christina and built a church in Crucenacum still known as "Christina's Chapel."

There is a good road leading across the plateau westward from Fels.

A three-mile walk over an island in the air brings one to Mysembourg, a château which in the olden days was the center of a wide domain and the seat of a powerful house.

A great castle stood there in the twelfth century—had been standing for centuries prior to that, perhaps—and remained for two hundred years as a menace to the peace

THE LAND OF HAUNTED CASTLES

of the country-side. It was destroyed by fire in the sixteenth century in a "private war" and rebuilt to be a target for Boufflers in 1684.

Baron Christophe d'Arnoult put up a modern palace in the ashes of the old, prior to the French Revolution. Then the sansculottes seized it and sold it to Monsieur Antoine, Barone de Casal de Fischbach, who paid a price of nearly a million francs for it. Inasmuch as the franc had dropped at that period to the modest retirement now claimed by the German mark, the consideration was n't so large as it might seem.

At present the estate is owned by the d'Arenberg family. Charles, who purchased it, married the widow of Prince Michael Obrenovitch of Serbia, who was killed by an assassin in 1868.

The castle looks more like a French château than a survival of Luxemburg's medievalism. It stands at the edge of a wooded park close by a little mirror of a lake.

The feudal town that surrounded the old castle or castles has completely disappeared. The villagers, oppressed by the alien lords who bought the place a number of decades ago, emigrated en masse to America. The lord of the manor, far from mourning their defection, tore down the buildings of the village and extended his formal gardens over the acreage they had occupied.

The wandering road leads back through a private avenue between thick forests to the highway at Angels-

CHRISTNACH AND MYSEMBOURG

berg,—a village where live the kindliest, happiest people in all Luxemburg. There should be a legend about Angelsberg. But the town is just a homely little farming hamlet on the edge of a precipice. It has no ruins if one excepts a rusting traction-engine in the burgomaster's front yard and an ancient who tolls the bell at the parish church. It has no story save the unromantic tale of daily decency which is too real ever to be the subject of folk-lore.

Angelsberg—some linguist can guess whence comes its name—is the village of Grandpré before the coming of the English and the dispersing of the Acadians. The hobnailed boots of the invader have not crushed out its hospitality and an excellent opportunity for profiteering has not destroyed its inbred generosity.

Over the hill the Rollingerbach dives down through a widening V into a tree-lined gorge. The road follows uncertainly through curves blasted out of the rock at the side of it. Steadily down it goes, with not a break in the gradient until it straightens out to cross a railroad. Beyond rises the Byzantine tower of Mersch.

CHAPTER XXVIII
PASTELS

The People of the Toy Kingdom

The poetry of earth is never dead.
—Keats.

CHAPTER XXVIII

PASTELS

THE toy kingdoms are vanishing. The Ruritanias, Transylvanias, Hentzaus, and Graustarks of yesteryear have gone to make larger maps for Germany, France, and Italy. New republics have sprung from the ashes of petty courts, but progress, the great leavener, has made one of them look much like all the others. Concrete and steel are replacing the ancient impractical but characteristic national architectures with the pillar-like designs of modern buildings. Easy transportation is leaving the imprint of Parisian style upon the remotest hamlets,—a dozen or more years late in some instances but still sufficiently recent to obliterate the eye-catching varieties of color and buttons and queer cuts that once figured in the community's official costume.

But apparently the Ardennes will always be the Ardennes. All of the processes of assimilation and extermination of a thousand years have failed to rob it of an iota of its individuality. Its colors have been blended, perhaps, in a rich, marvelous tapestry, but they are still its own colors. Its customs have persisted through ages

THE LAND OF HAUNTED CASTLES

beset by fire, famine, pestilence, and war. The identity that has persevered against the opposed envies of the Germans and the French is evidenced from one end of the duchy to the other in its towns, farms, mills, stores, beliefs, and mode of thought. The cock-sure nationality of Luxemburg is ingrained in every civilian and stamped in brilliant patterns on every gendarme in the land.

"We would remain just as we are," declares the Luxemburg national hymn, with an air of defiance. And every official Luxemburger is a walking proof that the people believe in the spirit of their song.

All of the elements of romance are found in the country, from the comely princess at the helm of state, to the *Krummerweg*,—the crooked way where men with crooked minds hatch dark plots against the state.

The opera-bouffe setting which we, since childhood, have been accustomed to associate with beautiful princesses, intriguing esquires, and brilliant young commoners who always rescue the toy palace from the toy troops of a neighboring principality at midnight on Shrove Tuesday, is here at its brightest. There is an indescribable air of antiquity even about the more modern things in Luxemburg, not to mention the disintegrating walls that Siegfroid and his fairy wife built upon the foundations left by Rome. There is a suggestion of a gateway to the past in the palace arches modeled at

PASTELS

a time when the glory of Spain was emblazoned in characters of gold across the face of the world.

This is a country of tints.

Its distances as we behold them in winter dress are hazy greens and grays and whites, blended and vague. Its foregrounds are colorful but all pastels,—no bold strokes with elemental tones on a broad brush. The farm-houses are pinks and creams and baby-blues with window trimmings of light green and shutters of violet. Here and there this generation's application of tint has fallen off, disclosing in a peculiar sketchy fashion the decorations of other years.

The burgomaster's son passes up the street. A plaid cap is set jauntily on the side of his blond head. A green scarf is wrapped carelessly about his neck, the end flung over the shoulder of his gold-colored corduroy jacket.

By his side lumber two Belgian horses, huge beasts hitched in tandem to a creaking cart,—overgrown Shetlands with long manes and sad eyes, flecked and dappled like toys from the Schwarzwald.

A Minorca rooster dodges between the horses' feet, voices a raucous protest, and brings up pompously in the safety of a dooryard. A postman with a mantle of purple and a cape piped in red has come into the scene. His leather bag is the color of cordovan with wax and wear. He is quarreling with a wolf-dog. Evidently the

THE LAND OF HAUNTED CASTLES

argument is of long standing, for he shows no hesitation in driving a clumsy boot into the gaunt gray creature's ribs. The dog snarls and disappears through a stone gateway. The ornate postman adjusts his elegant accoutrements and goes his way.

In the distance a whistle shrieks,—a tiny sound like the escaping plaint of a toy balloon. Over across the Alzette, under the dim buttresses of the pine-covered hills, wind a toy locomotive and a procession of toy coaches. One cannot hear the noise of the flat wheels nor of the steam that leaks from the pistons. But one can see the train as plainly as a pictured train in the cinema—ten coaches, short, fat little things, drawn by a pompous little engine—all silhouetted against a white plume of steam.

There is this to be said of Truth crushed to earth and rising again in Luxemburg: The highly revered legends are ninety per cent. imagination and preposterous, but they somehow leave the impression that their foundation rests upon fact. Whereas many a simple recital of wide-spread custom may be entirely true and yet sound like legend.

Such is the case of the Pig Piper. I had lived in the vicinity of Mersch three months before I would believe that he existed. I might accept without comment the story of the Flying Horseman of Marienthal or the

PASTELS

Dicers of Vianden but the Piper was a creature too impossible to be countenanced even by a vivid imagination.

And he seems impossible still,—for all that I know now of the valuable services which he performs in many communities and of the long and honorable line of pig-pipers who were his ancestors.

A horn sounded. The hills, green with winter wheat and evergreen shrubs, threw back the echo.

Across the Alzette the church-bell was chiming. A gendarme in gorgeous uniform lolled over the stone rail of the bridge, watching little Gretchen, the mercer's daughter, trying to sail a wooden shoe in the sluggish current. An ox-cart rumbled by along the main road to the capital. A still, peaceful scene, vivid, delightful.

The horn sounded again. There was a perceptible stir in the village street,—curtains drawn back, doors opened, female voices suddenly filling the air from everywhere and nowhere.

The echoing blast was not beautiful. It was a note long-drawn and dolorous, of a tone which in an American street would have brought much business to a fish-merchant. But obviously no mere fish-peddler could have produced such an upheaval in the staid life of Rollingen.

At the third note of the horn the player appeared. The stage-setting had not been wasted. He was truly a part of the picture.

THE LAND OF HAUNTED CASTLES

He was tall, thin, and dark, clad in wooden-soled, black leather boots, gray wrapped leggings, dark-blue breeches, a greenish coat that fitted up tight under his chin, and a fuzzy fedora hat with a bright red feather in it. A pied piper indeed, from rollicking, devil-may-care stride to the polished instrument under his arm.

It would have been no surprise had the old houses of Rollingen suddenly disgorged a regiment of rats and then a battalion or two of children to dance along in the wake of this strange being.

A door opened and I started involuntarily, wondering what would come into the street in answer to his trumpeted summons. And then I stared, scarcely believing my eyes. Never did a Pied Piper tread the streets of Hamelin Town with a stranger concourse at his heels than that which followed the youth with the red feather into the crooked lanes of Rollingen.

Two fat pigs, pinky white and far too clean for normal porkers, strolled into the street and grunted along in his wake. Then another and another stepped from roadside sties to join the march. Behind them trotted a bristly dog which prevented straggling, by nipping a curly tail every time the column threatened to lengthen out.

The piper raised the horn and sounded another ear-splitting blast. A barn-door at the head of the street was pushed back and an unseen housewife pushed a

PASTELS

fifth pig into view. The dog chased it into line with the others.

So the procession continued, slowly, sedately, down the street, another pig joining the ranks at every stop. A dozen or more were waddling at the piper's heels when he reached the opposite side of the village. There he turned about and led the strange parade back, returning the porkers to their proper owners.

A parting blast of the doleful horn and he was gone, swinging down the road toward Beringen with the fuzzy dog trailing after him. Street-cleaning and pig-exercising had been finished in Rollingen for another day.

A bell rings down in the valley. There is an answering echo from a spire in the gray distance on the hills. Then chimes from the depths of nowhere at all and a rolling clangor that swells and diminishes without beginning and without end. For the villages are close together, perched on sandstone cliffs or buried in narrow cañons, hidden in pine forests or teased by the four winds on tiny plateaus. On Sunday morning when the bells begin to ring, one must know the tone of his own to pick it from the iron chorus of the clustered towns.

Our village is always deserted until the warning call is sounded half an hour before the time set for mass. Then, before the last echoes of the final bell in the valley below have ceased to sound, little Gretchen sticks an unusually clean and surprisingly red face through the café door and surveys the empty street. It is always Gretchen. She has an eager disposition and an investigative turn of mind.

Rain or snow or wind fails to keep her indoors once this preliminary survey is completed. She steps into the street, a doll-like creature of fluffy blonde curls, striped calico frock, with lacy under things always too long and always getting into her way, bare knees, knitted stockings, and wooden-soled shoes. Somehow the cold does not seem to affect her in spite of her lack of heavy wraps. She has the constitution of an arctic explorer.

She stands with her thumb in her mouth, expectant of company and ready for adventure. Once she missed mass altogether because she found a strange and interesting soldier clipping a delightful mule. She might have missed her dinner, too, had not the soldier returned her to the arms of her anxious parents at noon. But usually she does not stir from her father's dooryard until the church-goers begin to pass by. Then she attaches herself to the first party that appears, and goes to church. Her parents may come later if they choose; obviously a young lady of three can't be bothered with the care of them.

Presently the town turns out,—a surprising town to one who has seen it only in workaday garb. It throngs to church with a quickened step, somber in the dark hues of Sunday clothes, plainly self-conscious in its unaccustomed finery.

It is a surprisingly well-dressed village. Here and there one catches a glimpse of a Parisian hat; four years old at least, it must be, since the war did not admit of more recent importations, but still as chic and jaunty amid the lesser creations as it was when it left the Rue de la Paix. And there are furs innumerable and beyond price,—mink and civet and martin and mole and blue wolf and sable,—an array passed down, no doubt, to the daughters of this toy village from the trousseaus of great-grandmothers long since dead.

The men are inevitably drab creatures, slightly bent with the routine of the fields, painfully ill at ease in their highly polished footwear, spotless linen, and seldom-worn accoutrements. Some of them, many of them, wear stiff collars of linen or German celluloid and pay the penalty of torture for their vain display. A few fly in the face of convention by appearing in the week-day costume of knickers and spiral puttees. But not many. Sunday is a day apart and its demands must be rigidly respected. This village which goes to church is a different one entirely from that which goes into the fields on week-days.

There is never an impulse to look twice at Frau Raths in sabots and soiled skirts, a shapeless figure scrubbing the blue-tiled hallway of her home on Saturday evening.

But Widow Raths neatly corseted, shod in patent-leather pumps, well gowned, and half concealed in a cloud of black veil, is a living mystery when she steps up the center aisle on Sunday morning.

Peter Hartman, who once worked in London, is a farmer lad for six days and an obvious "toff" on the seventh.

Hans the blacksmith is a picturesque figure in the uniform of his trade and a sad, uneasy, misfit sort of being in the mournful raiment of the day of rest.

One would have difficulty in recognizing, in the well-washed angel who follows her mother with an uncertain step over the cobbles from the pink house at the end of the street, the dirty little wretch whose companions yesterday were the soiled pigs in her father's barnyard.

It is a serious sort of holiday. Smiles seem to be meted out according to a set measure. The quaint carelessness of habit that has made the town a living picture is shrouded in a stiff covering of studied artificiality.

By noon our village will be alive again. There will be laughter in the houses and neighborly confabs in the streets. For most of the Sunday finery will have been laid away in the chests where such gladsome raiment is kept. Only a heavy gold-plated watch-charm or a button of honor for signal service rendered the fire-department will remain with the emancipated male to remind him that it is still Sunday.

PASTELS

The peasant, whatever his crudities, is a natural sort of soul. Clothes, even among his women-folk, are for modest concealment rather than attractive display. The village in Sunday dress knows that it is on parade and falls ready victim to its own self-consciousness.

CHAPTER XXIX
THE FIREMEN

Guardians of Society

And so sepulchred in such pomp dost lie,
That kings for such a tomb would wish to die
—Milton

CHAPTER XXIX

THE FIREMEN

ONCE there was a fire in a Luxemburg village, —a real fire in which the ancient rafters of weathered oak proved to the assembled throng that despite their age and appearance they were really wood and not the black basalt that they so closely resembled in color and texture. It was a terrible thing. There had been other fires, of course. There was that fire in 1812 which wiped out an entire village in the valley of the Alzette and numerous others before it. It is true that the fire of which we speak was not so momentous of those of the great Louis which Boufflers, his torchman, lighted from one horizon to the other. But it was a disastrous fire, none the less, Monsieur. A family named Birchen was made homeless. A fine dwelling-place valued at a thousand marks was destroyed,—all except the walls and part of an upper floor. It was truly a grand sight.

The fire-department turned out in full uniform and fought the flames gallantly. They came running up with their pump amid rousing cheers and dropped a hose into a well. But the hose was not long enough. So they could get no water. Only that it began to rain they might have had difficulty in extinguishing the fire. But eventually the flames died out and the fire-department received a diploma from the Government for efficient service. It is still to be seen in their meeting-rooms at the *Mairie*.

Almost in these words Herr Muller described to me the valor of an organization which, strangely enough, has not been properly celebrated in song and story. I decided that here was a matter worthy of closer attention.

In every Luxemburg community the fire-department is the chief social organization. The trend to uniformed grandeur, so evident in the gendarmerie of the grand duchy, finds its civil expression in a *Bund* exclusive in its membership and active as a secret society.

Where under a different plan of organization a country might find personal aggrandizement in a militia company, Luxemburg must content itself with the peaceful drills of the fire-fighters. And because they are essentially a peace-time organization, their uniforms are no more military than those of the Prussian guard on dress parade.

Gold braid, that shames the less brilliant brass gilt and nickel of the gendarmes, shines on their red or mauve or buff breast-shields. Patent-leather boots, dark trousers with wide red stripes, brilliant belts, and bur-

THE FIREMEN

nished buttons make the fire-fighters the most resplendent group of burghers within the boundaries of the duchy. But the crowning glory of the picture is the helmet that completes the uniform.

This head-piece differs in various localities, but in its main essentials it is the same throughout the entire federation of fire-departments. It is a casque of nickeled brass, plumed or spiked, depending upon whether the sympathies of the community in which it is worn are Prussian or French.

The models range in period and method of construction from the era of Julius Cæsar to the bright hour of William the Damned.

The glories of the helmet are displayed only upon very important occasions. Other parts of the uniform may be worn at affairs of no great importance, such as band concerts, etc. But the full dress from plume to boots is the mark of an event.

The firemen are social tyrants of a high order. No Indian caste nor ancient European aristocracy is more conscious of superiority nor more proud of its honorable connections.

The fire-department in the smaller towns is at once the police force, chamber of commerce, theatrical society, musical club, lodge, and social court of the community. It is the gage of public culture, a board of local improvements, and a city-beautiful commission. Indirectly it has a bearing upon the matrimonial prospects of many a fair damosel and her swain. For its fire-proof nose is in everybody's business and, though it grieves us to say it, it has been known to spread scandal. It brands the pariah and keeps him efficiently ostracized from decent society.

Herr Muller was a member of the Keispelt fire-department. On state occasions he would bring from a musty bureau drawer his grand collection of badges and honors conferred upon him as a pipeman or pumpman or trombone-player in that select group.

No Grand Army man recounting the prowess of his regiment could review with greater enthusiasm the doughty deeds responsible for each honor.

"This," he said, displaying a purple ribbon the gilt lettering on which had been corroded to a black rust, "was given the Keispelt fire-department for their gallant appearance at the Doomsday Fair in the capital. I was with them on that day, younger than now and quite able to wear a uniform, sir. The young women threw roses to us as we marched to the Grand Rue.

"Our helmets were gilded and our plumes were crimson. It was a noble sight, sir, a noble sight.

"We walked of course, from here to the Stadt Luxemburg, through Kopstal and Rollingergrund. I should not wish to take the walk now. But what are fifteen kilomet' to youth! We were a bit dusty when we arrived

THE FIREMEN

but gay—oh, so gay! And the grand-duke clapped his hands as we marched by the palace. Never shall I forget it."

Herr Muller had many such badges and many such reminiscences. The only peculiarity in his endless recital was that his fire-department seemed never to have meddled with a fire. It was created for higher things.

Do you remember the ancient vaudeville joke of Sweeney, the American fireman who died and became famous because his mourning comrades sent to his widow a floral piece with the inscription: "Gone to his last fire"?

I was forcibly reminded of this mortuary jest when Keispelt assembled to pay its last respects to Bernard Weiss, a member of the fire-department and an elector of the commune, who had acquired typhoid and died.

An undertaker brought a coffin from Mersch and laid out the late Barney on two chairs in the bare little front room of his home. Because of the throng that came to do honor to his memory, the coffin was pushed over well against a side wall and the tall tapers threatened momentary damage to an atrocious lithograph apprising the world in mouth-filling German polysyllables that Knorr soup was the world's greatest life-lengthener. It had not occurred to the mourners to remove this anomaly for the funeral.

A few roses and field flowers had been brought to deck

the casket, but the work of funereal decoration that attracted the attention of the neighbors was a marvelous *couronne mortuaire*—a beaded wreath, stiff, grim and ugly—that lay at the widest spot atop the hexagonal coffin lid. The couronne mortuaire, it seems to me, is typical of the stoicism with which the nation unconsciously regards death. The beaded wreath has no charm of its own. It is death's own label and trade-mark.

Pagan as may be the custom of flowers at a funeral, flowers serve at least the Christian purpose of reminding survivors of the naturalness of death. The flowers seem to establish a link between the life of the growing fields from which they come and the death within the chamber where the candles flicker and women converse in awed whispers. A couronne mortuaire comes as a shock. It is like nothing in nature, neither in the air above nor the earth beneath nor in the waters under the earth. It is a tabloid of selfish mourning, a concrete image of depression.

The widow sat in a corner near the three-decked stove, weeping as widows have always wept, deeply sensible of the loss that the man's own sons did not seem to feel.

There was chill in the house, the chill of Spring, heavy with the moisture of melting snows and sickly sweet with the perfume of early cherry blossoms. The cherry perfume seemed to turn back from the doorway of the house, unable to overcome the scents that are always part of

THE FIREMEN

an old house,—the pungence of stale wood-smoke; the faint, acrid taint of moist plaster.

A crone sat near the widow, murmuring over and over again: "It is too sad—that he should go. He was so good. Only last week—he was well. To-day he is dead. It is too sad!" There was little variation in her facial expression as she intoned her chant. A little girl, presumably the granddaughter of the departed fireman, sat stiffly on the edge of a rush-bottomed prie-dieu across the room, sobbing bitterly. But there was no other sign of heartfelt grief. The neighbors were sober, stiffly so, as if conscious that a long face was part of the essentially religious ceremony incident to death.

Even the sons and daughters of the old man who lay in the yellow casket seemed to have little concern with his passing. Their philosophy was written in their casual greeting to friends, their solicitude for the pot-au-feu stewing in the kitchen, and their wholly unsentimental comments upon the prospects of their house. They recalled the excellent funeral that Cousin Marie of Arlon had had the year before. They spoke feelingly concerning the profiteering tendencies of undertakers. They discussed the uses to which the dead man's fields north of the town could best be put. And all of this was with no apparent disrespect for the dead.

Death was an incident, like mass on Sunday. It was to be expected. It could not be forestalled, and now it had come. A good man was gone and a hard worker had been freed from toil. Why worry about it?

How much of this attitude was due to their faith and the consoling thought of life after death and how much to the hereditary familiarity with the Destroyer in all his varied forms, it would be impossible to say.

The Luxembourgeois display little of the avarice that plays a large part in peasant funerals in many districts in France,—the avarice that places prospect of inheritance above any sense of loss. The people are not lacking in filial devotion for all that they take their funerals philosophically.

Presently came the priests of the village attended by black-robed acolytes. The procession passed sedately and in stately dignity from the church upon the gently sloping hill, headed by a standard-bearer with the black-and-silver banners of church societies. Two censer-bearers preceded the celebrant and deacons, contributing a bit of fragrant mist to the morning haze.

It is a beautiful custom, this welcoming of the dead by the church, a bit more consoling than our ceremonial of carrying the corpse suppliant to the altar as to a seat of judgment. In Luxemburg it pleases the mourners to believe that a child of God has gone home. Elsewhere in Europe a funeral is a sinner's march to his last tribunal.

The priests crowd into the front room. The casket is

THE FIREMEN

closed. The rosary is recited. The firemen join the cortège.

No one seems to take it amiss that the firemen should contribute a bit of pageantry to the procession. The departed burgher was a fireman himself. What more natural than that his companions in this the greatest social order in all the duchy should lend an aristocratic atmosphere to the obsequies?

Outside the door, Herr Glaetzner is tuning up a battered trombone. Its sputtering bass notes blend weirdly with the moaning responses to the prayers of the priests. The rest of the orchestral choir has pushed with some show of importance into the little front room, crumpled brass horns and all. The firemen, proud and dignified, doff their tin helmets and stand in defiance of death itself against the wall.

Prayers are completed and the procession starts. Once more the banners are to the forefront, then the priests, the firemen, the casket, the mourners. Six stalwart burghers—members, of course, of the fire-fighters' guild—carry the coffin to the church. The whole town has mobilized for the funeral. For deaths are a community affair, a matter of concern to the entire electorate.

Save for the firemen there is little of the picturesque in the long procession. The mourners—relatives, friends, or merely neighbors of the decedent—are in black because black is the usual costume in the district.

THE LAND OF HAUNTED CASTLES

The vestments of the priests are black and white because that is prescribed in the ritual of the Catholic Church. The fire-department, hampered by no such rules, is a long streak of red-and-gold brilliance.

The band plays a dolorous air, faintly reminiscent of the German *Lieder* and astonishingly suggestive of an Hawaiian plaint. But the Hawaiian element is speedily suppressed in the blasting of the bass and an amazing indisposition on the part of the treble instruments to play any given note in unison. But there is something impressive in the solemnity of the thing. The procession will furnish a topic of conversation in the town for weeks, until the fire-department is turned out for another funeral or for a kermess.

The corpse is carried into the church. An admiral, in a red robe with a plumed hat and carrying a long brazen staff, meets the cortège with due solemnity and escorts the pall-bearers to the bier in front of the altar.

There, when the casket has been placed between the tall candles, the couronne mortuaire and the helmet and baton of the departed are laid at the head and the requiem proceeds amid Gregorian dirges the more awesome because rendered without the accompaniment of organ or other instrument.

During the mass the friends of Herr Weiss pass up behind the altar and back to their pews again, depositing, during their passage, numerous French sous, German

THE FIREMEN

pewter pfennigs, or the washer-like minor currency of the duchy. These offerings are to insure the saying of masses for the repose of the fireman's soul.

After the services the musicians, standard-bearers, and ornate fire-department file out of the church in the order of their entrance and stand about the grave in the nearby cemetery while the cracked bell in the spire tolls its last message of sympathy.

The casket is lowered. The firemen doff their helmets and bow their heads. Each in turn marches past the grave and throws in clods of earth.

Formerly it was the custom to bury with the deceased fireman his brass hat and other ceremonial accoutrements,—a survival, perhaps, of ancient Frankish rites. But a variety of causes prompted an end to this waste of ornament. Now the helmet goes back to a rack in the fire-department's hall for issuance to the next new member.

The mist has lifted from the hills as the cortège winds out of the cemetery. There is a more tangible scent of cherry blossoms in the heavy, soothing air. The tang of the cold is gone from the sunlit spaces.

Similarly the mourners have thrown off the burden of their grief as they pass through the old stone gates of the churchyard. Death has come; it will come again. And in the meantime there is Life!

At the late dwelling-place of Herr Weiss there is a

THE LAND OF HAUNTED CASTLES

dinner spread for the intimates of the family—a sedate, dignified feast at which the departed member of the household is represented by a vacant chair. As an invisible guest he is now attending his own strange obsequies just as he sat at the funeral table of his father before him. He would not begrudge those whom he has left their surcease from mourning.

CHAPTER XXX
MARRIAGE

The Bride and Her Garter

Honi soit qui mal y pense.

CHAPTER XXX

MARRIAGE

FRAU MULLER met me, as I came downstairs into the kitchen one day, and announced impressively:

"Katrina Spiess is about to marry herself."

"So?" I inquired with the interest that this important statement seemed to merit. "When does the event occur?"

"Oh, that is not known yet," declared Frau Muller. "They have just signed the contract." She babbled on in the usual gossip of weddings the world over,—the desirability of the favored youth, his possible inheritance in lands and cattle, the scandalous habits of his great-grandfather, the amount of the bride's dowry, her youth, and bits of her family history. Only the smoke rising from the *Eisenkuchen* interrupted the discussion.

She continued as she laid the steaming waffles on the plate before me.

"She is a very pretty girl," declared the good dame.

I remembered Katrina as a petite blonde, too young to have lost the blooming freshness that Europe's peasant women soon sacrifice to the necessities of hard labor.

"Yes," I agreed, "she is very pretty. But young, is she not?"

"Sixteen," returned the Frau. "Young enough and old enough. She should wait a while, however. She should learn more of hard work; for that, after all, is what makes married happiness. A pretty face soon goes. It is only the strong back that keeps a family prosperous and a husband contented. Ah, when I was married, I was as slender as a willow! And the young men of the neighborhood crowded our house until my mother ordered them all out. I do not say it boastingly, mein Herr. It is the truth. In Mersch and Gosseldange and Lintgen and Kehlen and Steinfort and Kopstal and Kapellen, even in the capital itself, I had many admirers."

The madame breathed a bulky sigh.

"A girl likes to know that she is popular, even though it excites jealousy. We women are very vain. I wonder if women are like that in America."

Apparently she concluded that they were, for she went on without waiting for a reply.

"But the time came when I must go to marry myself, so I chose John Muller. And I have been happy. It was a good choice. John had this house with six rooms. He owned also the farm to the west of here, and two good horses and a cow. I should have liked to marry Michael Molitor, who became a gendarme and looked very beautiful in his splendid uniform. But I was a practical girl, sir. I foresaw that if I married I should have children, and I wished to be sure that they would be fed and clothed."

"You loved John?" I inquired, a bit puzzled.

"Of course. He was a fine man and good to me. Why shouldn't I love him? But, then, had I married Michael I suppose I should have loved him, too.

"I am no longer as slender as the willow and I know that I am not beautiful. But John respects me. He knows that there is no woman in all of Luxemburg who can work more steadily. My house is clean. I can cook without extravagance. I can feed the stock and care for them, and milk the cow and churn butter, and I can do a man's work in the fields.

"I do not say this boastingly, mein Herr. You have lived here long enough to know that it is the truth. I mention it only because Katrina will have to do the same things. And she is now but a child with a pretty face."

I wondered if the little blonde Katrina would ever be able to tramp all day behind a plodding Belgian horse, plowing a stubborn field. And I decided that she would not. If physical strength were considered the prime requisite in a wife, I feared for Katrina's future.

But by that time I had learned that in Luxemburg female farm labor is not so general as it is in other parts of Europe. The congestion of population and the small size of the farms have brought about a balance between labor and workers. The woman is still a drudge who starts her chores in the barnyard at daylight and finishes them in the kitchen late at night. But her lot has been considerably improved. She is not a work-animal, as in parts of France, or a slave as in parts of Germany.

Any one who doubted woman's position in the household had only to look at the case of Frau Muller herself. John might be head of the house. The Government recognized him as such, but when she made a suggestion he complied with it. When she spoke he jumped. It was obvious that any labor she might do in the fields would be a task of her own choosing.

Katrina's wedding, despite the advice of crones who counseled a delay of a year or more, was celebrated a month afterward. I attended with the Mullers and nearly all the rest of the village.

The bride and her attendants might be heard running about the upper floor of the house. Their tense whispers and hysterical laughter sifted through the unplastered ceiling. Downstairs the bridegroom, looking like a picture of death and devastation, sat near the door, as languidly as a pair of tight black trousers would permit. On his knees dangled the duchy's badge of holy matrimony, a borrowed silk hat that bore sundry and divers dents from previous ceremonials.

FROM THE RAMPARTS OF HOLLENFELS
Hundreds of feet above the spot where the toes of the castle crag dip into a little river

MARRIAGE

His festive friends, showing all the humor that is customary at serious affairs in which some one else is to be the victim, made loud personal remarks of somewhat broad interpretation that caused many of the chubby damsels to hang their heads.

Promptly on time—mark this greatest of marvels—the bride came down the stairs. On her father's arm she set out for the church with scarcely a glance at the bridegroom. He and his widowed mother followed. Then came other members of the family and a number of self-conscious men and awkward girls, the remainder of the wedding-party.

The bride was clad in white muslin and veiled in the same material. Her simple coiffure was finished with a wreath of wax flowers that probably had been doing duty at all the weddings in the community for the past ten years. Her wooden-soled shoes peeped comically from beneath her long gown. But her golden curls, wayward and unwilling to stay pent beneath the veiling, distracted the attention of those who would have criticized her feet. Somehow she had the appearance of a very pretty and ingenuous little goddess whose baggage had gotten mixed with that of a slattern on her journey to earth.

The nuptial service at the church was in no way different from that of France. It was sedate and solemn. There was no wedding-march from Lohengrin, but the

THE LAND OF HAUNTED CASTLES

bridegroom lost the ring and the bride became very much excited. None would have doubted that this was a wedding.

Afterward the newly married pair set out for their home, followed by the long procession of friends. The entire village added to this part of the festivities. Many a farmer quit work to greet the bride as she left the church and drink her health in weak beer or villainous *Quetsch* in one of the three inns.

The husband picked up his bride at the entrance of the house and carried her over the threshold, a custom almost as old as marriage itself. The reason for this—according to Frau Muller, my mentor—is to outwit the evil spirits that would rob the poor girl of her happiness at the very outset of her wedded life. Should she trip on the threshold as she entered her own home it would be a terrible omen. So the wily burghers forestall the operation of any such curse by making it impossible for her to trip. Should the man stumble in carrying her, it would make no difference. The patron demon of ill luck would be beaten on a technicality.

Marriage is an all-day affair in Luxemburg. Though the wife may never have time to celebrate again during her life, she cannot say that merriment was lacking on her wedding-day. She is seated at the head of a long table about which have gathered friends and relatives, all of them in their funereal best, each with a stock of

MARRIAGE

pleasantry that he must recite at once. The heroine of the piece would be deafened were she not used to the Teutonic method of polite conversation.

Little Katrina looked very demure and startled as she sat down beside her husband at the banquet-table. All of this was a fairy tale to her,—a fairy tale, I thought, which was quite likely to have an unhappy ending. She said very little, even when spoken to, and ignored the coarse jests of her bridesmaids.

It was about ten o'clock when the wedding-party sat down to eat. Few of the attendants had eaten breakfast, so the earliness of the hour was no barrier to appetite.

Soup,—immense quantities of the homely *potage fermière*,—roast ducks, three or four of them; roast pig, spiced and sugared; baked ham whose mahogany color testified to long months of seasoning in the great chimney of the kitchen fireplace; smoked, fried and boiled sausages; steaming bowls of café au lait; and great pans of *gateaux* of all sizes, shapes, and flavors, some of them coated with quantities of real chocolate,—all were piled upon the table at once. Banquet etiquette in Luxemburg does not overlook the fact that the main essential of eating is to eat.

After the café au lait had disappeared came the second and last course, a barrel of *vin rouge*, which was rolled up close to the table to save steps in the serving.

THE LAND OF HAUNTED CASTLES

From that time on this festival would have given pleasant employment to Gargantua himself.

Speeches followed, of course. Speeches and red wine seem to be correlated. Choral activities developed early in the proceedings and continued until music had been smothered by vinous incoherence.

The bride was spared one ancient French custom that still may be found in parts of the Ardennes, the singing of the "Song of the Bride" by a group of toothless hags who make a business of this sort of minstrelsy. "The Song of the Bride" is a recitative of her life history and that of her husband, rendered in a cacophonous monotone. It is a dreary thing even in its happier passages, and calculated to drive all the joy out of even a Luxemburg wedding. Fortunately it is disappearing.

So far the wedding of Katrina had proceeded with much the same routine as that which governs in towns along the Meuse. But local custom was still to collect its due. The first instalment of the debt to tradition was paid when a basso-profundo outcry filtered up from under the table and a group of laughing youths dragged out Henry Riefschneider, holding his eye. He blushed, sat down, and drank deeply of the vin rouge while the crowd jeered at him.

All this was a mystery that to the crowd seemed to be no mystery at all. They seemed to understand perfectly why Heinrich had dropped under the table and how it

MARRIAGE

had come about that he was nursing a swelling over his eye. But there was no explanation for another half-hour. Then a second tumult arose from the cavern below the feast. Wilhelm Meisterheim emerged as had Heinrich. There was a livid streak across the back of his hand and he was a bit angry.

"It is not fair," he declared cryptically. "She wears pins. I scratched myself."

No one sympathized with him. The puzzle was passing beyond my comprehension when the bride gave a frightened little shriek and leaped up from her place. She stood upon her chair, holding her skirts tight about her ankles and looking down at the floor as if frightened by a mouse.

The wedding-party seemed to have gone wild. The men and women all were standing and screaming excitedly and the acme of din seemed to have been reached. It seemed impossible that human voices could create a greater volume of sound. But then Teutonic guffaws gave way to Teutonic cheers and the very rafters shook.

Johann Weber, dusty and flushed, had crawled out from under the table and was holding aloft a strange trophy,—a woman's garter. One had only to look at Katrina to realize where he had obtained it.

By way of forfeit he claimed a kiss from the bride. But he did not return the garter. Instead he carried it in triumph to Marie Dufour, the little French girl who had been his partner in the procession.

Laughingly she raised her skirts and lifted her foot. Laughingly he snapped the circlet about her knee. Then he kissed her and both sat down. The great event of the wedding celebration was over.

Frau Muller had difficulty in explaining all this to me. She was not certain of much of it, herself. But some of her neighbors were better informed and willing to talk.

The theft of the bride's garter has been a custom in the duchy since women began to wear garters. Originally it probably had no significance except as a trick to plague the bridegroom and tease the bride. With the years, however, it began to take on mystic connections. Success in the theft of the garter came to be looked upon as an omen of good luck in marriage for the youth who had stolen it and for the young woman upon whose leg he should place it. The bestowal of this "order of the garter" did not necessarily presage marriage between the donor and recipient, but frequently it had that result. Inasmuch as the youth invariably would give the coveted trophy to the lady of his choice, it is not to be wondered at.

Teuton, French, and native oddities mark marriages in the duchy. Along the Moselle and Our many villages still celebrate *Polterabend*—the night before the wed-

MARRIAGE

ding—by breaking glass and chinaware on the threshold of the bride's new home. This is distinctly a German custom in which the object is the pacification of the *Poltergeist*, a goblin whose sole purpose in existence is to maintain a sort of perpetual charivari. About Diekirch, where the Druid ruins bow to the east, one may view marriage rites more ancient. Young couples laughingly plight their troth by clasping hands through the arch in the Deivelselter ("Didos Altar"?), not knowing that they are observing a custom which the Breton peasants consider peculiarly their own.

In the rocky Ardennes one may still see the "testing of the bride," another ceremonial almost as ancient as Eve. The bride-to-be drops a pin from her bodice into a well or a stream. If it floats her fiancé knows that she is virtuous. If it sinks he casts her off.

This appears to be a severe test if one has never seen it performed. Actually it does not interrupt many marriages. Whatever may be a Luxemburg woman's knowledge of her own integrity, she learns in childhood that pins have a way of sinking. So she takes no chances. The pin that she drops into the water, here as in Brittany, is usually a long thorn, delicately carved and useful as a bodice ornament but still unsinkable.

Childish as may be all these wedding ceremonials they certainly produce permanent weddings. Women who marry in Luxemburg stay married. Illegitimacy is virtually unknown in the duchy.

CHAPTER XXXI
A FAMOUS VICTORY

"We Are the Salt of the Earth"

"But what good came of it at last?"
  Quoth little Peterkin:—
"Why that I cannot tell," said he,
  "But 't was a famous victory."
                —Southey.

CHAPTER XXXI

A FAMOUS VICTORY

OLD KASPAR sat by his cottage door repairing a strip of decrepit harness. There was a smell of pot-au-feu in the evening breeze that swept up from the cool reaches of the Kopstal ravine, and a rattle of pots and pans echoed in the street. A blue twilight was settling down over the purple crevasses beyond the town and the day's work was done.

There was an open space before Kaspar's doorway, —an open space between two tinted stone houses that stood like the sides of a great picture-frame, a crude setting for a wonderful landscape. Red roses in the foreground, dark rocks blending into cool green where the cliff dipped down to the Mamer; and beyond, the square-cut forests, a dim mysterious pattern where the slope arose again to the sky.

Sharp against the horizon stood the point of a German triangulation station and farther on, in dim outline, the crest of another craggy hill. The glow of the Steinfort furnaces was against the twilight in the distance at Kaspar's right.

There is idyllic beauty in Luxemburg in mid-spring.

THE LAND OF HAUNTED CASTLES

Sheltered by its own hills from the northern blasts that would seem to be a part of its climate, it bursts into bloom quickly after the melting of the snows. Its slopes are steep, its drainage rapid. Its thread-like streams swell to mountain torrents and presently the promise of a new harvest is in the fields.

A shrill voice from inside the cottage rose above the banging of ironstone china. The conversation was in the strange language of the duchy,—part French, part German, part Spanish, part Celtic,—but the tone was that of the aggrieved wife of any country.

Madame Kaspar was incensed because old Kaspar had tracked up the clean blue tile of her hallway with his muddy boots. It seems that the world over, so long as men shall live in houses and wear boots, they must track mud upon clean floors and hear about it from their wives.

Kaspar answered with the patience of admitted guilt. He stated that presently—as soon as he had finished saving four marks in the repair of the outworn harness—he would consent to do the menial work himself, a concession that silenced if it failed to appease the wrath from within.

"She speaks of mud on the floor," said Kaspar, with a half-smile as he made room for me on the door-step. "Mud on the floor, and a year ago a section of American artillery was quartered in her house! They thought nothing of mud nor of clean floors. Before them for four long years we had the Prussians. The Prussians owned the country then, Monsieur, and we were very sad. For it seemed that they would always own it. Women forget these things. They turn readily to the needs of peace without a thought of the troublous times that were just yesterday. Eh bien! That is the trouble with humanity. It forgets! If it remembered there would be no more wars.

He glanced toward the south, where the flashes of red from the steel-mills increased in brilliancy as the twilight gloom deepened.

"I sat at this very door and heard the roar of the guns at Verdun, Monsieur," he said. "Always—morning, noon and night—there was a rumble of death in the air, and our windows rattled and our floors trembled.

"We were unprepared for war when it came. There had been no lack of farm labor that year. French and Germans both swarmed the duchy in nineteen-fourteen and worked willingly for a few sous a day. Then the papers told us of the trouble in Austria. The trouble seemed to us to be very remote. War, in spite of our long acquaintance with Prussia, seemed to be impossible. One day the laborers disappeared.

"It was as if they had received a signal. At night they were here. In the morning they were gone. My cousin who lives in Arlon came over to say that the French troops were concentrating near Longwy and that some railroad tracks between Luxemburg and France had been torn up at the frontier.

"That was serious, of course, but the papers still told of parleys. It was not to be expected that there would be another eighteen-seventy merely because an archduke had been shot at Sarajevo. We were still confident that good sense would prevail, when we awoke one morning to see the roads dim with Feldgrau. From here, Monsieur, if your eyes are good, you can see three roads,—the one before the house here, the one in the valley, and the one over on the opposite crest. Over all three the Prussians were marching toward France.

"I have a niece in the capital, Monsieur. Her husband was a chemin-de-ferist. She came here one evening to tell us that a million men were to be engaged in the war and we smiled at her. It seemed so childish. Why should the Germans send an army of that size across Luxemburg when they could strike through Alsace as they had done in the war of eighteen-seventy? It did not seem right. But she said that the troops were pouring toward the border, not by mere divisions but by army corps.

"The chamber of deputies had opposed the invasion. They stood upon the rights of neutrality guaranteed to Luxemburg under the treaties signed at Vienna. But the Germans were all-powerful. They were determined

A FAMOUS VICTORY

to come through and the mobile forces of the duchy aside from those on duty at permanent stations at that time numbered just a few dozen men.

"There was a legend that Marie Adelaide had met a German staff officer's car as it came up the road from Treves and that she had thrown herself in front of it to prevent the Germans from passing. That is not true. I do not know whether *Sa Altesse* was in favor of the Germans as has been charged, or an ardent patriot as she afterward declared herself to be. But I do know that she was not foolish. Eh bien! What would have been the use of a young girl's trying to stop all that vast army?

"The German officers came into the capital and assured the president of the council that they were birds of passage and that they would not stay longer than necessary or put the people to any inconvenience. Mon Dieu! In two days the country was theirs.

"All day long at half-hour intervals the troop trains came down out of Prussia. Germany seemed to have gathered all the engines in the world, for few of them came back over our tracks.

"Then one morning we awakened to see the artillery coming through. It was a marvelous sight. Guns, guns, guns, on every hill-crest, in every hollow; splendid horses; fresh, healthy-looking men in new uniforms.

"Many of the soldiers were frightened. One officer billeted in this house told me that he had been expecting

THE LAND OF HAUNTED CASTLES

to be killed by French patrols as soon as he crossed the frontier into the duchy. The German staff had spread the reports that the French had taken possession of the fortress of Luxemburg and had manned it with mobile guns. The German soldiers were confident that nothing could defeat Germany, but they were very nervous nevertheless. They seemed to think that they had not long to live."

"The premonition was well founded," I commented.

"It was, Monsieur. The guns that passed through this town to the south are rust by now, and most of the men who took the road to Arlon are dust. So is the empire that drove them.

"There was fighting at Longwy, Longuyon, and Ethe. We heard about it from wounded men who came back. We were close enough to hear the guns. But the echoes were muffled. To us they seemed like the thunder of a summer shower. It was hard for us to imagine that such sounds could mean death.

"Then the French resistance stiffened. There was battling for the crossing of the Meuse at Stenay and there was bloody fighting in the Argonne forest. We received only slight information concerning all this. The Germans had taken over all the telephone lines for military purposes and the newspapers printed only such meager reports as were issued officially.

German artillery in retreat through Luxemburg city—November 1918

The German Retreat of November, 1918
LUXEMBURG CITY

A FAMOUS VICTORY

"The kaiser came to Luxemburg city with his whole staff. How long he remained there I do not know. A whole section of the city was roped off and placed under guard to accommodate him. That, Monsieur, did not endear the Prussians to us. It was a bit high-handed, coming as it did from a friendly power that had assured us that any violation of neutrality would be merely temporary.

"Then the troop movements became slower.

"The German advance was meeting some resistance in Lorraine and the artillery began to congest our roads. I have seen right here in this community miles and miles of cannon and hundreds of men asleep under them in the rain. The officers insisted that we turn out our own cattle and horses to give shelter to the horses of the army artillery. We had no choice! But no billets were asked for for the men. The answer was simple: A horse was worth four thousand marks. A man cost nothing except a mother's tears,—and there were plenty of those in Germany.

"I began to see what the war was going to be.

"There was much more of that later when the crown-prince's army was massing before Verdun. I believe that there were more German soldiers in the capital at that time than there were citizens in the whole duchy in times of peace.

"My niece brought reports that the French had struck

a counter-blow at Pont-à-Mousson and that the Germans were rushing troops to that sector. Her husband could see that from the manner in which the troop trains were being routed. We did not learn until long afterward that it was Joffre's feint at the east flank of his line to make the Prussians believe that it was there he had massed his strength. A Bavarian cavalry officer told me about it later.

"Then came the first Battle of the Marne. That did not affect us greatly, here. We knew, of course, that there had been a great battle and after a while we came also to know that the Germans had been defeated. But there was no immediate information.

"After that we were in the war and never had an opportunity to forget it. It seemed that we could never live through a year of it. But we did, somehow. We lived waiting for the inevitable advance of the Allies. For we realized that Germany could never win, when she had failed with the road to Paris open before her.

"The concentration directed against Verdun brought much hardship to the German soldiers who were filling our roads. The crown-prince established headquarters in Metz and there were many scandals concerning his activities. It is known that he made trips back to Luxemburg city repeatedly and the name of a certain Gräfin with an estate south of the capital was linked with his. Some of the Prussian hussars openly drank her health in stolen wine in this very house. It was nauseating.

"The snow came. But there was no change in the policy of billeting the horses and letting the men sleep in the roads. The troops that dragged their seventy-sevens down to Verdun were seasoned. Many of them had been wounded. They had seen war at close range and did not seem to mind the hardships of march. But pneumonia kept step with them as they passed through here.

"As for this poor land, its plight was indescribable. Prices began to go up out of all bounds. We were not under the marketing restrictions that applied in Germany. The Junkers who could n't buy what they needed in their own country soon discovered that the field was open on this side of the Moselle. So they came in here and bid against our own people for the necessities of life. I do not excuse our tradesmen for taking advantage of those prices. When they were getting fifty marks a dozen for eggs and sixty marks a pound for butter, they were taking those articles of food out of the home of some poor steel-worker who could n't afford to pay such prices even on a salary of five hundred marks a month. And yet it was natural. When there are buyers ready to pay an outrageous price, there will always be some one to sell to them.

"White flour got beyond all reach. I have seen Eisen-

THE LAND OF HAUNTED CASTLES

kuchen selling for three marks each. And those who could afford to pay for such a luxury as candy, paid as high as forty marks a demi-kilo for it.

"The farmers prospered. They had to pay a devil's price for sugar and a few things such as that, but they got it all back, out of eggs and grain. But in the city was starvation.

"It is always the cities that feel such conditions. They have no reserve and their poor people are poorer.

"Our youth went off to the war,—most of it with France, although sentiment was divided. The rest of us stayed home and tried to keep on good terms with our uninvited guests. It was a hardship, Monsieur. We knew that if Germany won, the doom of our country as an independent nation was sealed. We knew that we should become merely another province under the broad boots of Prussia. We prayed that the Allies might win. But we dared not say what we thought.

"Salaries at the iron-mills were raised. Many a ton of German munitions came out of Luxemburg ore. There was much bitterness over it. You could hardly expect a man with a son under the tricolor to feel enthusiastic about the increased wages of a neighbor who made shells for the seventy-sevens.

"Our mode of living approached savagery more closely every day. The soap-shortage was the cause of keen misery. Like Germany, we soon began to suffer from a

A FAMOUS VICTORY

lack of fats. Mathilde, my wife, managed to save up a bit of butter now and then in spite of the agents of our government after we had been placed on a national rationing-basis. She made soap of butter and wood-ashes. It was very expensive soap, but it sufficed.

"Shoes were rationed out to us by the pound,—two hundred grams per head, per family, per month. At that rate the women and children of the family would have to go nearly barefooted so that the workers could be sufficiently well shod for their work. Leather was worth its weight in German paper and just about as durable.

"Wool was as scarce as leather and it got to be the custom for our women to ravel out their old stockings and petticoats and knit new ones of the yarn. Our clothes never seemed to wear out. We could not afford to let them wear out. As a nation we were becoming wealthy. Whatever may be the criticism directed at the ethical standards of our tradsmen, it cannot be denied that their German custom brought them riches. Our farmers, who concealed flour and dairy products from the governmental agents only to turn over this food to Prussians, were merely smugglers. But they were well paid. Our steel-workers were receiving more for their work than they had ever dreamed possible. And for all that we were poverty-stricken.

"Money becomes useless when it will not buy necessities.

THE LAND OF HAUNTED CASTLES

"In November, 1918, there were many rumors that the war was nearing its end. But where these rumors originated we had no idea. We knew that things had been going badly for Prussia. The thundering of the artillery seemed to come from the west instead of the south and ambulances filled with wounded passed straight through Arlon without stopping. The whole policy of the war seemed to be changing. There were big guns at Montmedy. They had been brought out of the Argonne forest, crossing the river at Stenay on November 5th. The war was moving back to its old fields and we wondered what was to become of us.

"Even though the Germans were in retreat, we could not realize how badly beaten they were. That army that had passed through here in 1914 had seemed so strong, so splendid! We believed that this change of front was just another Prussian trick, that somewhere the Allies would step into an ambush that would end the war.

"Then the roads were dim with Feldgrau once more—dirty, stained Feldgrau that told the story of the useless struggle and the terrible retreat. We learned that history was repeating itself,—that fighting was in progress before Sedan, and that the fate of a million German soldiers in Belgium depended upon the holding of the Metz-Mézières Railroad, which at that point came close to the Meuse. Now, we figured, the Prussian will estab-

A FAMOUS VICTORY

lish his lines; we shall be the headquarters for his reserve and know the hell of close contact with war. But it was not so. The movement of troops continued. The men were like dumb brutes from lack of sleep, but they brightened when they spoke to us. They laughed and joked a little and told us that Prussia was finished. They actually laughed, as if the smashing of an empire was all part of the fortunes of war.

"They said that the Americans, of whom we had been told there were only a handful in all France, had driven them out of the Argonne.

" 'The tanks! The tanks!' they told us. 'There are millions of them and all the artillery in the world. They fire a dozen shells to our one, and the seventy-five does not make mistakes.

" 'The war will be at your doors in a day or two. They will knock down your houses, murder you in your beds, and carry off your women. They are like the wild men of the cinema.' That is what they told us, Monsieur, although of course we knew then and we know now that it was not true.

"On November 11th, at noon, there came a wonderful calm. The rumble on the west and south ceased and our windows rattled no more, after four long years. Some one in the village had lifted the telephone at the mayor's house just a little and he had heard that an armistice had been signed. The war was over. The Feldgrau flowed

THE LAND OF HAUNTED CASTLES

on over the hills toward the east. Few horses were with the artillery now. In some of the transportation units the men themselves dragged their own wagons. They were ashamed that Prussian soldiers should be put to such work. Near Eisch a photographer attempted to take their picture as they trudged along like beasts in the harness. A lieutenant knocked him down with a sword.

"In a few days we heard that the Americans were coming to occupy Luxemburg and the Rhineland. We felt pleased at that, because so many of our people have gone to America. And we were anxious to see these men who had driven the Prussians out of the Argonne.

"Herr Wagner and I went down to the frontier near Arlon on November 20th. But we saw no Americans. We came home that evening and found the infantry of the First American Division scattered all over our hills. The next day there was a formal entry into Luxemburg city,—a gala occasion on which all the city turned out to welcome them. And after that they became a part of our lives.

"In spite of ourselves we had been picturing the Americans as somewhat like the cow-boys of the American cinemas. It was a surprise to us to see them as they were. For the most part they were boys who looked very tired. Those that we saw first seemed to be a little bit more ragged than the retreating Germans. And they were friendly. It was surprising to think that less than two weeks ago they had been cutting a path through human flesh in the Argonne.

"At first I was a bit doubtful of them; they were so utterly unlike what I had been led to believe a conquering army would be.

"One evening little Gretchen Weinkoop, whose sweetheart was a machine-gunner in the German Army, began to sing 'Die Wacht am Rhine.' Oh, Monsieur, how I was afraid! Had one sung the Marseillaise when the Prussians occupied the duchy he would have been shot. But the Americans! There never shall be any understanding them. A big sergeant joined in the chorus, mimicking her, and all the others laughed. Gretchen blushed and went to her room.

"We miss the Americans here. They cleaned up a lot of spots about the town and kept things in repair. We who live here are apt to forget that our houses sometimes wear out. The children loved them and wept when they went away."

Old Kaspar paused. From the mist in his eyes it appeared that he, as well as the children, might have wept when the Americans went away. A kindly old man, he was, and I could easily believe him when he said:

"The American boys seemed to be very fond of me."

Any one would have been fond of him.

His name is not really "Old Kaspar." It is John

THE LAND OF HAUNTED CASTLES

Muller. He is a citizen of high standing in Keispelt and a member of the fire-department, but not generally rated high as a military expert.

And yet through the simple resignation that governed his tone throughout his story of those four dread years I realized, as never before, the futility of war. As he spoke I seemed to see the picture of Peterkin and Wilhelmine looking at the skull that they had found upon the field of Blenheim and unconsciously I repeated to Old Kaspar little Peterkin's query:

"What good came of it at last?"

He straightened suddenly.

"I should like to know that myself," he declared. "Prussia tore Christ down from His cross and drowned Him in blood. And for what? For whose profit? Certainly not her own: the allied troops are seizing her cities to force her to pay an indemnity that will not begin to compensate for the war. Certainly not France's: France gets a little territory and a few pennies of recompense at the price of her very soul. Certainly not England's: England is half starved and miserable and strangled by debt and the memory of her dead sons. Austria is a rotting corpse. The Balkans are a volcano. Russia is a hell.

"Kaiser Wilhelm said to his troops: 'We are the salt of the earth.' At the time he said it Belgium was a Sahara. Mon Dieu! what mockery!

A FAMOUS VICTORY

"What good came of it at last? Ah oui! what good?

"What of us? We are French now. We have been French before, just as we have been German, Belgian, and Spanish. What is to become of us? Only the good God knows.

"This war has ended only as a furnace fire dies down when the embers are banked to flare up again in the morning. There will be new wars. And our neutrality will mean no more in the wars to come than it meant in this last one. Always, Monsieur, we have been a slaughter-house for nations with grievances; and I suppose it must always be so. But when I hear my children at play in my kitchen I am glad that I cannot look into the future."

CHAPTER XXXII
THE END OF THE ROAD

Phantom Counselors

Ancestral voices prophesying war
—Coleridge

CHAPTER XXXII

THE END OF THE ROAD

WERE I "Old Kaspar" I know that I, too, should hesitate to think of Luxemburg's future. What it is likely to be, is pictured too vividly in its past.

But I went away from the duchy with that message of his echoing in my mind. The grim foreboding of it has never left me. Luxemburg has always had a part to play in the world's affairs and will again, and I cannot but think that its people have earned the right to the fruits of peace which they probably never will learn to enjoy.

Its people, who have gone quietly to work, are adjusting themselves to their new environment. The peasants are pursuing their unchanging routine in the fields, the artisans are manufacturing "three-decked" stoves and plows where once they turned shells for the seventy-sevens. The capital is struggling to shake off the influence of Berlin that made its cafés notorious.

"We would remain just as we are," is once more the typification of the national spirit as well as the national hymn. And if inbred fortitude amounts to anything, as the Luxemburgers are they probably will remain.

THE LAND OF HAUNTED CASTLES

The ghosts of the ancients sit in the councils of their descendants. The spectral guardians of the illustrious county gather in the ruins of Esch-le-Trou. The Templars watch from the heights of Fels. And Mélusine stands sentry upon the rock of Siegfroid.

THE END

www.ingramcontent.com/pod-product-compliance
Lightning Source LLC
Chambersburg PA
CBHW021756220426
43662CB00006B/79